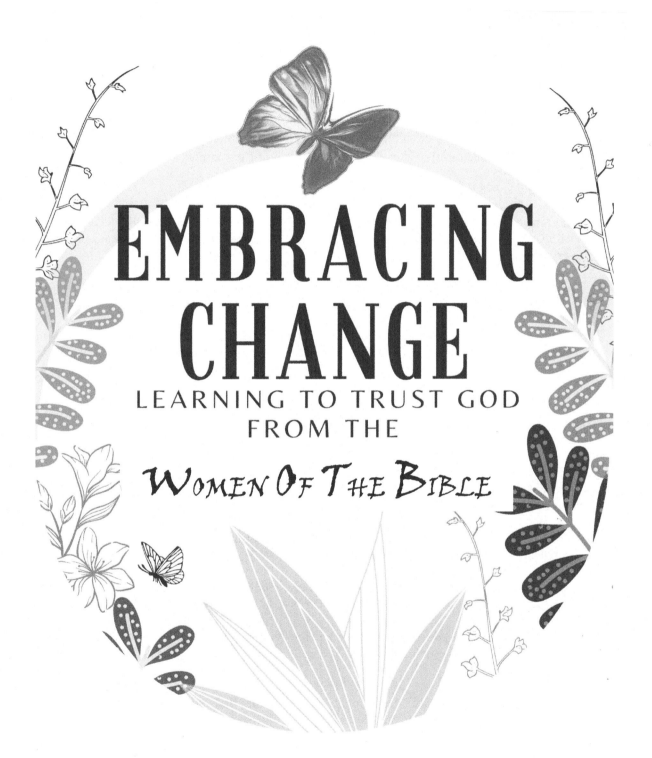

EMBRACING CHANGE

LEARNING TO TRUST GOD FROM THE

Women Of The Bible

PENNY NOYES

Published by Open Door Publishing

Hendersonville NC

Copyright 2015, 2022 Penny Noyes http://pennynoyes.blogspot.com/

ISBN Number 9780615698663

Table of Contents

INTRODUCTION

ABOUT THE STUDY

ACKNOWLEDGEMENTS

Check out our Digital Discussion Group

I've started a blog at pennynoyes.blospot.com so that you can share insights and comments with me and with other people who are also doing the study. My hope and prayer are that people all around the world will be blessed by the study and will also be able to bless others through sharing their godly wisdom and spiritual insight in the blog.

Thanks so much,

Penny

Introduction

While writing *Responding to God* about King Hezekiah and his mentor Isaiah, I started asking older women and younger women about their mentoring relationships. I wanted to learn about how women applied Titus 2: 3-5, "Likewise, teach the older women to be reverent in the way they live, not to be slanderers or addicted to much wine, but to teach what is good. Then they can train the younger women to love their husbands and children, to be self-controlled and pure, to be busy at home, to be kind, and to be subject to their husbands, so that no one will malign the word of God."

I was surprised by the responses from many of the "older" women to the idea of mentoring. Since most women don't think that they were "old," they didn't think this passage applied to them! These women were growing and learning, and they knew they didn't have all the answers regardless of their age. Many doubted that their perspective and life experiences would help another woman. Other women found the idea of "mentoring" intimidating because of the time commitment. They were so busy with careers, children, senior parents, and other responsibilities that they didn't think they had the time to invest in another relationship as a mentor to a younger woman.

Church programs are often segregated by age. When my parents were in their mid- 50's, they attended a church where they were some of the youngest congregants. My family attends a younger church that was established as a church plant ten years ago. Nearly 80% of the congregation has school-age children. In churches with more diverse congregations, there is often a divide between the older women who either maintain the status quo or simply retreat to senior activities and the younger women, including young moms, singles, and teenagers, who are often focused on connecting with others in the same life stage. I hope that this study will bridge the gap.

We may not have older women in our lives who will take us under their wing, lead us, and mentor us; however, by studying these women's lives, they can be our mentors. Whatever stage of life we are in, we can learn from how these women responded to change; and share what we have learned with others.

With love,
Penny

About the Study

If you want to embrace change, you have to trust God;

If you want to trust God, you have to know God;

If you want to know God, you have to know His Word.

Embracing Change- Learning to Trust God from the Women of the Bible is a nine-chapter Bible study that examines the lives of nine women in the Bible who are described as "old." All the women in this study have a lifetime of experiences that we can learn from and apply to our lives regardless of our current age. We will be challenged to trust God through all the stages of our lives by learning from these women's successes and failures and applying God's principles in our own lives. Our understanding of God's character revealed through time and history will help us to embrace change.

In each chapter of the study, we will explore each woman's life through scripture reading and interactive questions that facilitate better biblical understanding and life application. Our study of each woman's story starts by looking at her background and place in time. During the remainder of the chapter, we will examine four key areas.

- We'll explore her key relationships with her family and other women.
- We'll seek to understand her view of God by studying the names she uses for God and how that influences her ability to trust God.
- We'll learn from how she adjusts to change.
- We'll look for principles and wisdom that we can learn from her story.

You will notice that each chapter is divided into nine four week-long sections, so the study can be finished easily in nine months. For more of a challenge, you can complete the study in nine weeks and do four days of homework each week. My personal recommendation is to do the study in twelve-weeks; for the first three chapters take two weeks because they are very long and then finish by doing a chapter a week for the final six chapters. Questions that have bullet point (*) by them are good questions for group discussion.

On the title page of each chapter is a key scripture for the chapter. These are great scriptures to memorize and share with others. I highly recommend getting familiar with helpful online Bible study resources like www.biblehub.com and http://www.blueletterbible.org. I used both websites to look up different scripture versions and the Hebrew meaning of words.

CHAPTER I

Eve

SUITABLE HELPER

MOTHER

For God so loved the world that he
gave His one and only Son, that whoever
believes in him shall not perish but have
eternal life.
John 3:16

Week 1

Eve

Eve had it all; a perfect husband, a man without sin who had the perfect relationship with God; a perfect body, time and sin had not ravaged her flesh; and the perfect home with a beautiful garden. Life was perfection in every way. Eve had it all and blew it for all of us! Maybe that is why I kinda don't like her.

I put off writing this chapter until the rest of the study was finished because I just didn't want to think about why we have pain in childbirth and women get blamed for sin. But I kept coming back to her because her story connects all of us, and it helps explain some of our deepest longings, desires, and weaknesses. Plus, she certainly lived long enough; if Adam was 130[1] when his son Seth was born, then Eve had to be one of the oldest women in the Bible. Adam lived to age 800 and had other sons and daughters, which means that Eve possibly lived into her hundreds, and she may have lived longer than Adam!

Eve's story is vital understanding who God created us to be and why we long for perfection in our homes, oneness in our relationship with our spouse, and true intimacy with God.

Eve's story is vital to understanding who God created us to be and why we long for perfection in our homes, oneness in our relationship with our spouse, and true intimacy with God. For a moment in time, Eve had perfection in all these areas. Our deepest longings are evidence that God intended us for so much more.

Reading about Adam and Eve and their perfect life in the garden makes me wonder what could have been. What would life have been like pre-fall? What would the relationship between a husband and wife look like? What would it be like to walk with God without the cloak of sin blinding us to His glory and love? In this chapter, we will answer those questions and learn about God's plan to set us free from the curse, His plan for marriage, and the perfect home He has planned for us.

A little background: We find Eve's story in the book of Genesis, the first book of the Bible. We get the English word "Genesis" from a Greek word that means "origins." The Hebrew name for Genesis is בְּרֵאשִׁית which translated means "In the beginning."

---

[1] Genesis 5:3,4

Genesis is the first of five books called the Pentateuch. The Pentateuch consists of Genesis, Exodus, Leviticus, Numbers, and Deuteronomy. These five books are called the Torah and are treated as a unit in Hebrew. The Pentateuch is also referred to as the Book of the Law of Moses or as "the Law" in the New Testament. Most traditional Bible scholars attribute the authorship of the Pentateuch to Moses because of multiple references in the text to Moses as its author, and references back to Moses by later biblical writers. We will learn a lot more about Moses during our study of Miriam, his sister, in Chapter 3.

Genesis tells the story of the origins of God's relationship with His people, starting with creation. The first chapter of Genesis details God's creation of the world "in the beginning." The second chapter begins the story of the creation of people and His relationship with humankind. Soon, Adam and Eve's sin and rejection of God's command results in a world in disarray and a flood that destroys most of creation. After the flood, Genesis' focus begins to narrow to the descendants of Noah's son Shem. Most of the book of Genesis focuses on God's relationship with a distant grandson of Shem named Abraham, his son Isaac, and his grandson Jacob. We will learn more about Abraham when we study his wife Sarah in the second chapter of this study. Moses wrote Genesis to tell God's people, the descendants of Abraham, Isaac, and Jacob (who were called "Israel"), about their beginning as a people, teach them about God, and show them how they could be in relationship with God.

Please read Genesis 1 and write down what God created on each day and if it was bad, good, or very good.

	What was Created	Bad/ Good/ Very Good
Day 1		
Day 2		
Day 3		
Day 4		
Day 5		
Day 6		

Genesis 1 records the creation of the world in 7 days. During the process, God is pleased with His world and declares it "good." On the 6th day, God created humanity both male and female. At the end of the sixth day, God declared His creation, "very good."

I find it easy to focus on the specifics of creation and then wonder how dinosaurs and Neanderthals fit in this picture. Bible scholars and skeptics have come up with many explanations and ways of qualifying the word "days" as epochs, distinct periods of time, or literally when sun-up/sun-down equals one day. However, I do know for sure that focusing on the days or the things that were created is missing the bigger picture. The point of this chapter is to show the people of God that everything we can and cannot see in the world, what is known and what is unknown, what we understand and what we don't understand, was created by God.

Please skim Genesis 1 again and pay attention to the word, "God" (Elohim in Hebrew). If you want to be amazed, highlight the word "God" in your Bible every time it occurs in this chapter. Please write out the Genesis 1:1 below and underline the word "God."

The focus of the first chapter of Genesis is God. The Hebrew word for "God" in this chapter is "Elohim." The word "Elohim" occurs 32 times in the first chapter of Genesis!

ELOHIM- GOD אלהים 'elohiym

"Elohim is the plural form of El-one of the oldest designations for divinity in the world. The Hebrews borrowed the term El from the Canaanites. It can refer either to the true God or the pagan gods. Elohim is used more than 2,500 times. Its plural form is used not to indicate belief in many gods but to emphasize the majesty of the one true God. He is the God of gods, the highest of all. Christians may recognize in this plural form a hint of the trinity- Father, Son and Holy Spirit." [2]

In the Bible, names contain meaning and give insight into the character of the one with the name. Every time you read the word God in the Bible, think "Creator." John 3:16 is a well-known verse that starts out "For God so loved the world." This verse takes on new meaning when you realize that God, the Creator of the World (His special creation), loves it so much.

The first chapter of Genesis introduces God as the Creator of the world and everything in it. Elohim is a name that highlights the relationship between all of creation and its Creator, its sole source of life, and its owner. Everything belongs to God because He made it. Everything is under His dominion. Everything is subject to His plan and design. He is sovereign. He is Our Creator. He knows us intimately the way that a craftsman knows His creation. He gives life. He looks at what He has made, including you and me, and says, "It is good."

What is some evidence of God the Creator in your life and in the world around you?

---

[2] Spangler, Ann *Praying the Names of God*. Zondervan Grand Rapids MI 2004. 17

*How does knowing God as the Creator help you trust Him?

LORD GOD

In the second chapter of Genesis, another name for God is introduced. Please read Genesis 2:4-22. Pay attention to the name of God and His relationship to His creation. Describe what you think is the difference between "God" in the first chapter of Genesis and the "Lord God" in the second chapter.

יהוה Yĕhovah אלהים 'elohiym- Yahweh- LORD

The second name for God introduced is Lord. The distant Creator of Genesis 1 has become a Lord, intimately involved in His creation. The meaning of the word LORD is one who has power or authority. The LORD God was not only the Creator of the universe and everything in it, but also had all power and authority over it. Jehovah Elohim אֱלֹהִים יְהֹוָה is the title used that is translated in English as LORD God. In English, the transliteration of LORD is "Jehovah" or "Yahweh."

> "The word Yahweh occurs more than 6,800 times in the Old Testament... As the sacred, personal name of Israel's God it was eventually spoken aloud by only the priest worshipping in the Jerusalem Temple. After the destruction of the Temple in A.D. 70 the name was not pronounced. Adonay was substituted for Yahweh whenever it appeared in the biblical text because of this the correct pronunciation of this name was eventually lost. English translations of the Bible usually translate Adonay as "Lord" and Yahweh as "LORD." Yahweh is the name most closely linked to God's redeeming acts in the history of His chosen people. We know God because of what he has done."[3]

The title LORD also conveys the idea of a relationship. Just as you would have a relationship with your boss, God is the LORD of creation and has a relationship with people. "God wants us to know him. If we had only a distorted and corrupt view of God there would be no impetus to know him or to enter into relationship with him. The name LORD also denotes the "covenant-making and covenant-keeping God, specifically as the God who made promises to the patriarchs of Israel ...Lord is more than a word; it indicates a relationship. The lordship of God means His total possession of me and my total submission to him as Lord and Master."[4]

---

[3] Spangler, Ann *Praying the Names of God*. Zondervan Grand Rapids MI 2004. 74
[4] Arthur, Kay *LORD, I Want To Know You*. Waterbrook Press Colorado Springs CO 2000 Pg. 42

One of the most significant events in my spiritual life was when I made the choice to accept God as LORD of my life. Though I believed in God at a young age, it took me until I was 17 to acknowledge God as my Lord. Even as a kid, instead of singing "Trust and Obey," I would sing "Trust and hmm." I intentionally resisted God's authority. For most of my teen years, I had an attitude toward God that basically said, "You're not the boss of me." However, my ability (actually inability) to manage my life always left me wanting more. I was never satisfied or complete. Mercifully, at 17, I decided to trust God and let him be LORD of my life. I decided that I would do things His way and seek first His kingdom and righteousness. It was transformational.

If you have not prayed and asked God to be the LORD of your life, take a minute to pray and invite Him to be the boss. If He is the LORD of your life, write down a prayer of praise for His dominion and power.

Week 2

FROM NOT GOOD TO VERY GOOD

Last week in our introduction to Eve, we looked at two names used in the first chapter of Genesis; Elohim, which we translate as God, and Yahweh, which we translate as LORD. Understanding the meanings of these names will add depth to the rest of our study of women in the Bible. In this chapter, we will examine the creation of Adam and Eve and God's design for marriage to help understand Eve's role as Adam's helper.

Genesis 2 begins to amplify the story of God's relationship with His people through the story of the first man, Adam. Please read the entire chapter of Genesis 2 and write out Genesis 2:18 below.

Genesis 2 tells the story of a time of perfection. Though we now live in a world full of sin, conflict, pain, and suffering, studying this passage will open the door to understanding what life could be like without sin. How relationships with our husbands could be different and how true intimacy with our LORD God would look. It even provides a view into the future to a time when sin is no more, Satan is defeated, and we will live in harmony with God and each other. It was an innocent time when Adam walked with His LORD God in the garden, when God's love and perfect plan resulted in a suitable helper for Adam, and when Adam and Eve were one flesh. Before sin, conflict, pain, and toil entered the world; it was a brief time when life on Earth went from good to very good. In Genesis 2:18, the LORD God declares, "It is not good for man to be alone." This provides an interesting contrast to the repeated statements of creation being "good" in Chapter 1.

Our study of Genesis 1 introduced the creation of people created in the image of God, both male and female. Though the 6th day ended with the declaration, it was "very good," Genesis 2:18 records that there was a moment in time during the creation of people that God said "It is not good" because man was alone.

*Why do you think it is not good for man to be alone?

We find the answer to this question in God's solution to the problem of man being alone by providing a helper suitable for him. "The last part of v. 18 reads literally, 'I will make for him a helper as in front of him (or according to what is in front of him).' This last phrase, "as in front of him (or according to what is in front of him)" (*kenegdo*) occurs only here and in v. 20. It suggests that what God creates for Adam will correspond to him. Thus, the new creation will be neither a superior nor an inferior, but an equal."[5]

God created Eve out of Adam's side. In Genesis 2:21-22, it is interesting to note that the Hebrew word, "*tsela*" translated as "side of a body," in these two verses is most frequently translated as the side of the building and the side of the altar. Misunderstanding this passage led to an ancient urban myth that said men and women have a different number of ribs. This is false. Based on both x-rays and cadavers- both men and women have the same number of ribs. Understanding this passage in light of the word "*neged*," translated as "suitable," helps clarify that Eve was close to, parallel to, and corresponding to Adam. Their similarity, in a sense, made them two halves to a whole; they weren't complete without each other.

---

[5] Hamilton, Victor P. "The Book of Genesis Chapters 1-17." *The New International Commentary on the Old Testament*, ed. R.K. Harrison (Grand Rapids MI Eerdmans, 1990), 175.

God's original plan for the relationship between a man and a woman was a suitability that meant they weren't identical, but they completed and complemented each other. Who would have thought, "You complete me," that famous line from the movie *Jerry Maguire* had a connection to God's plan for marriage!

God knew the potential He had created in Adam; man by himself was good, but had the potential to be very good. So, God's solution to Adam's problem of being alone was to make a helper suitable for him. Adam and his wife would complete each other just as a hamburger and bun make a great meal on the Fourth of July. Each piece is different and good in its own right but together, they create something better.

God's original plan for the relationship between a man and a woman was a suitability that meant they weren't identical, but that they completed and complemented each other.

The Biblical view of a wife, as a helper and an equal, contrasts to a corrupted cultural view of marriage that led to the mistreatment of women in history. As a result, discussing roles in marriage can trigger confusion and hurt based on personal places of pain. Despite our past experiences, other people's sins, and misinterpretation of the Bible, the truth is that God created men and women equal though we have different emotional and physical dispositions; one is not better than the other, just different. We are designed to complement the other and express the completeness of God.

*God's solution was to create a "helper" suitable for him. What do you think it means for the woman to be a helper?

The Hebrew word (*'ezer*) is translated as "Helper" (NIV) and "Helpmeet" (KJV). This word is used twice to describe the wife of Adam in Genesis 2:18, 20. "This new creation which man needs is called a helper (*ezer*), which is masculine in gender, though here it is a term for woman. Any suggestion that this particular word denotes one who has only an associate or subordinate status to a senior member is refuted by the fact that most frequently this same word describes Yahweh's relationship to Israel. He is Israel's helper because He is the stronger one." Being a helper does not mean that God intended Eve to be subordinate to Adam. The verb root of "*ezar*" is "*azar*" which means "succor," "to save from danger," and "deliver from death." This word is most often used to describe God's relationship with His people in the Bible.

Please look up these verses and write out how God is our helper.
Deuteronomy 33:29

Psalm 33:20

Psalm 121:1-2

In addition to these three verses, nineteen other verses use the word "*ezer.*" These verses provide a view of the power of God to defend and protect His people. This word is found in Psalms in the phrase "he is our help and our shield, God is our help and our deliverer" and in Psalm 121 which declares "my help comes from the Lord, the Maker of heaven and earth."

God created Eve to be a helper, just as God is our helper. He created Eve out of Adam's side so that the two sides would correspond and complete each other. How does knowing this change your view of God's original design for marriage and the woman's role in marriage?

Marriage has come under attack. Going back to Genesis 2 provides us with the foundation of God's plan for marriage and the family. This is such an important passage that Jesus referred to Genesis 2 when skeptics questioned him about divorce. Jesus prefaced his view on divorce in Mark 10 with, "But at the beginning of creation." In Matthew 19:4, he said, "Have you not read that he who created them from the beginning, made them male and female."

By going back to the beginning, (a reference to the name of Genesis in Hebrew), Jesus was reminding the people of God's (Elohim, Creator) plan to make His creation complete and perfect. Jesus continued, ""For this reason a man will leave his father and mother and be united to his wife, and the two will become one flesh.' So, they are no longer two, but one flesh. Therefore what God has joined together, let no one separate."[6] The problem with divorce is that it separates people from each other and leaves them alone, which undermines God's plan to bless us and bless the world through children and marriage. Divorce is an attack on God's plan for people to be complete.

Genesis 2:18 states that "it is not good for man to be alone;" this provides insight into the way God created people and as a result, has relevance to our contemporary discussion of marriage. We are created for connection with others. No one wants to be alone, and many on the side of an inclusive definition of marriage bring up the argument of love being the foundation for all relationships, straight or gay.

The inherent problem with definitions of marriage that differ from God's plan is that they are not complete, just as a lawn chair without legs isn't very comfortable; it is just not as good as it could

---

[6] Mark 10:5-9

be. Fundamentally, God designed us for so much more. Unfortunately, many of us settle for less than God's best by cohabitating without a covenant or homosexual relationships. Just as God made the judgment call that it is not good for man to be alone, anything other than God's plan for marriage isn't very good.

After I wrote the sentence about a lawn chair without legs not being comfortable, a single friend was upset by the idea that she was less than complete and not very good without a husband. She wanted me to make sure that I didn't exclude the single ladies (and guys) out there; so, let me clearly state, "Because we are created in the image of God, all of us, male and female have wonderful attributes and gifts that we can use to glorify God and bless others, whether we are married or not." Some of us, like Paul, are called to singleness.[7] Regardless of our marital state, single, married, divorced, or widowed, we have a purpose of glorifying God by loving God and loving others with our heart, soul, and mind. My intention is not to make people feel bad because they are not married but to show that marriage, with all of its flaws and challenges, is a part of God's plan to experience fully His grace and blessing in our lives.

> *Regardless of our* **marital state, single, married, divorced, or widowed, we are created to glorify God by loving God and loving other people with our heart, soul, and mind.**

THE TWO BECOME ONE FLESH

I have heard people describe our culture as "sex-saturated." Write down some words to describe the cultural view of sex?

Would you use the same words to describe a biblical view of sex? Why or why not?

As you'll read below, the biblical view of sex includes words like "very good, blessing, and fun." Were any of these words in your answer? Unfortunately, we have been deceived by Satan into a distorted perspective and lost God's view of sex in marriage as a blessing.

Let's continue our study of Eve in Genesis 2:23 - 24, when Adam names the woman who was taken from his flesh, and they become one flesh. In God's design, the man and the woman together made something very good; a synthesis occurred that joined the man and the woman and made one flesh. Both the man and the woman were good, but when God joined the man and the woman

---

[7] 1 Corinthians 7:7

together, something mysterious occurred that was greater than the sum of its parts. This joining allowed the man to fulfill God's first command in Gen 1:28, "Be fruitful and increase in number; fill the earth and subdue it," but it also allowed him to experience the blessing from being fruitful that was intrinsic in the command. Carrying out this command to multiply and have children (which God commanded even before sin entered the world) is physically impossible without a father and a mother. For many of my friends, conceiving children has been very difficult, and this is a heart-breaking topic, but I do believe there is still a huge blessing in being married and joining with your husband whether or not you will get pregnant. Enjoy the physical benefits of your marriage; it is God's plan for sex to be fun; babies are the second half of the blessing.

God desires to bless us. To receive the blessing that He intended for marriage, husband and wives become one flesh so that the sum of the two parts makes something new requires doing things His way. When we settle for less than the very best in our relationships, whether it is through homosexual relations, premarital sex, or physical or emotional adultery, we are being disobedient to God's command, and we are being robbed of the blessing that God meant for all of us.

> *Following God's plan* and timing in this area has led to the greatest blessings in my life.

Much of the cultural conflict in our society goes back to our resistance to God's command to be fruitful and increase in number. For me personally, one of the most significant areas of putting my faith into action was trusting God's plan for marriage and children. I grew up thinking I didn't want ever to get married, and I certainly didn't want kids. Both seemed to be a lot of work without a lot of rewards. I gradually realized that fully trusting God in my life included getting married, but I still clung to my birth control. Then, one day, I felt God ask me, "Do you trust me?" I knew if I answered "Yes," I had to trust His plan, which included the possibility of having children. Though I was terrified of getting married and having kids, following God's plan and timing in this area has led to the greatest blessings in my life.

We all come to places in our relationship with God where we have to answer the question, "Do you trust me?" Are there places where you are resisting God's plan and His best by trying to control things?

WHAT TO LEAVE AND WHAT TO HOLD ON TO

God often makes passages of scripture alive in various ways and through different situations in our lives. I've found applying another principle from this passage to be life changing. Recently, I have been dealing with the communication patterns that my husband and I both picked up from our parents. As I have thought about Genesis 2:24, "Therefore a man shall leave his father and his mother and hold fast to his wife, and they shall become one flesh," I have realized that God is calling both of us to leave the unhealthy patterns we inherited from our parents and become one flesh, a new creation that is greater than the sum of our individual halves.

As God has been showing this pattern to me, I've realized the most practical way I can apply this passage, "to leave his father and mother," is to leave behind the unhealthy communication patterns that I learned from my parents. This has been a process because I don't always realize my unhealthy habits because they are so ingrained. Recently, I have been praying for God to bring these unhealthy patterns to light. I have had to humble myself and repent of my sins. I asked God to create a new flesh between my husband and me, one that is healthy, free of the curse of previous generations' sin, and that will start a pattern of blessing and honor for our children and a thousand generations.

Are there ways that God has shown you that you should cut unhealthy ties or patterns from your family and cling to your husband by creating a new healthy, complete flesh?

In 1 Cor. 6:16, Paul cites Gen. 2:24 "the two shall become one flesh (*sarka mian*)." This verse was quoted in the New Testament to show the covenant of marriage and the new covenant between Christ and His bride, the church.

Paul quotes Genesis 2:24 in Eph. 5. Please read Ephesians 5:31-32. Why do you think this idea relates to the church?

Whether or not we are married, this concept applies to all believers. The Apostle Paul's interpretation of Genesis 2:24 expanded the application of this passage from a husband-and-wife relationship to include our relationship with Christ. In Ephesians 5:32, he wrote about being one flesh, "This is a profound mystery—but I am talking about Christ and the church." God's design for marriage was not only to create one flesh out of two but also to model the transformation that occurs between Christ and the church.

This amazing picture of the church as the bride of Christ gives us hope in our places of incompleteness. Each of us who long for perfection in our spouse, home, and bodies can look forward to one day when we will be perfect as the bride of Christ, in heavenly bodies in a heavenly home. Our desire for "more and better" clothes, kids, money, jobs, food, houses, husbands, furniture, and bodies is a symptom of a foundational need that goes all the way back to creation when Eve had the perfect body, perfect relationship with Christ, and a relationship of perfect balance and equality with her perfect husband. We want these things because God made us for perfection. However, the only way we will ever be satisfied is to become one with Christ, who is perfect.

Please look up Matthew 5:47-48 in the www.blueletterbible.com. Then, click on the Strong's number G5046. This will take you to the Greek word "*teleios.*" Please write out the definition from the outline of Biblical usage.

Do you think that it is possible to be perfect? Why do you believe that Jesus commands us in Matthew 5:47 to be perfect?

After studying this, I realized that my definition of being perfect was very different from biblical usage. I thought it was fascinating that being perfect also required a certain amount of maturity. When Jesus commands us to be perfect, He is telling us to be complete. However, we define perfection, it is an elusive goal, but it is easy to see when something is complete and whole. I realized that I don't have meet a human standard of perfection. Instead, I need to strive to be like Jesus because my desire for "more and better" is always a desire for God. As we grow closer to Christ, we will grow more and more like him because when "perfection comes, the imperfect disappears."[8]

We covered a lot this week—Take a minute to review God's plan for marriage, your view of God being our helper, and the wife's role as a helper and a shield. Are there areas in your life that you want "more and better?" How does knowing these are only satisfied through Christ change your perspective?

Take some time to pray and ask God to create new family patterns of blessing and grace.

---

[8] 1 Corinthians 13:10

Week 3

THE BEGINNING OF THE END

Eve's story quickly turns into a tragedy in Genesis 3. Life changed from bliss to pain, from perfect communication and harmony with God and her husband to unhealthy desire and subordination. One of my friends compared Eve's deception in the Garden of Eden to a scene in a horror movie where the girl opens the door to the basement and blithely begins to walk down the dark staircase. As you are watching the scene, every part of you says, "No, don't do it!"; "Get out now!"; or at least, "Turn on the light, you idiot!"

To understand how this happened, let's read and compare Genesis 3:1-7 and Genesis 2:16-17. Then, to make sure we know the truth, please write out what God said to Adam in Genesis 2:16-17.

Here's a quick context note regarding the serpent in Genesis 3. I had trouble with understanding how people could make the jump from a talking snake, the "Serpent" in this passage, to Satan. As I was researching this, I found a verse that clarifies this connection: Revelation 12:9 says, "The great dragon was hurled down—that ancient serpent called the devil, or Satan, who leads the whole world astray. He was hurled to the earth, and his angels with him." This verse explains that the serpent was Satan, who as we will read is a liar and the father of lies.[9]

What did the serpent Satan say that God said? Genesis 3:1

What did Eve say to the serpent? Genesis 3:2-3

What was the serpent's response? Genesis 3:4-5

---

[9] John 8:44

Satan is a liar. Satan takes God's Word, and he challenges, distorts, and abbreviates it. A slight twist of God's Word and Eve's misunderstanding of God's command led to the beginning of the end. Satan attributes characteristics to God that are the opposite of the reality of who He is and how much He loves us. One of the most powerful reasons to study the Bible is so that we know the Word of God. Hosea 4:6 presents a chilling picture and a warning to each of us when God declares, "My people perish from lack of knowledge." Eve's fatal choice was based on believing the lies that Satan told her. Throughout this study, we will study the names and character of God so that we can believe His Word and trust Him in every aspect of our lives.

Let's take a minute to apply what we learned about the characteristics of God (Elohim) and LORD. Flip back to the first week's work on pages 4 - 5 and review these two names. How would understanding the meanings of these titles help someone deflect Satan's lies?

Reviewing the names and character of God reminds me that He is my Creator, and He loves me. He knows and wants what is best for me. He is LORD and desires a relationship with each of us. He is our Master.

We can trust God and rebut Satan's attacks on His character and His Word when we know God. Second Corinthians 11:3-4 contains a warning to believers. "But I am afraid that just as Eve was deceived by the serpent's cunning, your minds may somehow be led astray from your sincere and pure devotion to Christ. For if someone comes to you and preaches a Jesus other than the Jesus we preached, or if you receive a different spirit from the Spirit you received, or a different gospel from the one you accepted, you put up with it easily enough." Paul is concerned that these believers will be persuaded away from the truth just as Eve was in the Garden. Therefore, we must study the Word of God, and we must hold up the shield of faith[10], which comes from knowing God so that we can deflect the attacks of Satan.

Jesus modeled the proper response to Satan's attacks and lies in Matthew 4:1-11. Though Satan tried many ways to deceive Jesus and even quoted scripture, Jesus refuted Satan's attacks with the truth in God's Word and sent him away with the command, "Away from me, Satan! For it is written: 'Worship the Lord your God, and serve him only.'"[11] The antidote to Satan's lies includes commanding Satan to leave us alone, worshiping God, and serving Him only.

---

[10] Ephesians 6:16
[11] Matthew 4:10

If we worship anyone or anything else, we will be deceived, and we will not experience the abundant life that Jesus has secured for us. The death that came through the sin in the Garden of Eden was spiritual. It caused a break in our connection with God. But thanks be to God, Jesus forever fixed the disconnection between people and God through His death and resurrection. In John 10:10, Jesus states, "The thief comes only to steal and kill and destroy; I have come that they may have life, and have it to the full."

Salvation means **not just knowing that you are saved and that one day, you will go to heaven; salvation is a taste of heaven on earth!**

God's best and most perfect life for us is secured through our salvation in Christ. Salvation means not just knowing that you are saved and that one day, you will go to heaven; salvation is a taste of heaven on earth! Salvation is living every day filled with the blessings that God has given us by worshipping Him and carrying out His purposes.

DON'T DO IT!

In ninth grade, I fell in love with Greek tragedies. Something about the inevitability of the tragedy in Oedipus Rex stuck with me. So, in the style of a Greek tragedy, I can't help but wonder whether the fall was preventable or was it inevitable that the serpent would deceive innocent, gullible Eve. Could it have been prevented? Where was God, and better yet where was Adam?

Genesis 3:6 contains the answer to the question, "Where was Adam?" Please fill in the blanks. When the _____ saw that the fruit of the tree was good for food and pleasing to the eye, and also desirable for gaining wisdom, she took some and _____. She also gave some to her husband,_____.

Adam was there! Argghh! Eve was deceived by Satan and seduced by her need for food, her eyes, and her mind's desire for wisdom, so she took some and ate it. How was it possible that this woman, who had it all, was persuaded to want more and doubt God, who had already provided everything she needed?

I think that one answer is that Eve was distracted. Eve allowed her focus to be shifted from the beauty and majesty of God to the temporal beauty of the fruit. She let her hunger for God be replaced by a longing for earthly food. She substituted her inherent desire for wisdom and knowledge of God with a false desire to be like God.

* What are things that distract you from God?

I am easily distracted. So often, the things of this world are so much easier to focus on than God. I get distracted by my needs like food and shelter, dirty laundry, birthday presents, health issues, children, TV shows, and my desire to be the boss. It really doesn't take much for me to lose sight of God's provision, His wisdom, and Lordship in my life. The deception I face is that I have to take care of myself, my kids, and my world and that I can't trust God. This is a lie that goes all the way back to the Garden; it wreaked havoc back then and will continue to destroy relationships unless we continually "seek first the kingdom of God and His righteousness"[12]

One of the most eye-opening parts of this passage about Eve is the sentence, "She also gave some to her husband, who was with her, and he ate it." Get this, Adam was standing next to Eve as the serpent talked to her! She wasn't all alone dealing with the lies of Satan. Adam was by her side. So why didn't he stand up to Satan's lies? Why didn't he quote God's Word, since God said directly to him before Eve was even created, "You are free to eat from any tree in the garden; but you must not eat from the tree of the knowledge of good and evil, for when you eat from it you will certainly die."?[13] I don't know, but the consequences were immediate and severe.

As a result of their sin, shame came into the world. In Genesis 2, Adam and his wife were both naked, and they felt no shame.[14] Still, after eating the fruit, they realized they were naked, so they made clothes out of some fig leaves.[15] That evening, when they heard the Lord God walking in the Garden, they hid because they were afraid.[16] In addition to shame, the relationship between God and mankind was damaged. The relationship between a husband and wife morphed from balance and harmony (two halves of a whole) to blame and inequality.

Jeff VanVonderen writes about this in his book ***Families where Grace is in Place***. Though this is a long quote – this book was eye-opening and was life-changing for me.

"After the fall, we see how drastically things changed. Adam and Eve became afraid of God and wanted to hide from Him. In relationship to themselves as individuals they carried shame. And in relationship to each other they began to blame and condemn.

"But there is an even more serious ramification affecting male/female relationships. In Genesis 3, we find what is traditionally called the curse. In this passage God said to the woman, "your desire shall be for your husband, and he shall rule over you. (v.16) First came the impulse to blame. Then God simply revealed the self-centered core than began to motivate each of them: The woman would continue

---

[12] Matthew 6:33
[13] Genesis 2:16-17
[14] Genesis 2:25
[15] Genesis 3:7
[16] Genesis 3:8-10

to try to draw life and nurturing from a man who was not capable of filling these deep needs-never was and never will be. And the man would be forever trying to rule over the woman, either aggressively or passively trying to keep her quiet about his inadequacy to fill her needs. Each would demand love, respect, nurturing from the other. And as generations of their children passed, men and women would forget that they were never supposed to draw their life from each other."[17]

"Curse-full relationships have many characteristics and the one that we will focus on here is our underlying tendency to usurp God's role by trying in futile and powerless ways to control.

To help us see this more clearly, I will develop my thoughts around the acronym- C.U.R.S.E. Each letter happens to stand for a primary aspect of curse-full relationships.

They are
C-Controlling
U-Unforgiving
R-Reactive
S-Shaming
E-Ego-Driven

Controlling

"If our sense of well-being and value stem from the behavior of another person instead of God, we will always be giving off messages that say to others: You'd better perform right. The innate problem is that no human being is capable of performing well enough to establish another's self-esteem, that person's behavior will always fall short at some point. If the other person is not willing or able to change their behavior fast enough or in the "right way" to meet our needs, most of us decide that their behavior is an issue we must do something about."[18]

Unforgiving

"When I say that curse-full relationships are unforgiving, I am not simply talking about a lack of forgiveness for a given incident. I am talking about a lack of forgiveness for things that happened years and even decades before. This can be

---

[17] Van Vonderen, *Families Where Grace is in Place.* 20-22
[18] Ibid 28

seen by the amount of time and energy used to rehash old issues for which there is still no forgiveness.

For some people, unforgiveness has a very practical purpose. One reason why people don't or won't forgive is because it is a way for them to have the upper hand over another; it holds the other in a position of owing a debt they cannot repay. And feeling held in a constant state of being unforgiven keeps people scrambling to discover what good behavior it will take on their part to make up for what they have done wrong. In a very real and devilish sense, unforgiveness becomes an effective tool to control another's behavior.

Reactive

People who are in curse-full relationships have not learned how freeing it is to respond to someone else's behavior. Healthy responses are based upon what is true, what is beneficial and what is appropriate. People who are not free react in order to control the situation. When your sense of well-being comes from the performance of another, in fact, you are assigning that person a lot of power over you. Their words and behavior have the power to indict or vindicate. The other person has the power to establish your self-esteem or to destroy it. Consequently, when that other person acts in a way that is bad "public relations" for you, you must react immediately in order to get on top of the situation. Under the curse the byword is control or be controlled.

What a sad contrast to Paul's description of love in 1 Corinthians 13! Paul says that love "is not provoked." This means that when we learn to rest in God's love, outside factors do not control our response-love does. Love is also patient- which means slow to anger – but curse-full relationships are often full of angry reactions of either the icy or heated varieties. In either case, love frees- while living under the curse traps us in our own reactions.

Shaming

Shame is the painful sense that you lack value as a person. It is the belief that you are defective, worthless, and unlovable. It is not simply that something is wrong with your behavior; it is that something is wrong with you as a person.

Shame is often used by people as a means of placing themselves over others. When I give you the message that you are bad or defective, I am placing myself in the position of being more valuable or more powerful and the judge of your value as a person. Shame is also used as an attempt to control the behavior of others.

How would you respond, for example, if someone said, "What's wrong with you-why can't you be like your brother?" If you react by trying harder to be like your brother, than that person has succeed in shaming you- that is playing on a sense of defectiveness- and controlled you to change your behavior to escape the feeling of worthlessness."[19]

Ego-Driven

"People in curse-full relationships are ego-driven (That is the fancy psychological equivalent of being selfish.) Beneath their line of conscious or stated, reasoning lies another layer of thought where the truth is hidden:

- I want my children to dress a certain way because of what people will think of me.
- I want my spouse to go to church because of what people might say about me, if he/she doesn't go.
- I need you to cater to me so I can feel important.
- For you to want to do something other than what I want means I must not matter to you.
- For you to give someone else attention instead of me means something is wrong with me.
- Behaviors in these relationships are so ego-driven that even apparent selflessness masks underlying selfish motives:
- I must please my spouse in every way and meet every need so I can feel like a good spouse.
- I must speak kindly to my children in public so others will see me as a good parent.
- I must never say no when asked to do something in the church so others will see me as a dedicated Christian."[20]

Reading through Jeff VanVonderen's description of how the CURSE plays out in families today shook my core because I could see how this pattern had perpetuated in my life and my relationships with others. I realized that I had focused on a performance-based relationship with myself and others rather than receiving the grace that Christ has shown me and giving it to others.[21]

---

[19] Ibid 29-31
[20] Ibid 32
[21] Van Vonderen's book is a practical guide to understand how families can give grace.

Has God revealed areas in your heart where you need to break the curse (Controlling, Unforgiving, Reactive, Shaming, and Ego–Driven behaviors) in your life? If yes, name them, pray for them to be removed entirely from your life, and ask God to replace them with His grace, love, identity, peace, forgiveness, self-control, and gentleness.

If God revealed places where the curse has a foothold, I have good news because you don't have to live like that any longer. Jesus has broken the curse. All you have to do is acknowledge the sin, repent and claim the truth that you are set free, receive His amazing grace, and then share it with others. Then, the curse can stop with you for your life and for generations to come.

Week 4

THE NEXT GENERATION

People often tell my boys how much they look like my husband and me. My oldest son has my husband's blue-green eyes, and my younger son has golden-hazel eyes like mine. Just as my husband and I have passed down our eye color to our two boys, Adam and Eve passed down their damaged relationship with each other and with God to their children, Cain and Abel.

Please read Genesis 4 and write down what happened and your thoughts.

Though their sin had resulted in eviction from the Garden, God had given Eve an amazing blessing. Imagine Eve's hope and love when her precious baby, a gift from the Lord, was given to her. Even after the pain of childbirth and labor – she knew that the Lord had given her a little man. According to the NIV Bible note, Cain sounds like the Hebrew for brought forth or acquired.[22] This precious baby was a gift from the Lord. Soon after, she gave birth to a second son. Abel was a double blessing, and both boys grew up together and had a relationship with the Lord.

---

[22] http://www.biblegateway.com/passage/?search=Genesis%204&version=NIV#fen-NIV-81b

However, the curse that Adam and Eve lived under transferred to their sons. These young men, who were only one generation from the perfection of the Garden of Eden, struggled with sin. Cain mistakenly believed he would feel better if he took out his competition by killing Abel. He blamed his anger and sadness on his brother just as his parents blamed their shame on each other and the serpent. He tried to control the people around him rather than realizing the problem was his, and he had a choice to do what was right or to let sin master him. It is possible to get confused and think that Cain's choosing to "do right" meant that his performance could earn God's favor; instead, Cain's choice was about who would be his Master: God or his sinful nature.

God highlighted this struggle when He spoke to Cain in Genesis 4:7; He said, "If you do what is right, will you not be accepted? But if you do not do what is right, sin is crouching at your door; it desires to have you, but you must rule over it." The same word for "desire" is found in the curse when God tells Eve her desire will be for her husband. This destructive pattern of sin is a result of the fall. In this verse, sin is not just a concept; it is an aggressive creature crouching at his door. Cain had a choice; let sin take over his life like a lion overtaking its prey or break the sin pattern inherited from his parents by doing what was right. Unfortunately, Cain chose the wrong path; he killed his brother, and as a result, he was cursed and exiled from his family.

All of us can learn from God's dialogue with Cain. Like Cain, we can choose what is right or allow the curse of sin passed down from our families to overtake us as a lion devours its prey. God has shown me that I need to choose to do what is right, and specifically, I need to take God up on His offer to break the curse of sin in my family. As a bonus, God will not only break the curse, but He promises us blessings, which are the biblical opposite of curses, for a thousand generations if we obey Him.

When God reveals patterns of sin in my life or my children's lives, it is my responsibility to repent of that weakness. Next, I claim Jesus' victory over that sin in my life and my kids' lives because, as Galatians 3:13 says, "Christ redeemed us from that self-defeating, cursed life by absorbing it completely into himself. Do you remember the scripture that says, "Cursed is everyone who hangs on a tree"? That is what happened when Jesus was nailed to the cross: He became a curse, and at the same time dissolved the curse." (MSG) Whenever God showed me patterns of sin (like miscommunication, abuse, desire for control and status, selfishness, disrespect, self-righteousness, and covetousness), I prayed and repented of them in my life. Then I asked God to forgive me for these sins and to break the pattern of the specific sin in my family, in my children, and grandchildren for a thousand generations.[23]

---

[23] Deuteronomy 7:9

If you see any patterns of sin that are common in your life and your family, *stop right now and pray.* Repent of any sinful thoughts and behaviors.

> Ask God to forgive you for the sin and break that unhealthy pattern of sin in your family.
>
> Ask God to replace the curse with blessings like His protection, love, and healing. Ask for the opposite of the sin: humility instead of pride, peace instead of fear, joy instead of anger, a thankful heart instead of ungratefulness, and grace that covers a multitude of sins.
>
> Ask for these gifts to be sealed according to His good and perfect will.

Please read Ephesians 3:16-19 as a prayer for you, your husband, and your children. Please underline the last sentence.

"I pray that from his glorious, unlimited resources he will empower you with inner strength through his Spirit. Then Christ will make his home in your hearts as you trust in him. Your roots will grow down into God's love and keep you strong. And may you have the power to understand, as all God's people should, how wide, how long, how high, and how deep his love is. May you experience the love of Christ, though it is too great to understand fully. Then you will be made complete with all the fullness of life and power that comes from God." (NLT)

A NEW FAMILY PATTERN

The story of Cain and Able is heartbreaking to read, but it was even more devastating for Eve. I can't imagine the grief of losing both of your precious sons because one brother killed the other in a fit of rage and jealousy and then never seeing the living son again because he was banished. Heartbreaking.

God, in His mercy, gave Eve another son. Genesis 4:25 gives us insight into Eve's heart. She named her new baby boy Seth and said, "God has granted me another child in place of Abel since Cain killed him."

Why do you think Eve gave credit to the "Lord" when Cain was born in Genesis 4:1, but Eve said that "God" granted her another child when Seth was born? (Genesis 4:25)

I am not sure what Eve was thinking, but we often use the names of God based on how God has revealed himself to us. Cain was born soon after Adam and Eve's exile from the Garden. The Lord's supremacy over every living thing, including their lives, was probably top of mind. Seth's birth may have reminded her of the time in the Garden when they walked with their Lord God, their Creator, and Provider, Designer, and Master.

Seth was a special child. Please read Genesis 5:3-4. How old was Adam when Seth was born?

Adam was 130 years old when Seth was born. After Seth was born, Adam lived 800 years and had other sons and daughters. So, Eve was probably a very, very old mom!

Genesis says that Seth was a son in his likeness, in his own image, a phrase that was also used when God created people. Genesis 1:27 says, "So God created human beings in his own image. In the image of God he created them; male and female he created them." (NLT)

Seth's birth was the beginning of a new relationship with God and a new generation of believers in God. Genesis 4:26 says, "Seth also had a son, and he named him Enosh. At that time, men began to call on the name of the LORD."

A new family pattern had begun; it would eventually bless the entire world. Please skim through Luke 3:23-38. Please use Luke 3:38 to fill in the blanks "the son of Enosh, the son of_____, the son of _____, the son of God.

Though sin came into the world, God provided His son, Jesus Christ, the great,… great-grandson of Eve, to reconcile us with God and each other. Though Eve's story started with a tragedy, God created a new life in her, and through her descendant Jesus, we all are redeemed because "God so loved the world that he gave his one and only Son, that whoever believes in him shall not perish but have eternal life." John 3:16

HOW HAVE YOU LEARNED TO TRUST GOD THROUGH STUDYING EVE?

CHAPTER II

Sarah

BEAUTIFUL PRINCESS

IMPATIENT WOMAN

Lived about 2,000 BC

For this is the way the holy women of the past who put their hope in God used to make themselves beautiful. They were submissive to their own husbands, like Sarah, who obeyed Abraham and called him her master. You are her daughters if you do what is right and do not give way to fear.
1 Peter 3:5-6

Week 1

Sarah

I was done, bored, and ready to try something new. After three years working in marketing for a small insurance firm, I was ready to look for another job. Two of my best friends had decided to pursue other opportunities, and I knew we wouldn't make our bonus goals that year. Why stay? I sent out resumes to several firms, and I was super excited to be contacted by a growing law firm specializing in new technology. It was a fantastic opportunity. The interview went well, but I had a pit in my stomach as I was driving back to work. At that instant, I knew that God's will was for me to stay in my current situation. Though my friends had left, and my pay would be less, there was no doubt in my mind that God's best for me was staying put.

Years later, I can look back at my decision to stay at that small company as a pivotal point in my life. Soon after, our firm was bought by a large bank which increased my career options. But even more importantly, I started meeting twice a month with a friend to do Bible studies together. I firmly believe spending that time in God's Word prepared me for writing Bible studies and helped me grow. In addition, because my two friends had left the company, I got to know a sweet girl named Dawn, and through our friendship, I was able to introduce her to Jesus, the greatest friend of all.

I wasn't happy in my job, but by being obedient to God's will, I was able to experience unexpected blessings in my life, introduce a dear friend to Jesus, and begin a foundation that has led to writing multiple Bible studies. If we are faithful to trust God despite our circumstances, God can use challenging situations to bless us and bless others through us.

Sarah's faithfulness in challenging situations is a model for all of us. As we learn about Sarah in this chapter, you also will learn to see God as your Lord and Almighty God. Sarah teaches us how to trust God in the face of fear, submit to God by submitting to our husband, trust God in impossible situations, and know God's plan in challenging circumstances. No one is perfect, including Sarah. Hopefully, we will also learn from her mistakes. We will see that when she didn't trust God and made decisions out of impatience, it led to significant problems in her relationships with others, including her husband.

SARAH'S BACKGROUND AND HISTORY

Sarah is a fascinating woman. She was born nearly 4,000 years ago in Ur, a thriving city on the edge of the Euphrates River. Sarah lived to be 127 years old (the only instance in the Bible where a woman's age is recorded.)[24] She was beautiful, impatient, and was probably a Daddy's girl. When she was born, she was named Sarai, which means "my princess." Her family included three brothers and her father, Terah, who had at least two wives. In the awkward way of royalty and ancient civilizations, Sarah was both the wife and the half-sister of Abraham.[25] Abraham was ten years older than Sarah.

To begin, let's start with a quick overview of her life. Sarah's early life involved moving from Ur, a civilized town on the banks of the Euphrates River, to rural Haran. When Sarah was 65 and Abraham was 75, they left Haran to go to Canaan in response to a promise from God.

A detour through Egypt resulted in Sarah briefly becoming a member of the Pharaoh's harem. A year later, Sarah, Abraham, and her Egyptian servant Hagar left the land of Pharaoh and returned to Canaan. Ten years after leaving Egypt, by age 76, Sarah had grown impatient with God because of her barrenness, and so she gave Abraham her servant, Hagar, to father a child.

Thirteen more years passed. When Sarah was 89 years old, she had a personal message from God, who changed her name from Sarai to Sarah. Sarah means "princess for all the races." God told Abraham that she would be the mother of nations and kings of peoples would come from her. At the same time, God changed Abram's name to "Abraham" which means "father of many nations." In Hebrew, adding ה, shown by "H" in their name is an indication of the spirit of God. I will call them Sarah and Abraham throughout the entire chapter for ease of reading. Quotations from scripture may use the names Abram and Sarai. When Sarah was 90 years old and her husband was 100, she gave birth to a precious baby boy named Isaac.

> *Sarah* was a remarkable woman. Though she struggled with impatience, she was a woman of faith who did what was right and did not give in to fear.

Over the course of this chapter, I hope that you will find that Sarah was a remarkable woman. Though she struggled with impatience, she was a woman of faith who did what was right and did not give in to fear. Sarah was commended for submitting to her husband. Submission is a complex topic for some, so I pray that you will study God's perspective on this topic with a heart to trust God in every aspect of your life. I know He will show you how to apply this in your life according to His will. As we study Sarah, we will look at how she handled a long-distance move to an unknown place and her relationships with Abraham and another woman. By examining the names that she uses for God, I hope we will expand our view of God as our Lord, God Most High, and God, Creator of life.

---

[24] M.G. Easton M.A., D.D., *Illustrated Bible Dictionary*, Third Edition, published by Thomas Nelson, 1897.
[25] Genesis 11:29; 20:12

LEAVING HOME

"And Terah took Abram his son, Lot the son of Haran, his grandson, and Sarai his daughter-in-law, his son Abram's wife, and they went forth together to go from Ur of the Chaldees into the land of Canaan; but when they came to Haran, they settled there."[26]

Sarah and Abraham's hometown was Ur of the Chaldees. Here's how it is described by the Amplified Bible in a footnote for Genesis 11:28.

"As the result of extensive archaeological excavations there by C. Leonard Woolley in 1922-34, a great deal is known about Abraham's background. Space will not permit more than a glimpse at excavated Ur, but a few items will show the high state of civilization.

The entire house of the average middle-class person had from ten to twenty rooms and measured forty to fifty-two feet; the lower floor was for servants, the upper floor for the family, with five rooms for their use; additionally, there was a guest chamber and a lavatory reserved for visitors, and a private chapel.

A school was found and what the students studied was shown by the clay tablets discovered there. In the days of Abraham the pupils had reading, writing, and arithmetic as today. They learned the multiplication and division tables and even worked at square and cube root. A bill of lading from about 2040 B.C. (about the era in which Abraham is believed to have lived) showed that the commerce of that time was far-reaching. Even the name "Abraham" has been found on the excavated clay tablets (J.P. Free, Archaeology and Bible History)."(AMP)

Based on what you just read, what type of life do you think our Princess Sarah lived?

Until I started researching Sarah and Abraham, I had no idea that Sarah was an ancient princess who probably lived in a house with 14 to 20 rooms, servants, and a lavatory. Scholars estimate that Ur had a population of 65,000 in 2030 BCE making it the largest city in the world.[27] Ur was in a lush, prosperous area. Leaving this place of civilization and extended family must have been difficult.

*Have you had to move to a new town or home to follow a new job opportunity? How would you respond if your husband said God told him to leave your home and go to a place that He would show him?

---

[26] Genesis 11:31
[27] http://geography.about.com/library/weekly/aa011201a.htm Four Thousand Years of Urban Growth: An Historical Census by Tertius Chandler. 1987, St. David's University Press.

Abraham and Sarah's move from Ur of Chaldees was the beginning of a long journey physically and spiritually for both of them. Their view of God became immensely personal when God called Abraham to a new land and a new opportunity with a great promise recorded in Genesis 12:1-3.

> The LORD had said to Abram,
>
> "Leave your country, your people and your father's household and go to the land I will show you.
>
> I will make you into a great nation and I will bless you;
>
> I will make your name great, and you will be a blessing.
>
> I will bless those who bless you,
>
> and whoever curses you I will curse;
>
> and all peoples on earth will be blessed through you."

In this passage, God said several specific things He would do for Abraham. Please write down the specific blessing that God said He would give Abraham if he left his country to go to the land that God would show him.

This was an amazing blessing, particularly for a man who had no children. God told Abraham to go to Canaan, that He would bless Abraham and make him a great nation. Wow! I'd even be willing to move after such a great promise in verses 2-3.

How would this blessing affect Sarah? Sarah left her home and everything she knew because of her husband's calling to Canaan. What hope did she have in moving?

Sarah was 65 and barren. They both hoped moving to the place that God told them to go to would result in a child. Sarah hoped to establish her home in Canaan and have a baby to hold.

It seems like good things are about to happen to Abraham and Sarah; let's find out what happens next, "So Abram left, as the LORD had told him; and Lot went with him. Abram was seventy-five years old when he set out from Haran. He took his wife Sarai, his nephew Lot, all the possessions they had accumulated and the people they had acquired in Haran, and they set out for the land of Canaan, and they arrived there."[28]

---

[28] Genesis 12:4-5

Sarah and Abraham's journey to the Promised Land required a lot of traveling. Please draw a line on the map starting with her journey from Ur to Haran, then continue the line tracking her journey throughout Canaan to Egypt, based on the following passage.

"Abram traveled through the land as far as the site of the great tree of Moreh at Shechem. At that time the Canaanites were in the land. The LORD appeared to Abram and said, "To your offspring I will give this land." So he built an altar there to the LORD, who had appeared to him. From there he went on toward the hills east of Bethel and pitched his tent, with Bethel on the west and Ai on the east. There he built an altar to the LORD and called on the name of the LORD. Then Abram set out and continued toward the Negev. Now there was a famine in the land, and Abram went down to Egypt to live there for a while because the famine was severe."[29]

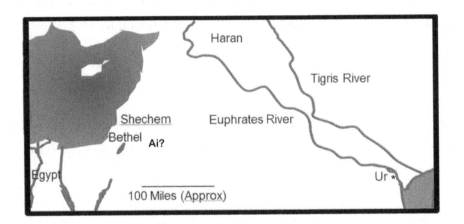

Sarah's daily reality of traveling from town to town during a famine was dramatically different from her dreams of a home and a family. Even when we think we know God's plan and timing, our journey is often different than we expect. Imagine her heartbreak as her dreams were crushed every month of this challenging journey when she realized she was not pregnant. Even though God had directly communicated to Abraham that He would make Abraham a great nation, the day-to-day reality of their situation was in direct contrast to the Word of God. Yet, Sarah had faith despite her circumstances. Hebrews 11:11 says, "It was by faith that even Sarah was able to have a child, though she was barren and was too old. She believed that God would keep his promise." (NLT)

---

[29] Genesis 12:6-10

Change is risky and hard, but it is just as risky not to change and potentially much harder. Only God knows the future and the plans that He has for you.

Embracing change means trusting if God calls you to do something, even if it is hard; it is better than any other alternative. Living in God's will may be challenging, just as traveling through a foreign land with no hotels, restaurants, or air-conditioning was difficult for Sarah and Abraham. But just as God promised blessings to Abraham and Sarah, God has amazing blessings for you if you stay in His will. We can learn from Sarah how to believe God would keep His promise.

> Change is risky and hard, but it is just as risky to not change and potentially much harder.

We must base our faith in God on His faithfulness rather than our circumstances. Please write down the following scriptures about God's faithfulness.

Deuteronomy 7:9

2 Thessalonians 3:3

1 John 1:9

God is Faithful! Take a minute to pray and thank God for His faithfulness. We all slip, fail and doubt. But God is faithful to forgive, love, strengthen, and protect us. If you are struggling to trust God in an area of your life, ask Him to increase your faith. You can pray like the father in Mark 9:24, "I believe, help my unbelief."

Week 2

SARAH'S RELATIONSHIP WITH HER HUSBAND

An area that I frequently struggled with when I first got married (and still do at times) is the idea of submitting to my husband. I resist in the little things of submitting to my husband's opinion of what type of coffee we buy or how often I give my kids vitamins. I also struggle in significant areas of submitting, like how we spend our time and money. I am an independent, intelligent woman. So, submitting to another imperfect human, my husband, didn't make sense to me. Yet my heart desires above all to submit to God, and God calls wives to be submissive to their husbands. Sarah was commended as a woman who put her hope in God because she was submissive to her husband. Let's find out more about what that means.

Please read 1 Peter 3:5-6 and write it down.

This verse encourages modern women to model themselves after women in the past. "For this is the way the holy women of the past who put their hope in God used to make themselves beautiful. They were submissive to their own husbands, like Sarah, who obeyed Abraham and called him her master. You are her daughters if you do what is right and do not give way to fear."

From Sarah, we can learn two foundational concepts to understand this complex subject, first, to do what is right and second, to not give way to fear. Let's examine some other places in the Bible that also include these two phrases.

DO WHAT IS RIGHT

Each of the following verses contains the phrase, "Do what is right." They show why this is important and the blessings of doing what is right. Please underline the benefits of doing right. Choose one verse that you want to apply to your life. In the margin, write a note about why you chose this verse.

Genesis 18:18-19 "Abraham will surely become a great and powerful nation, and all nations on earth will be blessed through him. For I have chosen him, so that he will direct his children and his household after him to keep the way of the LORD by doing what is right and just, so that the LORD will bring about for Abraham what he has promised him."

Deuteronomy 6:17-19 "Be sure to keep the commands of the LORD your God and the stipulations and decrees he has given you. Do what is right and good in the LORD's sight, so that it may go well with you and you may go in and take over the good land that the LORD promised on oath to your forefathers, thrusting out all your enemies before you, as the LORD said."

Proverbs 21:3 "To do what is right and just is more acceptable to the LORD than sacrifice."

Jeremiah 23:5 "The days are coming," declares the LORD, "when I will raise up to David a righteous Branch, a King who will reign wisely and do what is just and right in the land."

Daniel 4:27 "Therefore, O king, be pleased to accept my advice: Renounce your sins by doing what is right, and your wickedness by being kind to the oppressed. It may be that then your prosperity will continue."

Acts 10:34-36 "Then Peter began to speak: "I now realize how true it is that God does not show favoritism but accepts men from every nation who fear him and do what is right."

Romans 12:16-18 "Live in harmony with one another. Do not be proud, but be willing to associate with people of low position Do not be conceited. Do not repay anyone evil for evil. Be careful to do what is right in the eyes of everybody. If it is possible, as far as it depends on you, live at peace with everyone."

Romans 13:2-4 "Consequently, he who rebels against the authority is rebelling against what God has instituted, and those who do so will bring judgment on themselves. For rulers hold no terror for those who do right, but for those who do wrong. Do you want to be free from fear of the one in authority? Then do what is right and he will commend you. For he is God's servant to do you good. But if you do wrong, be afraid, for he does not bear the sword for nothing. He is God's servant, an agent of wrath to bring punishment on the wrongdoer."

1 John 3:7 "Dear children, do not let anyone lead you astray. He who does what is right is righteous, just as he is righteous."

Based on these scriptures, how would you define what it means to "do what is right?"

DO NOT GIVE IN TO FEAR

Peter commends Sarah because she did not give in to fear. Without a doubt, fear keeps me from trusting God and from being submissive to my husband. Sometimes my fear is based on selfishness and a need for control; I am afraid that if I do what God wants, I won't get what I want. Sometimes my fears have to do with consequences I don't like. I also struggle with fears that my husband could be wrong, my kids would be hurt, or I would lose myself and my identity. Other worries have to do with the future; I am afraid that bad things will happen to my children or something I love.

Have you struggled with fear?

Are there fears that keep you in control and keep you from submitting to God and your husband or parents?

Fear is a powerful motivator. One of the most damaging results of unbridled fear is letting our fears control our thoughts and actions rather than allowing God to control us. Our greatest fear should be for God because He is more powerful than anything else. Sarah is commended because she did not give in to fear- she was afraid- but she did not let her fear control her. Instead, she chose to let God control her, and she did what was right even though she was scared.

Becoming woman who "does not give in to fear" requires trusting God. Each of the following verses has an antidote to fear to help us not be afraid. <u>Underline how we cannot give into fear.</u>

Isaiah 12:2" Surely God is my salvation; I will trust and not be afraid. The LORD, the LORD himself, is my strength and my defense; he has become my salvation."

2 Timothy 1:7 "God has not given us a spirit of fear but of power, love and a sound mind." (KJV)

1 Peter 3:13-16 "Who is going to harm you if you are eager to do good? But even if you should suffer for what is right, you are blessed. "Do not fear what they fear; do not be frightened." But in your hearts revere Christ as Lord. Always be prepared to give an answer to everyone who asks you to give the reason for the hope that you have. But do this with gentleness and respect,"

1 John 4:16 "And so we know and rely on the love God has for us. God is love. Whoever lives in love lives in God, and God in them. This is how love is made complete among us so that we will have confidence on the Day of Judgment: In this world we are like Jesus. There is no fear in love. But perfect love drives out fear, because fear has to do with punishment. The one who fears is not made perfect in love."

Hebrews 13:5 -7 "Keep your lives free from the love of money and be content with what you have, because God has said, "Never will I leave you; never will I forsake you." So we say with confidence, "The Lord is my helper; I will not be afraid. What can mere mortals do to me?"

* Focusing on God's word through meditation and memorization will take our minds off our worries. Choose one or all of these verses to write out on an index card to put on a mirror or in your Bible as a bookmark.

In the midst of your places of fear- who do you need God to be?

Knowing God helps us embrace change and stand against fear.
Whatever we fear, God is the antidote.
God is love, and perfect love casts out fear.
God has given us power, love, and a sound mind.
God is always with us. He is our helper, and He will never leave us or forsake us.
He is our Salvation, our strength, and our defense.
Hold fast to Him. He will heal you, protect you, guide you, love you, empower you, help you, and defend you.
Keeping God's Word in our hearts will help us trust him, just as hearing the voice of a loved one can comfort us.

An Extreme Example of Submitting

While I struggle to submit in many of the minor daily areas of life, Sarah faced much more significant challenges when it came to submitting to her husband, Abraham. Genesis 12:11- 20 tells a particular story of when Sarah submitted to her husband. Keep in mind that Sarah was at least 65 years old[30] when this story takes place.

---

[30] Genesis 12:4

Please read Genesis 12:11-20 to answer the following questions.

What word is used to describe Sarah?

What motivated Abraham to give Sarah up?

What happened to Pharaoh?

What happened to Abraham after Pharaoh found out who Sarah was?

Sarah must have been stunningly beautiful since she was at least 65, and Abraham thought that the Egyptians would kill him for her! Though we just read that Sarah was commended as a woman who did not give in to fear- the same couldn't be said for her husband. Abraham was motivated by fear. For Abraham, the fear of being killed loomed larger than his faith in God's promise. Though logically, God's promise that Abraham would be a father of nations couldn't be fulfilled if Pharaoh killed him. But in Abraham's panic-stricken mind, they were mutually exclusive.

In contrast, Sarah showed radical faith by submitting to Abraham even though he made decisions out of fear and not faith. As a result, Sarah was taken into Pharaoh's harem and treated as one of his concubines. But God miraculously delivered Sarah from the harem by inflicting severe diseases on Pharaoh. As a result of Sarah's faithfulness, Abram even acquired sheep and cattle, male and female donkeys, menservants and maidservants, and camels.

Sometimes I tell my boys the Bible is "R-Rated." This is one of those stories. Can you imagine if your husband told you to lie and then expected you to join another man's harem? How would you feel?

Wow! This is an extreme example of Sarah's submission; it goes way beyond my struggles of where to get my hair cut or whether to put Starbucks or Dunkin' Donuts coffee in the coffee maker. Obviously, there is a lot of weird stuff going on here, and we need to make sure we understand what "submit" really means as 21st-century women.

In your opinion, should you submit to your husband? What do you think it means to submit?

"Submit" in the www.blueletterbible.com lexicon for this verse had the following Greek word and definition. Submit - Strong's G5293 – hypotassō - ὑποτάσσω Pronunciation hü-po-tä's-sō (Key) 1) to arrange under, to subordinate, 2) to subject, put in subjection, 3) to subject one's self, obey, 4) to submit to one's control, 5) to yield to one's admonition or advice, 6) to obey, be subject

This word was a Greek military term meaning "to arrange [troop divisions] in a military fashion under the command of a leader." In non-military use, it was "a voluntary attitude of giving in, cooperating, assuming responsibility, and carrying a burden."[31] I like this picture of carrying one another's burdens. If you think about a military mission, everyone has a job to do, and the entire team is working toward the same goal. That's how our marriages should be. At a Family Life Marriage Conference, I heard it described as a situation where two equal ranking military leaders work together on a joint mission when one "ranks down" to let the other leader be in charge. It is important to note that our ultimate commander is God. In God's eyes, we are all equal, both male and female. Our mission is to carry out his will.

Here is another verse to think about- Please look up and write out this scripture.
Ephesians 5:21

Ephesians 5:21 is a verse that specifically deals with mutual submission to one another by church members. The previous verses in Ephesians talk about submitting to others in the church, just as Christ loved the church and gave himself up it, by walking in the way of love, abstaining from obscenity, foolish talk, coarse joking, and other inappropriate behavior. If you and your husband are believers, you are *both* called to submit to one another as you would submit to a leader in your church like a pastor or elder. Biblical submission isn't about someone making another person submit, but it is about the choice of one person to submit to the other.

Ephesians 5:22-32 adds more specific information on how this relates to husbands and wives.
Please read this passage and explain how these could apply in your life.

Please read 1 Peter 3:5-7, and in light of what you just read in Ephesians 5- what are we called to do?

---

[31] http://www.blueletterbible.org/lang/lexicon/lexicon.cfm?Strongs=G5293&t=KJV

We are to submit to our husbands and those in authority over us. However, if you are like me, this is easier said than done because of sin in my heart and my husband's. He's not perfect any more than I am, so my natural response is to question why I should submit to him. I so strongly want things done my way that I struggle to submit even if my husband's way is actually better. Several years ago, my husband gave me a gift certificate to get a haircut and pedicure at a lovely salon. Rather than appreciating such a wonderful gift, I was upset about the cost and didn't want to go. However, once I chose to submit and go to the salon, I had a wonderful time, I felt relaxed and pampered, and I was blessed by following my husband's will.

My first response is often driven by fear but what comes out is anger as I question God about why I even need to listen to my husband.

I struggled to submit in this small area of where I got my hair cut. Submitting is much more difficult when I disagree or think my husband is making a decision that may cost us financially or result in something I don't agree with. My first response is often driven by fear, but anger comes out of me as I question why I should listen to my husband. If God wanted me to be a robot that does everything my husband says why did He give me a brain and free will? My attitude and resistance to submitting to my husband mirrors my resistance in submitting to God in all areas of my life. I have the same questions regarding submitting to God. I ask God "why" a lot. I question if His way really is the best and I fail to follow through on things that I know He has called me to do because I think I've got a better handle on the situation than God. Obviously, my ways are not better than God's ways and my thoughts are not superior to His. However, in many areas of my life I stumble along thinking that my way is better than God's way.

Through trial and error, I've learned God's ways are always the best. I can look back on dating relationships, financial decisions, and life choices to see evidence in my life when I made choices based on my will or when I made choices based on God's will. Without a doubt, the greatest joys and blessings in my life have come from choosing God's will over my own. On the surface, God's will may appear more complicated or difficult to obey, but when I decide to do things my way, I have found that life gets really, really hard. It's like swimming upstream against a flash flood—difficult, dangerous, and futile.

Here's what I've learned: God's will is for wives to submit to their husbands. If I am not willing to submit to God's will in my relationship with my husband, I am not submitting to God. The same logic holds true for kids obeying their parents. When kids choose to disobey their parents, they are disobeying God, who commanded children to obey their parents.[32] Single women also fall under the authority of their parents. As a result, a lack of submission to parents or our husbands is a sin because we are not submitting to God. (I talk more about obedience to parents in my books, *Responding to God, Learning from the Life and Legacy of Hezekiah,* and in *Seeing Value, A Biblical perspective on Intrinsic Value.*)

---

[32] Ephesians 6:1-3

Important exceptions are in situations of abuse and outright sin. Physical abuse distorts the marriage covenant between a husband and a wife. Just as if a platoon leader started attacking a soldier under his command, spousal abuse violates the marriage vows. Abuse is the opposite of the meaning of Ephesians 5:25-28, "Husbands, love your wives, just as Christ loved the church and gave himself up for her …. In this same way, husbands ought to love their wives as their own bodies. He who loves his wife loves himself." If you are in an abusive relationship, it is critical to seek help from a pastor or a domestic violence hotline (1-800-799-7233.)

Submission to parents and our husband does not remove the fact that God is our ultimate authority in all areas of our lives. We must do what is right. In situations of outright sin, such as a husband asking a wife to commit fraud, join a brothel, steal, or do drugs, we have a resource that Sarah did not have; we have the Holy Spirit, who will instruct us in the way we should go. *Each of us is individually accountable to God for our actions.* God must be the ultimate authority in our lives. Putting another person's opinion above God's Word is a form of idolatry.

Henry and Richard Blackaby captured this idea in this paragraph about spiritual authority, "Christians are commanded to voluntarily submit to those in authority because God has, out of his sovereignty, allowed those leaders to hold office (Rom 13:1-1). But people are not to obey leaders blindly and unquestioningly, simply because of the position they hold. Scripture is clear that all must give an account to Christ for everything they have done, regardless of who told them to do it. (2 Cor. 5:10) Christ does not need a mediator to exercise his lordship over people. The Holy Spirit dwells within each believer, leaders and followers alike, guiding, teaching, and convicting every Christian… While God may choose to work through leaders to accomplish his purposes, obeying a leader is not necessarily equal to obeying God; God will tolerate no substitutes for a personal relationship with him. He exercises his lordship directly over his followers. People who obey leaders as though they were responding to God are in danger of committing idolatry."[33]

> **Submission to parents and to our husband does not remove the fact that in all areas of our lives, God is our ultimate authority.**

Submitting to our parents when we are young and submitting to our husbands after marriage is a training ground for submitting to God. It is much harder to submit to an authority that we can't see than one we live with.

When we train our children to submit to our authority as parents, we are ultimately teaching them to submit to God. When we as wives submit to our husbands, we are modeling for our children how to submit to God. So, here's a bit of advice to all the single girls out there—don't marry someone you cannot/ will not/ do not respect enough to submit to.

---

[33] Blackaby, Henry and Richard, *Spiritual Leadership: Moving People on to God's Agenda.* B&H Publishing Group Nashville TN 2001. 91.

But you may say it's too late for me, I am married, and my husband, unlike God, is not perfect. You are right; no husband is perfect, no parent is perfect, and neither are you. No one is perfect- yet God commands children to obey their imperfect parents and all of us to submit to those flawed people in authority over us.[34]

Our submission is ultimately not to our husband or our parents but to God. Here's how Voddie Baucham explains this concept, "Your submission is not about how you feel about your husband. You're not submitting to your husband because he's worthy of your submission. You're submitting to your husband, in spite of the fact that he will never be worthy of your submission. Show me a woman who is waiting for her husband to be worthy of her submission and I'll show you a woman who has no intention to submit. You submit to your husband "as to the Lord." Your submission to your husband is a picture of your submission to Christ. If you are not submissive to your husband, you are not submissive to Christ! You don't have a man problem; you have a worship problem!"[35]

Submission isn't trusting that our husband will do the right thing or make the right choice as much as it is believing that God is all-powerful and can change a bad situation for good. Romans 8:28 says, "And we know that in all things God works for the good of those who love him, who have been called according to his purpose." In tough and challenging times, God will work things for your good as you love Him and follow His purpose. Another great verse on this topic is from 2 Peter 2:9, "… the Lord knows how to rescue the godly from trials and to hold the unrighteous for punishment on the Day of Judgment." Just as God rescued Sarah from Pharaoh's harem, God knows how to save you. God is full of mercy, but he is also a just God. Trust that God will hold the unrighteous for punishment.

Submission... **is trusting that God is all powerful and can change a bad situation for good.**

If we trust God to take care of us, we also need to trust that God will work in those who are in authority over us. Proverbs 21:1 says, "The king's heart is in the hand of the LORD; he directs it like a watercourse wherever he pleases." As I read this Proverb, I substitute the name for the authorities in my life, so when I read it, I think, "My husband's heart is in the hand of the Lord; God will direct his heart just as he directs the course of a river." God can change the way of a river through a flood, drought, or hurricane; in the same way, God can change the actions and hearts of those in authority over us. Our mission is to trust God and to get out of God's way by being submissive so that God can change the course of someone else's heart.

Take a minute to pray and aske the Holy Spirit to help you trust him and to protect you (and your kids) as you submit to your parents or husband.

---

[34] 1 Peter 2:13
[35] http://familylifetoday.com/program/the-value-of-submission/

SUBMITTING TO AUTHORITIES BY SUBMITTING TO GOD

How do we submit to God by submitting to authorities? That's a good question and the answer is not always the same, even in very similar circumstances. To explore the idea that circumstances do not determine God's will, let's compare two similar stories found in the Book of Acts: Paul and Silas in prison in Acts 16 and Peter's imprisonment in Acts 12. Let's start with the story of Peter's imprisonment. Here's some background, King Herod persecuted and arrested many followers of Christ, including James, the brother of John, who he had killed. These actions pleased the Jewish leadership, so Herod decided to arrest Peter. Herod intended to bring him out of prison for public trial after the Passover.

Please read Acts 12:6-11 and write a summary of Peter's situation and what God did. Did Peter stay or leave in the situation?

This is a remarkable story. Peter was in prison, and God miraculously sent an angel to deliver him from captivity. Peter wisely followed the angel out of jail. This story shows God's powerful ability to supernaturally deliver us from hopeless situations. Without a doubt, God can save us from the most miserable, painful problems. He has come to set the captives free and has paid the ransom for our freedom. Trust Him. But keep in mind—this doesn't always happen.

Please read Act 16 and summarize Paul and Silas' situation and what God did in this chapter. Did Paul and Silas stay or leave the situation?

Acts 16 tells the story of Paul and Silas, who were in Philippi sharing the good news of Jesus. Some people were upset with Paul and Silas, so they had them stripped, beaten, flogged, and thrown in prison. At midnight that night, God caused an earthquake to shake the jail so that the doors flew open, and the chains came loose. The jailer woke up, and when he saw the prison doors were open, he was about to kill himself because he thought the prisoners had escaped. But Paul shouted to let the jailer know that all the prisoners were still in jail. In amazement, the jailer rushed to Paul and Silas to ask them how he could be saved. Paul explained to him the way of salvation, his whole family, and he believed.

These godly men were in very similar conditions; they had all been imprisoned for doing what was right. Their situations were unjust and unfair. And God supernaturally intervened in both. He created an earthquake that removed Paul and Silas's shackles and opened the prison gates. To Peter, he sent an angel that miraculously removed Peter's chains and opened the doors.

While their circumstances appear very similar, God's will for these prisoners was very different. For Peter, God's will was for him to escape the prison. For Paul and Silas, God's will was for them to stay in this horrible situation so that the jailer and his family would be saved. Sometimes our freedom and comfort as believers is not as important to God as the eternal salvation of a person or an entire family.

These stories illustrate an important concept—our circumstances do not always indicate God's will in a situation. Just because God caused the earthquake and loosened Paul and Silas' shackles did not mean that they should leave the prison. They had to follow God's will despite what looked like the obvious answer to their prayers. As we strive to follow God's will in submitting to our husbands and those in authority over us, it is essential to remember this point: God's will for each of us is specific to our situation and the purpose He has for us. Sometimes God will remove us from a challenging situation, and other times God will call us to stay, regardless of our discomfort, so that His plan to save a family can be carried out. Without a doubt, God will sacrifice our short-term comfort and happiness for the eternal joy of another person's salvation.

Our comfort as believers is not as important to God as the eternal salvation of a person or an entire family.

Knowing God's will in any situation starts with knowing His voice. I frequently pray for God to give me ears to hear him. We get to know God's voice by praying, reading the Bible, and seeking him. God has given us the Holy Spirit to lead and guide us.

It is easy to know the voices of the people we love and spend time with. When my dad calls me on the phone, I don't have to check caller ID to see who it is; I know his voice as soon as he says, "Hi Penny, I was thinking of you." Just as sheep know and follow their shepherd's voice, we need to make sure that we listen to God and obey his voice in whatever situation we find ourselves.[36]

Other believers will try to give us advice based on their experience and understanding. False prophets and ungodly people will also weigh in on our situation. None of them are God. While it is wise to seek godly counsel, remember, the ultimate authority in our lives must be our LORD, Jesus Christ. Only God can tell us His will in any given circumstance.

EMBRACING CHANGE BY TRUSTING GOD

This week's lesson on Sarah provided a provocative perspective on submission. I can't imagine going through what she endured. Sarah was commended because she did what was right and did not give in to fear. We must believe that God is more powerful than anything in the universe. Giving in to fear keeps us from doing the right thing and indicates that we believe our fear is more powerful than God.

[36] John 10:14-15

God has given us the Holy Spirit, our counselor who will give us supernatural wisdom in seemingly impossible situations. Sometimes, the wisest thing is to get out of a bad environment as soon as God opens the door, just like Peter. Other times, God opens the door, but His best requires staying in a miserable place for the benefit of others.

If you or someone you love is facing a difficult situation, take the time to read the Bible and pray for God to open your eyes and show you His will.

Week 3

OUR PLANS VERSUS GOD'S PLANS

After Abraham and Sarah left Egypt with their animals, gold, and servants, including Sarah's Egyptian maid named Hagar, they traveled to the Negev and then to Bethel. After this the LORD expanded His promise to make Abraham a great nation, "Look around from where you are, to the north and south, to the east and west. All the land that you see, I will give to you and your offspring forever. I will make your offspring like the dust of the earth; so that if anyone could count the dust, then your offspring could be counted. Go, walk through the length and breadth of the land, for I am giving it to you."[37]

In the following passages underline the Name of God and note in the margin how God shows His lordship in these situations. (I completed the first one for you.)

Gen 12:7 "The <u>Lord</u> appeared to Abram and said, 'To your offspring I will give this land.' So he built an altar there to the <u>Lord</u>, who had appeared to him."

Said he would give land to offspring

Gen 12:17 "But the Lord inflicted serious diseases on Pharaoh and his household because of Abram's wife Sarai."

---

[37] Genesis 13:14-17

Gen 13:14-16 "The Lord said to Abram after Lot had parted from him, 'Look around from where you are, to the north and south, to the east and west. All the land that you see I will give to you and your offspring forever. I will make your offspring like the dust of the earth,'"

How does knowing that the Lord is sovereign over these areas help you trust Him?

Abraham learned that the Lord is master over the land and its resources, and the Lord has authority over diseases and healing. Abraham had grown up in a pagan society where the people believed in multiple gods, and each one had dominion over an area like land, fertility, or even water. The people who lived in the lands around Abraham had multiple gods. As Abraham was journeying to a land that the Lord would show him, he had to trust that the land belonged to the Lord and that the Lord would give it to his descendants. As Abraham and Sarah dealt with her continued infertility, Abraham learned that the Lord was sovereign over sickness, disease, and healing.

Abraham and Sarah's view of God was shaped by what they had personally learned about God through their life experiences and what they had been told about God. The creation story was passed down from the first man, Adam, to his descendants. They had heard about their Creator- Elohim, and their Lord- Yahweh (Jehovah). As Abraham and Sarah learned more about God and experienced His power in their lives, they trusted Him more.

A GREATER VIEW OF GOD

As Abraham grew to know his Creator and Lord, he understood that God was sovereign, ruler of all kings and peoples. Through this journey through the land of Canaan, Abraham's view of God expands to see God as the God of all other gods, the Most High God. Elyon was the name given to the highest of the Canaanite deities[38].

Please underline the name "God Most High" in the following passages.

> *God* אל *'el*
>
> *Most* עליון *'elyown*
>
> *High.* עליון *'elyown*

Gen 14:18 "Then Melchizedek king of Salem brought out bread and wine. He was priest of God Most High,"

---

[38] Spangler, 294

Gen 14:22 "But Abram said to the king of Sodom, "I have raised my hand to the Lord, God Most High, Creator of heaven and earth, and have taken an oath.""

How would knowing that God Most High was sovereign over all other gods and idols help Abraham? How can you apply this to your life?

IMPATIENCE LEADS TO "HELPING" GOD

A couple of years later, God spoke with Abraham again. Then the word of the LORD came to him: "This man will not be your heir, but a son who is your own flesh and blood will be your heir." He took him outside and said, "Look up at the sky and count the stars—if indeed you can count them." Then he said to him, "So shall your offspring be." Abram believed the LORD, and he credited it to him as righteousness.[39]" While Abraham believed the LORD, Sarah to doubt that she would have a son. Ten years had passed since leaving Egypt; Sarah was tired of waiting for the start of a new nation. She wanted children to make her descendants as numerous as the stars. But God had made promises to Abraham, not to her specifically. She was now 76 years old, she had probably started menopause, and realistically, she did not think she could have a child. So, she decided to help God along.

Even with the **best intentions we can absolutely go down the completely wrong path.**

Have you ever grown impatient with God's plan and timing?

Please read Genesis 16:1-6 - What was Sarah's plan?

After Sarah's plan backfired, who did Sarah blame for the problem?

Do you think this is fair or not? When have you had a similar reaction?

This story illustrates an important lesson; even with the best intentions, we can go down the completely wrong path. Sarah's plan involved giving Abraham her servant to see if she could have a baby. Abraham agreed to do what Sarah said. So, Sarah gave her Egyptian maid Hagar to her husband as a wife. After

---

[39] Genesis 15:5

Hagar learned she was pregnant, she looked down on her mistress. Sarah told Abraham, "It's all your fault that I'm suffering this abuse. I put my maid in bed with you and the minute she knows she's pregnant; she treats me like I'm nothing. May the LORD decide which of us is right."[40] Hagar's pregnancy confirmed a sad reality of Sarah's life: she was infertile. Abraham wasn't the problem; she was. Her grief magnified, and so she lashed out at Abraham.

I was surprised that Sarah blamed Abraham for Hagar's attitude toward her and that she told him God would decide who was right. This didn't seem fair to me. It was Sarah's idea. Then I realized that while Sarah had the idea, Abraham carried it out. He listened to what made sense rather than trusting what God had already told him. Our default must be to hold on to God's Word and his message to us rather than let public opinion or even our own limited understanding guide our steps.

The plan to make a great nation out of Abraham's descendants was God's idea. Don't you think that if God had wanted Abraham to take a wife other than Sarah, He would have told Abraham directly? Sarah probably had good intentions to "help" God fulfill the prophecy that Abraham would be the father of nations, but she gave bad advice based on her impatience with God's timing. Yet the responsibility for this wrong decision rests with Abraham. Abraham had heard from God on multiple occasions, but he didn't stop to inquire of the Lord in this instance. This is an important lesson for all of us- if God has told us something, we need to believe that God will carry it out. We don't have to "help" God; instead, we must be obedient by doing what God has told us.

We get trapped by what we see, what makes sense and what we can do, and so we limit God to what we know and understand rather than focusing on God's perspective, His Glory, His unlimited resources and what HE can do.

Sarah's idea to "help" God had dire consequences. The consequences reverberated through Abraham, Sarah's, and Hagar's lives and modern history. First, Sarah's relationship with Hagar was ruined. It is likely that Hagar and Sarah had become friends during Sarah's time in Pharaoh's harem. When Sarah left Egypt, she probably took Hagar with her as a servant and as a friend. Without a doubt, Abraham's sleeping with Hagar and Hagar's pregnancy changed the relationship for both women. Second, it changed Sarah's relationship with her husband. There was now "another woman" in the relationship, and after Ishmael's birth, Abraham's time was split between Sarah and his new son. Third, the consequences for all of us are ongoing. Sarah's decision to give Hagar to Abraham has led to generations of fighting between the Jews (descendants of Sarah) and the Arabs (descendants of Hagar.)

Our actions and seemingly small decisions can have huge ramifications. If Sarah and Abraham hadn't tried to "help" and had instead trusted God's timing and plan rather than doing what made sense at the time, the entire course of world history could have changed.

---

[40] Genesis 16:5 MSG

Isaiah contains a verse that puts God's ways and plans in perspective. Isaiah 55:9 says, "As the heavens are higher than the earth, so are my ways higher than your ways and my thoughts than your thoughts." We often get trapped by what we see, what makes sense, and what we can do, and so we limit God to what we know and understand rather than focusing on God's perspective, His Glory, His unlimited resources, and what HE can do. Trusting God means that we have to trust God's timing and have patience with His plan.

Abraham and Sarah thought that they would help God's plan along. However, there is a fine line between using the gifts and resources God has given us to carry out His will and coming up with our own solution. Trusting what God has told us and living it out while waiting on God is a difficult balance that can only happen when we focus on God's abilities, His provision, and His power.

What are your thoughts? Is there an area where God has called you to "go" like He called Abraham and Sarah? Is there an area where you need to trust God and wait?

Week 4

A NEW PERSPECTIVE OF GOD

The names people call us give insight into our relationship with them. To my sons, I am Mom; to the teller at the bank, I am Mrs. Noyes, and to the boys on my soccer team, I am Coach. To my husband, I am Sweetie, and my friends call me Penny. We use different names for God to denote our understanding of his character and our relationship with Him. As we will soon learn, God gave Sarah and Abraham new names to signify their changed roles in history as the father and mother of nations.

After many years of waiting, God finally addressed Sarah's question if she was to be the vessel for the promised child. In Genesis 17, God renews his covenant with Abraham, and He includes Sarah in the promise.

Gen 17:1 "When Abram was ninety-nine years old, the LORD appeared to him and said, "I am God Almighty; walk before me faithfully and be blameless. Then I will make my covenant between me and you and will greatly increase your numbers. Abram fell facedown, and God said to him, "As for me, this is my covenant with you: You will be the father of many nations. No longer will you be called Abram; your name will be Abraham, for I have made you a father of many nations." …. God also said to Abraham, "As for Sarai your wife, you are no longer to call her Sarai; her name will be Sarah. I will bless her and will surely give you a son by her. I will bless her so that she will be the mother of nations; kings of peoples will come from her.""

Please answer the following questions based on the passage you just read in Genesis 17. What name did God use for Himself?

God changed Abram's name to Abraham which means _____

God changed Sarai's name to _____ **which means** _____

What blessings did God say He would give Sarah?

In Biblical times, names were not just a way to identify someone but a way to understand who they were: their character and personality. The LORD (Master) wanted Abraham and Sarah to know more of his character, and so he told them His name of *El Shadday*, God Almighty. El Shadday means God, "the Mountain One."[41] God is seen as strong and unchanging just like the mountains. "Nothing can prevent El Shadday, our almighty God from carrying out his plans and pouring out his blessings on those who belong to him. Pain, confusion, struggle and difficulty are inevitable, but God can use even these to bless us as we trust in him.[42] God wanted Abraham and Sarah to know his power; He was able to carry out his covenant with them to bless them and make them into more than what they could be on their own.

God changed Abram's name which means "my father is exalted" to Abraham, "father of many nations." Sarai went from being "my princess" to Sarah, which means "mother of nations." Though

---

[41] Spangler, pg. 42
[42] Ibid pg. 48

Abraham and Sarah were too old to have a child on their own, Almighty God changed them from childless to being parents. God changed both Abram and Sarai's names because they were one. Together God would use them to bless the whole world as the father and mother of nations. When God changed their names, He changed who they were. Just as God changed Abraham and Sarah's identities, in Christ, you have a new identity, you are a new creation.[43] God has a mission for you and an identity in Him that goes beyond anything that you could do on your own.

NAMES SARAH USES FOR GOD

Sarah most often uses the name "LORD - יהוה Yĕhovah" meaning "the existing one." It is the proper name for God. It captures the idea that He was her LORD and Master.

Please underline the word "Lord" in the following passages. In the margin write what the LORD was responsible for.

Gen 16:2 "so she said to Abram, "The Lord has kept me from having children. Go, sleep with my maidservant; perhaps I can build a family through her." Abram agreed to what Sarai said."

Gen 16:5 "Then Sarai said to Abram, "You are responsible for the wrong I am suffering. I put my servant in your arms, and now that she knows she is pregnant, she despises me. May the Lord judge between you and me."

Gen 18:10-12 "Then the LORD said, "I will surely return to you about this time next year, and Sarah your wife will have a son." Now Sarah was listening at the entrance to the tent, which was behind him. Abraham and Sarah were already old and well advanced in years, and Sarah was past the age of childbearing. So Sarah laughed to herself as she thought, "After I am worn out and my master is old, will I now have this pleasure?"

Gen 18:13-14 "When the LORD said to Abraham, "Why did Sarah laugh and say, 'Will I really have a child, now that I am old?' Is anything too hard for the LORD? I will return to you at the appointed time next year and Sarah will have a son."

Do you view God as your LORD? How does that affect the way you live?

---

[43] 2 Corinthians 5:17

AT AGE 89, HISTORY REPEATS ITSELF!

Have you ever felt like you had to go through the same situation more than once? Poor Sarah! She had a moment of Déjà vu at age 89 when she and her husband moved to the Kingdom of Gerar, and she became a member of Abimelech's harem. First, she was in Pharaoh's harem. Fourteen years later, at age 89, she was in Abimelech's harem! As I continued to read her story, I thought she must have wondered, "Why do I have to go through this situation again? Didn't I do what was right the first time? "I am 89 and way too old for this!" This story isn't about history repeating itself but a reminder of God's protection, restoration, and the power of prayer.

Please read Genesis 20:2-18 and answer the following questions.
Vs. 2 What did Abimelech, King of Gerar do?

Vs. 3 What did God reveal to Abimelech?

Vs. 6 What did God do to protect Sarah?

Vs. 13 What did Abraham ask Sarah to say to show her love for him?

Vs. 16 What was given for Sarah to repay the harm done to her?

Vs. 17 -18 What did Abraham do and what was everyone healed from?

This story provides a remarkable contrast to Sarah's experience in Pharaoh's harem. Just as we learned from studying Paul and Silas in prison compared to Peter's imprisonment, sometimes God uses similar circumstances for different purposes. Though the situations seem very similar, this moment of Déjà Vu, which on the surface seemed like history repeating itself, was actually a means of blessing and healing for Sarah. God was doing something in both Sarah and Abraham's life. Because she was obedient to her husband, God protected Sarah and God made everyone so sick that Abimelech did not even touch her.

Just as God exposed the truth to Abimelech in a dream, He can supernaturally reveal the truth about any situation. He is not limited by anyone's faith or knowledge. Realizing God's sovereignty over all people and all creation allows us to trust Him in difficult situations. Abimelech gave Abraham 1,000 shekels of silver for Sarah- This is the equivalent of 25 kilograms of silver worth over $25,000 in current silver prices.

Get this—God didn't allow Sarah to be in this Déjà vu situation to punish her because she hadn't learned her lesson the first time. Instead, God allowed it because He wanted to bless her (give her $25,000) and heal her, an even more significant blessing, which we'll read about in a second.

In a dream, God told Abimelech to ask Abraham to pray for him and his household to be healed. This is the first time the word "pray" is used in the Bible. So, Abraham prayed; God healed Abimelech, his household, and Sarah.

Please write down what happened right after Abraham prayed in Genesis 21:1-2.

This is significant because there wasn't a break between the end of chapter 20 and the first two verses of chapter 21 when Genesis was written. Sarah's healing and Isaac's birth came because Abraham prayed. God used Abimelech to ask Abraham to pray for him to carry out God's plan in Sarah's life! We never know how God will use the situations and circumstances in our lives for our good and blessing.

Sarah's healing from infertility was supernatural. Isaac's birth was a miracle by any standard. Abraham was 100 years old, and Sarah was 90 when she gave birth to their son Isaac. Genesis 18:11 says, "Abraham and Sarah were already old and well advanced in years, and Sarah was past the age of childbearing."

> *We never know* how God will use the situations and circumstances in our lives for our good and blessing.

If Sarah were alive today, she would be in the record books as the oldest woman to give birth, and Abraham, her husband, would be in the record books as the oldest father.[44] God is not limited by our age, our resources, or our abilities!

Not too long ago, I was sharing this story about Sarah and Abimelech with a family friend who felt that a hard time in her history was repeating itself. I encouraged her to see that the situation was different, and this time, God had allowed her to go through it because "It's not a repeat. It's a complete." God was going to fulfill the promises He had made and bring about an amazing blessing.

---

[44] Abraham took another wife after Sarah died and she had six children Genesis 25:1-6

A NEW VIEW OF GOD

After Isaac was born, Sarah's view of God expanded from seeing Him as her Lord to understanding that he was God, her Creator. In celebrating the birth of Isaac, Sarah used the word אלהים' Elohim, which means "the creator, Almighty God, strong."

Please read the following verse from Genesis 21:5-6, "Abraham was a hundred years old when his son Isaac was born to him. Sarah said, 'God has brought me laughter, and everyone who hears about this will laugh with me.'"

Why do you think Sarah used God's name, which means Creator, instead of LORD after Isaac was born?

Before Isaac was born, Sarah's understanding of the nature of the Lord is expressed as one who knows the Lord is sovereign. Sarah knew if the Lord wanted to keep her from having children, he would. He was sovereign over relationships, so he would judge her husband for sleeping with Hagar. She understood that the Lord was involved with the lives of His people, just as a master or boss is involved with the lives of his servants. It is a relationship, but it is a relationship between the powerful one and the powerless.

When our life **has been changed by an encounter with God, our perspective of Him changes.**

After Isaac's birth, Sarah's perspective on God changed, and so did the name that she called him. She knew that only God, her Creator, could have given her a son. She had personally experienced God's creative power in her life. Sarah knew that God had created Isaac in her because it was impossible for her to have a child. Isaac's birth confirmed the miracle of all creation. Just like Sarah, we are transformed by experiencing God even more than through our knowledge of Him.

When our life has been changed by an encounter with God, our perspective of Him changes. My friend was healed from Multiple Sclerosis-like symptoms. When she talks about God, her Healer; she knows Him as Healer. A friend of our family was saved after a life of many bad choices, so when she talks about Jesus being her Savior, she knows Him as Savior. I grew up without a lot of money, so when I tell my sons that Jesus is our Provider. I know Him as my Provider. God wants us to know Him through experience that only comes from trusting him during uncertainty, impossible situations, and change.

How does sharing and hearing stories of God's involvement in our lives help us understand Him?

As we learn the names of God and share stories of God's involvement in our lives, our view of God expands. We can trust that the God who saved a friend can save an unbelieving husband or child. The God who created Isaac in Sarah's womb can create new life in us. We believe that God Most High is sovereign over all other gods and is greater than any addiction, false god or lie.

Sarah's life involved a lot of change. She was a princess and a Daddy's girl. She left her hometown and most of her family when she was old enough to join AARP. Her husband and her servant mistreated her. She went through the grief of infertility for 90 years and was blessed by the miraculous birth of her son Isaac. Hebrews commends her faith despite her impossible situation. Sarah is a remarkable woman who modeled how to trust God in the face of fear, how to trust God in impossible situations, how to trust God by submitting to our husband, and how to trust God in difficult circumstances.

HOW HAVE YOU LEARNED TO TRUST GOD THROUGH STUDYING SARAH?

KEY EVENTS IN SARAH'S LIFE

-Sarah Born in Ur of the Chaldeans (Her half-brother Abraham was ten years old.)

-Sarah Marries Abraham (Bible doesn't say the age they were married.)

-Sarah and Abraham move with their father Terah and nephew Lot to Haran.

-Age 65, Sarah, Abraham and Lot leave Haran to go to Canaan but because of famine go to Egypt where Sarah enters Pharaoh's harem

-Age 66, Sarah, Abraham and Hagar leave Egypt and return to Canaan

-Age 76, Sarah gives Abraham her servant Hagar to father a child

-Age 89, God changes Sarai's name to Sarah and Abram's name to Abraham. God promised in one year they would have a son named Isaac. Sarah and Abraham moved, Sarah joins Abimelech's harem.

-Age 90, Sarah gives birth to Isaac

-Age 127, Sarah died at Hebron

CHAPTER III

RESOURCEFUL BIG SISTER

LEADER AND PROPHETESS

Lived about 1,300 BC

Trust in the LORD with all your heart and
lean not on your own understanding; in all
your ways submit to him, and he will make
your paths straight.

Proverbs 3:5-6

Week 1

Miriam

Change is hard for me, even good change. Buying our house was a situation that showed my innate resistance to change. My husband and I had talked about moving to a home that would better fit our family and our plans to have another child. I had spent countless hours with real estate agents looking at houses, and I read numerous online listings, but a tiny part of me didn't think we'd actually move. I liked our house, my work commute was perfect, and I was comfortable with our mortgage payment. My husband had said that we would move, but I figured that it wouldn't happen anytime soon.

Then one day, my mother-in-law, who was helping us by evaluating house possibilities, found "the house." By the time I saw it, my husband had already decided it was the one. It had the rooms we were looking for, was in a great neighborhood, and was move-in ready. A month later, we were living in the house. It was so wonderful! It was more spacious, had an office for my husband, and was on a short cul-de-sac. It was so much nicer than our last house, but I was miserable. I mourned my old house; all I could focus on was what I didn't have. I missed my short commute and my second-floor laundry room.

Moving ten miles to our new house was a huge adjustment for me. As I began to learn about Miriam, Moses' older sister, I was struck by the fact that Miriam was in her late 80s when she moved over 33 times after the Israelites left Egypt! Every part of her life changed; she went from being enslaved to being free and from having a settled life in a place where her ancestors had lived for 400 years to a nomadic existence. How did she embrace such earth-shaking changes?

As we'll learn in our study, shifting from a place where we are comfortable to a new, better place is challenging, even if it means going from bondage to freedom, from a bad situation to a good environment. Every step of the way requires trusting God through obedience, believing that He will be our Provider, our Healer, our Light, and our Deliverer.

MIRIAM'S BACKGROUND

Miriam was born into slavery in Egypt nearly 3,300 years ago. Miriam's life is recorded in the books of Exodus and Numbers in bits and pieces, so to learn about her, we will be detectives as we piece together her story. Miriam is unique in our study because we can look at her life as a young girl and an older woman.

Miriam lived over 400 years after our princess Sarah. Abraham and Sarah's son, Isaac, married a lovely girl named Rebecca. Isaac and Rebecca had twin boys, Esau and Jacob. Jacob had twelve sons by his wives Leah and Rachel and two concubines. Jacob's sons became the twelve tribes of Israel.

Joseph, Rachel's oldest son, was sold into slavery by his brothers. Joseph became second in command to Pharaoh through God's divine plan and invited his father[45] and his family to live in Egypt to escape a famine in their land. The Israelites, Jacob's descendants, moved to Goshen, a fertile part of Egypt that was good for raising livestock. During the next 400 years of living in Egypt, the Israelites were fruitful, multiplied greatly, and became exceedingly numerous.

A new Pharaoh saw the multitudes of Israelites as a threat. He was terrified that the Israelites would band together with another nation and rebel against Egypt. So, to control them, he mandated infanticide and enslaved the people of Israel. "But the more they were oppressed, the more they multiplied and spread; so the Egyptians came to dread the Israelites and worked them ruthlessly. They made their lives bitter with hard labor in brick and mortar and with all kinds of work in the fields; in all their hard labor the Egyptians used them ruthlessly[46]."

Miriam's name means "bitterness" and is the root word for the names Mary and Marie. In Hebrew, this word means "bitter taste," as in the sentence, "This coffee has more bitterness than usual." Why do you think Miriam's parents gave her a name that means bitterness?

Life was bitter, and suffering was a part of every day. Miriam was born into slavery. Her name reflected the reality of her parents' lives. Miriam's family was oppressed and treated harshly by the Egyptians. Life was bitter and harsh. Just as you would ask a waitress to send back a bitter cup of coffee, they wanted God to change their situation.

Imagine being enslaved and raising a child in that harsh environment. Pause for a moment to think of how Miriam's parents must have felt when their baby girl was born. What would they have prayed and asked God to do for their daughter? Write down your thoughts.

Raising a child in a land where you were hated and feared would be very hard. It would be tough to believe in God and trust His promise to Abraham while being surrounded by Egyptian gods and their

---

[45] Joseph's father was Jacob. Jacob was a grandson of Abraham and the son of Isaac. God gave Jacob the name Israel in Genesis 32:28
[46] Exodus 1:12-14

power. As a parent during this time, trusting God would be very difficult but teaching your children about God and his power over all creation and other gods was essential for having hope amid suffering.

Though the Israelites had heard stories of the Creator and Lord Most High, the God of Abraham, Isaac, and Jacob, God felt far off and distant during their back-breaking everyday life. The land that God had promised Abraham and his descendants seemed like a fairy tale. Though they cried out to God during their slavery, it seemed as if God didn't care. God did care. But even the length of time the Israelites spent in Egypt was a part of God's design. His plan was sovereign, and their deliverance was destined long before Miriam was born.

Please read Genesis 15:12-14. What did God say to Abraham long before his grandson Joseph was sold into slavery in Egypt?

God had a plan for His people that stretched across centuries and two continents, 400 years and a journey from Egypt to the Promised Land. Even before Isaac was born, God knew that Isaac's descendants would be enslaved and treated harshly. God had not forgotten His people. When the time was right, He called Miriam's brother, Moses to lead the Israelite people out of Egypt, out of bondage and bitterness into the freedom and abundance of the Promised Land.

BIG SISTERS ROCK

Miriam played a significant role in the history of Israel because of her care for her youngest brother Moses. Miriam was the oldest of three children in her family. Let's learn a little more about her.

Numbers 26 contains a census of the Israelites. Please read Numbers 26:59 to learn about Miriam's family. Please fill in the blanks.
"The name of Amram's wife was Jochebed, a descendant of Levi, who was born to the Levites in Egypt. To Amram she bore _____, _____ and their sister _____.

Miriam was the sister of Moses and Aaron, who grew up to be spiritual leaders of Israel. Aaron was three years older than Moses, and Miriam was their older sister. Moses and Aaron's lives are well documented in the books of Exodus and Numbers and give us insight into Miriam's life.

Amram's family became the "first family" of Israel, but both Moses' and Aaron's birth and survival were miracles considering the infanticide that Pharaoh ordered to control the population of Israelites. Pharaoh commanded the Hebrew midwives to kill any baby boys that they delivered.

However, the Hebrew midwives feared God and did not do as the Pharaoh decreed.[47] To counteract the midwives' defiance, Pharaoh ordered that all Hebrew boy babies be thrown into the Nile River. This was a death sentence for baby Moses except that God protected Moses and transformed this evil act to turn it into good. Miriam's bravery and resourcefulness resulted in Moses growing up in the household of Pharaoh, the very man who ordered his death.

Please read the passage from Exodus 2:1-10 below and underline any mention of Moses' sister.

Exodus 2:1-10 "Now a man of the house of Levi married a Levite woman, and she became pregnant and gave birth to a son. When she saw that he was a fine child, she hid him for three months. But when she could hide him no longer, she got a papyrus basket for him and coated it with tar and pitch. Then she placed the child in it and put it among the reeds along the bank of the Nile. His sister stood at a distance to see what would happen to him.

Then Pharaoh's daughter went down to the Nile to bathe, and her attendants were walking along the river bank. She saw the basket among the reeds and sent her slave girl to get it. She opened it and saw the baby. He was crying, and she felt sorry for him. "This is one of the Hebrew babies," she said. Then his sister asked Pharaoh's daughter, "Shall I go and get one of the Hebrew women to nurse the baby for you?"

"Yes, go," she answered. And the girl went and got the baby's mother. Pharaoh's daughter said to her, "Take this baby and nurse him for me, and I will pay you." So the woman took the baby and nursed him. When the child grew older, she took him to Pharaoh's daughter and he became her son. She named him Moses, saying, "I drew him out of the water."

Based on this passage, how would you describe young Miriam?

This is such an exciting story about a brave little girl. As a big sister, I like to identify with Miriam. Miriam was resourceful, smart, discerning, and caring. She may have been as young as six years old, but she was obedient and did what her mother asked her. She was responsible for caring for her little baby brother who was only 3 months old and still at the "cuddling age." I also admire her bravery in approaching Pharaoh's daughter and her resourcefulness in asking the princess if she needed a nursemaid for the baby.

---

[47] Exodus 1:17

Even though she was a little girl, God used Miriam's resourcefulness, bravery, compassion, and care for her little brother; if you are a mom, reinforce the truth to your kids that God has given them amazing gifts and abilities, no matter their age, that they can use to bless others.

*If you think back to your elementary school years and what you loved to do, I bet you can see glimpses of who you have become. Like Miriam, even as a young girl, God gave you unique gifts, passions, and abilities that He intended you to use for His glory and bless others. Please write down some of your talents and passions and how you have helped others.

As a young girl, I loved flowers. I have so much joy making beautiful flower arrangements from flowers in my garden. As an adult, I used this gift first when my sister got married and most recently at my stepdaughter's wedding. Our age does not limit our ability to be used by God, whether we are six or 86. God has a mission for us to bless others and to use our life experiences—good and bad—for His glory.

As a result of Miriam's quick thinking, Moses was adopted by Pharaoh's daughter and was nursed by his mother. Then, when he was about two years old, he went to live with Pharaoh's daughter.

God allows us to go through many different situations to prepare us for the mission and for the blessing He has in store for us and for others.

While Moses was raised as the son of a princess, Miriam and her brother Aaron continued to live in Egypt in bondage. The Bible does not record specific details from the middle part of Miriam's life, but it was likely a time of suffering, pain, and hard work interspersed with moments of joy. Two ancient documents mention that Miriam was married, and one included that she had a son.[48]

Moses lived in Pharaoh's palace until he was 40 years old when he killed an Egyptian in a fit of rage and then fled Egypt. For the next 40 years, until he was 80 years old, he lived as a shepherd in the wilderness. God used the 40 years that Moses spent as a Prince of Egypt in the court of Pharaoh, learning to read, write, and lead people. Moses spent the next 40 years learning the nuances of survival in the desert to prepare him for his ultimate calling to lead the descendants of Jacob out of slavery and into the land promised to their ancestor Abraham.

God also allows us to go through many different situations to prepare us for the mission and the blessing He has in store for us and others. These times of preparation can be wonderful, like living in a palace, or miserable, like learning to survive in the desert. God used both the good and the bad to

---

[48] http://en.wikipedia.org/wiki/Miriam

prepare Moses for his purpose. Despite her situation as an enslaved person, God was also preparing Miriam through her unique life experiences, giftedness, and leadership skills for her role as a leader of women. In the same way, God has prepared you to use the life experiences and abilities that He has given you for the mission that He has for you.

*To prepare and equip us for His mission, sometimes God provides remarkable opportunities, and other times He uses difficult situations. Can you think of a situation (good or bad) that you have been through that God used to prepare you so that you could bless others? Take a minute to reflect and thank God for his faithfulness in all situations.

Week 2

OUR PATIENT AND POWERFUL GOD

This week's Bible study will be a little more involved and require more time than last week's work, but if you stick with it, I know you will be encouraged. I pray God will open your eyes to see His hand, His protection, and His presence in Miriam's journey and your everyday life.

The first 86 years of Miriam's life were bitter and full of suffering. For most Israelites, the one true God was a distant memory in a land where multitudes of gods, including Pharaoh, were worshiped. But God was waiting for the right time (prophesied over 400 years before) to bring a deliverer to His people, and when the time was right, He called Miriam's brothers to begin a historic journey that would set His people free.

Moses was 80 years old, when God spoke through a burning bush to call Moses back to Egypt after 40 years of exile.[49] While Moses was arguing with God about going back to Egypt, God told him that his 83-year-old brother Aaron was "already on his way to meet you, and his heart will be glad when he sees you."[50]

---

[49] Exodus 3 - 4
[50] Exodus 4:14

Stop for a moment and ponder this: these two brothers had not lived together since Moses was two years old and may not have been in contact with each other for the 40 years while Moses lived in the wilderness, but God directed them to meet in the middle of the desert at the right time and place. No cell phones, GPS, or text messaging, yet God brought these two brothers together. Moses and Aaron's story illustrates that whenever God asks us to do something, we need to trust that He has gone before us and prepared the way. Long before God had set the bush on fire and struck up the conversation with Moses, God had called Aaron, and Aaron was on his way. This is a powerful reminder of what God can do for all of us when we allow Him to direct our paths. Who knows what miraculous meetings and miracles are waiting for us?

* Have you experienced a time when God prepared you for a divine meeting?

ANSWERED PRAYER AND UNBELIEF

Miriam was at least eighty-six years old when Moses returned to Egypt. God sent Moses and Aaron back to Egypt to carry out a mission, to lead God's chosen people to a land of freedom and away from the slavery they endured in Egypt.

After years of slavery, heartbreak, and toil, God responded to the cries of the Hebrews with a life-changing message, "I am God. I will bring you out from under the cruel hard labor of Egypt. I will rescue you from slavery. I will redeem you, intervening with great acts of judgment. I'll take you as my own people and I'll be God to you. You'll know that I am God, your God who brings you out from under the cruel hard labor of Egypt. I'll bring you into the land that I promised to give Abraham, Isaac, and Jacob and give it to you as your own country. I AM God".[51]

Imagine being in a hopeless, miserable situation and receiving this message recorded in Exodus 6:6-8. How would you respond?

Exodus 6:9 tells us how the Israelites responded, "When Moses told this to the Israelites, they were too discouraged and mistreated to believe him."[52]

---

[51] Exodus 6:6-8 (The Message)
[52] CEV

Have you ever been in that place of being so beaten down, so heartbroken, so weak and discouraged that you can't even see the miracles that God is doing in your life, and you aren't able to believe that He will ever answer your prayers? What was that like?

It's okay- Just like the Israelites, you can find hope in this vital truth; *your inability to believe does not determine God's power!* As we learned in our study of Sarah and Abraham, God is Almighty. He is all-powerful. Omnipotent. Too often, our view of God is limited because we confuse our abilities with God's abilities. His power is not determined by anything we do or say. God, in His very essence and nature, is powerful.

God is all-powerful, just as a waterfall is intrinsically powerful. The first time that I saw Niagara Falls, I was amazed at the power of the water and awed that the water never stopped cascading into the pool below. Twenty-four hours a day, millions of gallons of water cascade over the Falls. My belief in the power of Niagara Falls does not affect how much water flows over the Falls. My understanding does not limit Niagara Falls, it is innately powerful. In an even more incredible, mind-blowing way, God is always powerful.

> *Even when we don't see* God at work, we need to trust that He is powerful and working in other people's lives just as he is working in our life.

One of the most remarkable features of His tremendous power is His patience with us in our weakness. God was patient with the Israelites, knowing that just as He would convince Pharaoh, God would convince His people to believe that He could set them free and bring them to the land He had promised to their ancestor Abraham. About 700 years before, God had prophesied to Abraham that his descendants would be in captivity for 400 hundred years.[53] As Moses revealed God's plan for His people, God was preparing the people of Israel for the journey ahead of them. In the same way, God is patient with us. He knows our hearts and our resistance to change, yet rather than forcing us to do His will with His power and might, He patiently woos and gently works in our lives for our good.

Please read 2 Peter 3:9 and circle the correct phrase below to fill in the blank
"The Lord is not slow in keeping his promise, as some understand slowness. _____, not wanting anyone to perish, but everyone to come to repentance."

A. He is angry with you

B. He is forgetful

C. He is busy with other things

D. He is patient with you

---

[53] Genesis 15:13

God is patient with us; however, it is not a passive patience. God is actively carrying out His will in our lives and the lives of others. So even when we don't see God at work, we can trust that He is powerful and is working in other people's lives, just as he is working in our life.

If you are frustrated and feel God is not working in your life or someone else's life, pray and ask God to open your eyes to see His hand at work. You will be amazed.

SIGNS OF ACTIVE PATIENCE

Moses to go to Pharaoh with a message, "Let my people go so they can worship me.[54]" Pharaoh stubbornly resisted God, so God performed signs and miracles to convince Pharaoh to let the Israelites leave Egypt. Exodus chapters 7-10 tell the story of the ten plagues God sent to Egypt. God turned the Nile River to blood, sent frogs to swarm the land, and turned dust to gnats so that the Egyptians and Israelites would experience God's power over all creation. For over a week, everyone in the land suffered. The Egyptians, Miriam, and all the Israelites smelled the stench of dead fish in the Nile; they felt the discomfort of frogs in their chairs, beds, and kitchens; and they experienced the annoyance of gnats in their eyes, ears, and mouths. For the Israelites, these signs made a difficult time even harder; and for the Egyptians, it gave them a taste of the misery the Israelites experienced as slaves.

Interestingly, the subsequent seven plagues afflicted the Egyptians but spared the Israelites. God sent flies to annoy all of Egypt, struck down their livestock and cattle, caused boils to cover their bodies, and then sent a hailstorm to crush their crops. Next, God sent locusts to devour any crops, plants or trees that remained behind after the hailstorm. Miraculously, during this assault, God kept the flies and hail out of the region of Goshen where Miriam and the Israelites lived, and He protected the Israelites' from boils and their animals from sickness. Even when God put a thick cover of darkness for three days over the entire land of Egypt, He spared where the Israelites lived.

The Israelites had been told stories about God, Creation, and their ancestors Abraham, Sarah, Isaac, and Jacob. How did the plagues in Exodus 7-10 show God's sovereignty over all creation and His faithfulness to their ancestors as relevant to their lives?

Why do you think God allowed the first three plagues to affect all the people in the land yet spared the Israelites during the last seven?

---

[54] Exodus 7:16

Throughout the plagues, God wasn't just working on Pharaoh's heart; God was also working on the Israelites' hearts so that they would believe and act on what God said to do. God used the plagues to show His power over the Egyptians' gods and their land and show the Israelites His sovereignty over creation and all people. He was Lord Almighty, Lord Most High, Creator, and their Deliverer.

After the plague of darkness, Moses went to the leaders of Israel and told them what the Lord commanded regarding the Passover. When he finished speaking, the people knelt and worshipped the Lord, and then they went home to do what the Lord commanded. This was a radically different response to Moses than when Moses initially told the Israelites God's message and "they were too discouraged and mistreated to believe him."[55]

God hadn't changed. He was powerful before he sent the gnats and hail, but they had changed because they had experienced His power. Our ability to trust God is related to our understanding of who He is and His power and might over every situation, person, and circumstance.

God required them to put their new faith into action because, in addition to preparing for the Passover meal, God had also asked them to ask their Egyptian neighbors for gold, silver, and clothes and told them to get ready to move in two weeks. Imagine knocking on your unbelieving neighbor's door saying, "Our Creator, God has told me we will be moving in two weeks. Would you give me some jewelry, money, and clothes?" Nerve-wracking for sure. But God had also been working on the Egyptian's hearts during this time to make them receptive to the Israelites. Amazingly, the Egyptians gave the Israelites clothes, gold, and silver.

While it was risky to ask their oppressors for these things, the reward was great. *The blessings of obedience dwarf the risks of following God. Whenever God calls us to do something, we need to remember that God has gone before us and has prepared the way to bless our obedience.* God is at work all around us. Before God had even spoken to Moses from the burning bush, God had already called Aaron to the desert to meet Moses. Later in Exodus 23, God tells His people, "See, I am sending an angel ahead of you to guard you along the way and to bring you to the place I have prepared."[56] In the same way, God has often been working for weeks or years, preparing us and those around us for the mission he has for us. Our responsibility is to simply do what He says.

Obeying God is often the most tangible way that we can show that we trust God. Ask God to reveal to you any areas that you need to act out your faith by obeying His Word.

---

[55] Exodus 6:9 CEV
[56] Exodus 23:20

THE BEST WAY IS NOT ALWAYS THE SHORTEST WAY

It was finally the right time for Miriam and the Israelites to leave Egypt. "At midnight the LORD struck down all the firstborn in Egypt, from the firstborn of Pharaoh, who sat on the throne, to the firstborn of the prisoner, who was in the dungeon, and the firstborn of all the livestock as well[57]." Pharaoh had reached his limit and the Israelites were convinced of God's power over life and death. They were ready to embark on their journey to the Promised Land. After the Passover, Pharaoh told Moses and Aaron that they could leave Egypt to worship their God. About six hundred thousand Israelites, not counting women and children, as well as many other people and a lot of sheep, goats, and cattle left Egypt that night.

Please read Exodus 13:17-18 below to answer the following questions.
"After the king had finally let the people go, the LORD did not lead them through Philistine territory, though that was the shortest way. God had said, "If they are attacked, they may decide to return to Egypt." So he led them around through the desert and toward the Red Sea. The Israelites left Egypt, prepared for battle.[58]

God led the Israelites _____.

      A. Shortest way   **B. Easiest Way**

      C. Around through the Desert   **D. Route to Starbucks**

God led them this way because He knew _____.

      A. They would follow Him anywhere   **B. They liked the long way**

      C. They might return to Egypt

God knew the Israelites' faith was not strong enough to face a battle. So, he led them the long way, around and through the desert, even though it was not the easiest or the shortest way because it was the best way to keep them on the path to the Promised Land. God's way is always the best way, even if it is not easiest. He knew their hearts and if they were attacked, they would just run back to slavery in Egypt. God knows our hearts; He will protect us from attack and guide us on the paths that enable us to follow him faithfully. Just as you would be patient with a toddler learning to walk, He is patient with us as we grow to know him more and to trust Him more.

Please write out Proverbs 3:5-6

---

[57] Exodus 12:29
[58] Exodus 13:17-18 CEV

This is one of my favorite scriptures. According to this Proverb if we trust God and don't lean on our own understanding, God will direct our paths and make our paths straight. This is a powerful promise given at a time when there were no paved roads or bulldozers. God can do seemingly impossible things.

Psalm 147:5 says, "Great is our Lord and mighty in power; His understanding has no limit." When I am tempted to trust what I know and have experienced rather than God, this reminds me that there is so much that I don't know and don't understand while God has unlimited understanding. We need to trust that the God who made the universe and each of us knows what is best for us. He knows our strengths and weaknesses, and He adjusts His plans to our level of faith. While it may seem risky to trust God, in reality, it is the safest, most logical thing to do.

Ask God to help you trust Him in the risky and scary places. He will help you and go before you to prepare the way according to His will.

FOLLOWING GOD

I love I love GPS. It might be because I struggle to distinguish between my right and left. (They both seem right to me.) Reading maps and giving directions is much more challenging because I am never quite certain if the turn is a right or a left. GPS reduces the stress out of long trips and takes the pressure off me to give accurate directions. Even though the Israelites didn't have GPS, God made it easy for the Israelites to follow Him. He created a proprietary "God Positioning System."

Please read these two passages and answer the question below.
"During the day the LORD went ahead of His people in a thick cloud, and during the night he went ahead of them in a flaming fire. That way the LORD could lead them at all times, whether day or night." Exodus 13:21 (CEV)

"All this time God's angel had gone ahead of Israel's army, but now he moved behind them. A large cloud had also gone ahead of them, but now it moved between the Egyptians and the Israelites. The cloud gave light to the Israelites, but made it dark for the Egyptians, and during the night they could not come any closer." Exodus 14:19,20

Based on these verses how did God lead His people through the desert?

During this pivotal time, God made His presence obvious and practical. God was not far off in space, letting them wander on their own. Whether it was day or night, they could see God's presence. At night, the fire provided light and a beacon for the nearly two million people that had left Egypt. He provided light during a time when there was no electricity. During the day, His presence was in a column of smoke so that all two million people who left Egypt could see and follow Him. God also protected the Israelites so that the Egyptians could not attack them at night.

God is practical and obvious. Just as God clearly led Miriam, Moses, and the other Israelites, He desires for us to follow him. If you are struggling to see and experience God in your everyday life, pray right now and ask Him to show himself to you. He will! (Make a note of your prayer in the margin and today's date so that you will remember this date.)

One of my favorite Bible studies is *Experiencing God* by Henry Blackaby and Claude King. It is about knowing and doing the will of God. One point they made is that God is practical. Here's a quote from this study, "When Jesus fed five thousand, He was being practical. The God I see revealed in scripture is real, personal, and practical. You can trust God to be practical and real as He relates to you too."[59] Throughout the Old and New Testaments, God's plan and provision are practical.

GOD'S UNIQUE MISSION AND PLAN FOR OUR LIVES

God considers our individual needs, strengths, abilities, and limits. He created you for a purpose with specific gifts and experiences to carry out His mission and plan. God will guide and direct where we live and what we do to prepare us to carry out his plan. Moses lived in the desert for 40 years before leading the Israelites out of slavery into the desert. At the same time, God also called Miriam to a leadership role. God explained to His people, "I brought you up out of Egypt and redeemed you from the land of slavery. I sent Moses to lead you, also Aaron and Miriam."[60]

God had prepared Miriam for her role as a leader by giving her unique gifts and abilities that she first used as a young girl to protect her baby brother, Moses and later used as a leader of women. In the same way, God has been practically preparing and equipping you to carry out His plan. When you devote your life to His plan, He will not let your experiences, passions, and gifts go to waste at any age.

After leaving Egypt, the LORD led the Israelites to the edge of the Red Sea and told Moses to stretch out his hand so that the Israelites could walk across the sea on dry land. Two million Israelites, including Miriam and her family, walked across the dry ground to the other side of the sea. When the Egyptians pursued the Israelites into the sea, Moses stretched out his hand, and the water covered the

---

[59] Blackaby and King, *Experiencing God* pg. 65 Lifeway Press, Nashville TN
[60] Micah 6:4

Egyptians and their chariots, and they drowned. "On that day, when the Israelites saw the bodies of the Egyptians washed up on the shore, they knew that the LORD had saved them. Because of the mighty power he had used against the Egyptians, the Israelites worshiped him and trusted him and his servant Moses."[61]

Exodus 15 records Moses and Miriam's song of praise and deliverance. Please read Exodus 15:20-21. What does this passage tell you about Miriam?

Miriam was a prophetess, a woman who spoke forth the Word of God. She was also a leader of women. God had given her a musical gift, so she used a tambourine and led the women in singing and dancing. Miriam sang to them: "Sing to the LORD, for he is highly exalted. The horse and its rider he has hurled into the sea."[62] This is an encouraging story of how God uses each of our gifts that is made even better by the fact that Miriam was 86 years old! Can you imagine leading dancing and singing at 86? Wow! Though she was definitely an "older woman," she hadn't stopped dancing, singing, praising God, or leading others in the worship of God. Psalm 92 says, "The righteous will flourish like a palm tree…They will still bear fruit in old age, they will stay fresh and green."[63]

While I don't have the gifts that Miriam had, I can't carry a tune and don't have the slightest bit of rhythm, God has given me a passion for reading stories that has grown into a passion for reading the Bible and sharing God's Word. Regardless of our age, God will use our gifts and abilities. My friend Joyce who is 92, has been a primary editor and sounding board for this book. One of my friends loves to sew. God allowed her to lead a ministry through her church that provided dresses for thousands of girls worldwide. High school kids in our church have blessed our whole family by serving as small group leaders for my two little boys. These examples illustrate that regardless of our age, young or old, we can be like Miriam and use the gifts God has given us for His kingdom and glory.

> *Regardless of* your age, young or very old, God has a plan for you to bear fruit and bless others.

A way to figure out your unique passions is to ask, "What do I love to do? What do I think is fun?" Take a minute to think about this and write down how God could use it to bless others.

---

[61] Exodus 14:30
[62] Exodus 15:20-21
[63] Psalm 92:12- 14

God gifted you so that you can use your gifts to encourage and bless others. The joy that Miriam had leading the women as they danced on the shore of the Red Sea can be yours when you use your gifts and passions for God. Ask God to show you areas you can bless him and bless others by sharing what you love with others.

AN EXPANDED VIEW OF GOD

After living decades in bondage, Miriam understood the LORD was different from a selfish, wicked Egyptian master. The LORD was a Master who took care of them and protected them. Her deliverance from slavery showed the dominion of the LORD. (יְהֹוָה Hebrew) Jehovah = "The Existing One." The LORD explained to Moses, when Moses asked his name, "I Am who I Am."[64] Whenever we experience God's presence and power in our lives, our view of Him expands exponentially. Miriam was able to learn and experience more about God through their deliverance from Egypt.

Please read Exodus 15:2.

> *Then she sang to them: "Sing praises to the LORD for his great victory!*
> *He has thrown the horses and their riders into the sea." (CEV)*

How did Miriam's and the Israelites' view of the LORD Jehovah change after crossing the Red Sea and seeing the Egyptian chariots and riders thrown into the sea?

How can you apply this insight about the LORD in your life?

Our LORD and Master is a mighty protector. He gives us victory beyond our abilities. He can defeat even our strongest enemies and turn our times of fear into times of rejoicing.

WATER YOU WANT TO SPIT OUT!

Miriam and all the Israelites left the Red Sea and went into the Desert of Shur. They traveled in the desert for three days without water.

"When they came to Marah, they could not drink its water because it was bitter. (That is why the place is called Marah.) So the people grumbled against Moses, saying, "What are we to drink?" Then Moses cried out to the LORD, and the LORD showed him a piece of wood. He

---

[64] Exodus 3:14

threw it into the water, and the water became sweet. There the LORD made a decree and a law for them, and there he tested them. He said, "If you listen carefully to the voice of the LORD your God and do what is right in his eyes, if you pay attention to his commands and keep all his decrees, I will not bring on you any of the diseases I brought on the Egyptians, for I am the LORD, who heals you."[65]

Based on this passage, what did the LORD reveal about Himself to Moses, Miriam, and the rest of the Israelites?

How could you relate this to your life?

One of the things that struck me about this passage is that "Marah" and "Miriam" have the same root word meaning bitterness – a disgusting taste. Bitter water is something you want to spit out of your mouth as soon as possible. Just as you would not wish to take another sip of bitter water, Miriam's parents were in a miserable situation that would leave a bad taste in anyone's mouth when she was born. Yet the Lord took the "marah" water, the bitter water, and turned it sweet, just as He took Miriam out of slavery and bondage and gave her the sweetness of freedom. He can do the same for you. He is the LORD that heals you. Whatever painful situation you have been experiencing, the LORD can make it sweet.

Pray and ask God to take the bitter places in your life and make them sweet. Dedicate the gifts and abilities God has given you (singing, sewing, teaching, cooking, dancing, writing) to God for His Glory. He has a sweet plan for every stage of your life. Trust Him.

---

[65] Exodus 15:23-26

Week 3

IF ONLY...

The Israelites continued on their journey around the Sinai Peninsula. Two and a half months after they left Egypt, their resources were exhausted. There was nothing left of the food they had packed when they left Egypt. The people were miserable, and they began to complain to Moses and Aaron, "If only we had died by the LORD's hand in Egypt! There we sat around pots of meat and ate all the food we wanted, but you have brought us out into this desert to starve this entire assembly to death."

The LORD said to Moses, "I will rain down bread from heaven for you. The people are to go out each day and gather enough for that day. In this way I will test them and see whether they will follow my instructions. On the sixth day they are to prepare what they bring in, and that is to be twice as much as they gather on the other days."[66]

Have you ever felt the need to complain about a change? Do you ever find yourself thinking that things were better off in the past?

As the Israelites, cried "If only," what did God reveal about Himself to Moses, Miriam, and the rest of the Israelites?

How could you relate this to your life?

Miriam and the rest of the Israelites were in a tough situation. They had been in the desert for two and a half months, and they had nothing left. They were "Hangry"! They were in the state of being hungry and angry. The Israelites rightly blamed God for their situation. This reminds me of when I took my youngest to the doctor for his shots; he got mad at me and blamed me for the pain. He was right; it was my fault. I did it for his good and benefit. Though I understood the process hurt him, I would do it again for the health benefits. The result was beneficial though the process was painful. God purposely

---

[66] Exodus 16:3-5

took His people out of Egypt and led them to where they were at the end of their resources. There is nothing wrong with letting God know that we are upset about a significant change or hard time in our lives. God is a Big God and can handle our expressing our hurt and frustration over situations outside of our control.

Just as I was ungrateful moving to our new house, the Israelites were ungrateful after leaving the bondage of slavery. In their ungratefulness, they became delusional about what they had left behind. We need to guard against the "If only's" in life. One of the most effective ways to do that is to give thanks.

When you find yourself in a place of doubt, saying, "if only…," do two things. First, give thanks by acknowledging God's sovereignty, deliverance, healing, and protection. This will refocus your mind from what you don't have and how bad things are to the absolute sovereignty of God in every situation.

Second, look for God's provision. He knows your needs even before you ask (whine or complain.) God even mandated a time of rest, no gathering manna on the Sabbath. Just as he sent down manna for the Israelites, he will care for you. He will give you what you need, and He will also provide the rest you need to appreciate His blessings.

One more important lesson to learn from this story is that God sent down the manna only after the Israelites had reached the limits of their resources. Sometimes the best way to fully embrace change and trust God requires coming to the end of our resources, so that He is all we have.

THE DANGER OF COMPLAINING

Over two years passed, and the Israelites grew tired of the same meal; morning, noon, and night! What had been a blessing and an answer to a cry for food became a source of discontentment. Numbers 11 tells the story of what happened when they became ungrateful for the blessing that God rained down on them every day, and they started to complain.

> "If only we had meat to eat! We remember the fish we ate in Egypt at no cost—also the cucumbers, melons, leeks, onions and garlic. But now we have lost our appetite; we never see anything but this manna!"… God said to Moses, "Tell the people: 'Consecrate yourselves in preparation for tomorrow, when you will eat meat. The LORD heard you when you wailed, "If only we had meat to eat! We were better off in Egypt!" Now the LORD will give you meat, and you will eat it. You will not eat it for just one day, or two days, or five, ten or twenty days, but for a whole month—until it comes out of your nostrils and you loathe it—because you have rejected the LORD, who is among you, and have wailed before him, saying, "Why did we ever leave Egypt?" '"But Moses said, "Here I am among six hundred thousand men on foot, and you say, 'I will give them meat to eat for a whole month!' Would they have enough if flocks and herds were slaughtered for them? Would they have enough if all the fish in the sea were caught for them?" The LORD

answered Moses, "Is the LORD's arm too short? You will now see whether or not what I say will come true for you."[67]

Numbers 11 continues the story of the deadly consequences of their complaining in verses 31-33. "Now a wind went out from the Lord and drove quail in from the sea. It scattered them up to two cubits deep all around the camp, as far as a day's walk in any direction. All that day and night and all the next day the people went out and gathered quail. No one gathered less than ten homers. Then they spread them out all around the camp. But while the meat was still between their teeth and before it could be consumed, the anger of the Lord burned against the people, and he struck them with a severe plague."

Based on this passage what did God reveal about Himself to Moses, Miriam, and the rest of the Israelites?

How could this relate to your life?

My pen pal Felicia shared an important insight from this passage, "We often don't view grumbling as a sin, but it's clear from the Bible that God doesn't like complaining." This quote was a wake-up call to me. I realized ungratefulness, grumbling, and complaining are often a rejection of God, my Provider, and LORD.

Focusing on our problems distracts us from seeing the blessings God gives us every day.

Ungratefulness distorts our perception. I've seen this pattern many times in my life where I've become ungrateful for the blessings that God has given me. I have friends who left their husbands, though on their wedding day, they were confident he was a gift from God. I know people who have praised God for healing and strength but are later ungrateful and focused on what they can't do. I know women who deeply wanted children but are frustrated and unhappy as parents. We can only focus on one thing. Focusing on our problems distracts us from seeing the blessings God gives us every day.

My son-in-law mentioned that he didn't complain or argue with his mom growing up. Wow! I was shocked and challenged; my life consists of much grumbling and complaining. As I pondered my complaining habit, I decided to make Philippians 2:14 my New Year's resolution, "Do everything

---

[67] Numbers 11:4-23

without complaining or arguing." This will be a challenge because I love a good complaint. But I know it is important to God, and I pray that I will be able to live out this verse through the power of the Holy Spirit.

"Do everything without complaining" seems simple, but what if you had to eat the same meal for two years, what if you had to live with the same husband for 30 years, and if you had to drive the same car for a decade? How can you acknowledge that you'd like something different to eat, a newer car, or your husband to change his behavior without grumbling or complaining? This isn't easy. For me, the answer is focusing on the sovereignty of God. He is your Provider, and He knows your needs before you ask.

The first step is praising God for who He is, how He has answered prayers in the past, and how he is in control of everything. Praise takes our focus off ourselves and our situation and realigns our hearts with God. The next step is to pray and ask God for His will in your situation. His will is good, pleasing, and perfect. He's God. He's got this. Trust Him.

Do you complain or grumble? Take a minute to pray and repent for rejecting God's provision.

Are there places where you need to seek God's will instead of complaining?

MISERY WITH A PURPOSE

Sometimes God allows us to become uncomfortable in a place because he is preparing us for something more. For example, the Israelites' discontent with the manna was a part of God's process to prepare their hearts to go into a land flowing with milk and honey. If they had been praying for God's will when the explorers later came back from exploring the Promised Land, their eyes would have been ready to see the grapes and food as the answer to their "no more manna" prayer.

Things had to get **very challenging before I was even willing to consider that God had something different for me.**

Before I retired from the corporate world, I was miserable, so I started praying a simple prayer, "God help me 'cause something's got to give." I was working on a complicated project, my husband's job was incredibly demanding, and the final straw came when my nanny quit. I could have found a new childcare situation or a new job; instead, I called out to God for His will and wisdom. I loved working and having an income, and my plan after becoming a mom was to continue working. However, things had to get very challenging before I was even able to consider that God had something different for me.

God used that time of discomfort to prepare me for the life change that came when I became a stay-at-home mom. As a stay-at-home mom, I've had a different set of challenges, but I have never doubted that I am in God's will, and when I look back on that time of misery, God uses it to remind me of how blessed I am.

Has God prepared you for a change by making you uncomfortable?

When we are in difficult situations, it is okay to acknowledge that we are miserable and would like a change, but we need to make sure that we do everything without complaining or arguing. First, we need to focus on God and His power and might; then, we seek His will. Finally, we will know we have found his will when we can give thanks. As 1 Thessalonians says, "Give thanks in all circumstances for this is God's will for you in Christ Jesus." Thanksgiving reminds us that God often uses places of discomfort to prepare us for future blessings or to bless the people around us.

WARNING- GOSSIPING AND CRITICIZING CAN LEAD TO BAD SKIN

Though Miriam was a prophetess, a musician, and a leader of women, she was also human and prone to fall into the traps that catch all of us when we criticize other people and gossip.

Miriam's big mistake is chronicled in Numbers 12:1-3.

"Although Moses was the most humble person in the entire world, Miriam and Aaron started complaining, "Moses had no right to marry that woman from Ethiopia! Who does he think he is? The LORD has spoken to us, not just to him." The LORD heard their complaint and told Moses, Aaron, and Miriam to come to the entrance of the sacred tent. There the LORD appeared in a cloud and told Aaron and Miriam to come closer. Then after commanding them to listen carefully, he said: "I, the LORD, speak to prophets in visions and dreams. But my servant Moses is the leader of my people. He sees me face to face, and everything I say to him is perfectly clear. You have no right to criticize my servant Moses."

The LORD became angry at Aaron and Miriam. And after the LORD left and the cloud disappeared from over the sacred tent, Miriam's skin turned white with leprosy. When Aaron saw what had happened to her, he said to Moses, "Sir, please don't punish us for doing such a foolish thing. Don't let Miriam's flesh rot away like a child born dead!" Moses prayed, "LORD God, please heal her."

But the LORD replied, "Miriam would be disgraced for seven days if her father had punished her by spitting in her face. So make her stay outside the camp for seven days, before coming back." The people of Israel did not move their camp until Miriam returned seven days later. Then they left Hazeroth and set up camp in the Paran Desert. (CEV)[68]

How did Miriam's view of God change after this encounter with God?

How did Moses show God's mercy to Miriam?

Miriam got an earful of the LORD's justice and judgment when the LORD spoke out of a cloud and plainly told her that she had no right to criticize his servant, and when the lecture was over she was covered with a horrible skin disease. I am sure this is a lesson on criticism that Miriam would never forget. Her complaining even led to a warning being written in Deuteronomy 24:9 "Remember what the LORD your God did to Miriam along the way after you came out of Egypt." Just as Miriam was faced with the consequences of complaining and criticism, each one of us will give an account of our actions to the LORD.[69]

Miriam had an encounter with the LORD that most of us would not want to replicate. He personally defended Moses against Miriam's criticism. God said to Miriam, "you have no right to criticize my servant Moses." In Romans 14:4, Paul asks, "Who are you to judge someone else's servant?" As I studied this passage, I learned that the Greek word for "judge" also carried the meaning of elevating oneself. The problem with judging God's servant is that we are elevating ourselves above God, not just the other person. One area that God has shown me to be careful is in criticizing or gossiping about our ministers. I need to trust that just as God is working in my life, He is working in their lives, as well. When we gossip, criticize and judge others, we are stepping out of line. We are elevating ourselves above God. Criticism destroys and demeans God's servants and complaining takes our focus off the good things that God has done for us.

The problem **with judging God's servant is that we are elevating ourselves above God not just over the other person.**

---

[68] Numbers 12:1-3
[69] Romans 14:12

Imagine if every time you criticized someone or gossiped, you broke out in a horrible skin disease. How would that change your interactions with other people?

God showed His justice in defending Moses, and He also showed His mercy to Miriam by answering Moses' prayer to heal her. When Moses prayed, "LORD God, please heal her." He was calling out to their Sovereign, LORD, Master, and the Creator of the Heavens and Earth and every person. I think it is worth noting that Moses, the object of Miriam's gossip and criticism, was the one who prayed for God to heal her. There is great power in praying for God to heal the hearts and minds of people who insult us, criticize us, gossip about us, and make fun of us.

Moses is a great role model for each of us when people gossip or criticize us. Rather than responding to them, we need to forgive them and pray for God to heal them. God will bring justice to our situation. Just as He humbled Miriam by declaring that she was to be outside of the camp for seven days, He will bring justice to those who elevate themselves by gossiping and criticizing. Our job is to humble ourselves under God and trust that He will take care of the people that attack us. A great verse to encourage you to trust God is 1 Peter 5:6, 7 "Humble yourselves, therefore, under God's mighty hand, that he may lift you up in due time. Cast all your anxiety on him because he cares for you."

If there is someone who has hurt you, criticized you or gossiped about you; forgive them and ask God to heal them. Just as God healed Miriam, He can heal them. Try it. It could change both of your lives!

GOD OUR HEALER- RAPHA EL

As she led Miriam experienced God's healing power when Moses cried out to the LORD, "Heal (Rapha') her, O God (El), I beg you!"[70] In Hebrew, the verb for "heal" in this passage is "Rapha." "The verb from which Raphe is derived occurs sixty-seven times in the Old Testament. Though it often refers to physical healing it usually has a larger meaning as well, involving the entire person. Rather than merely healing the body Yahweh (LORD) Rophe (Healer) heals the mind and soul as well. This Hebrew verb is also used in other ways; for example, God "heals" water, land and nations, and He "repairs" the altar. At other times this verb is used when God heals sin and apostasy. The Hebrew Scriptures link sickness and sin by presenting sin as the cause of illness just as it is the cause of death. In the New Testament, the corresponding Greek word is "iaomai" and it can refer to deliverance from death,

---

[70] Numbers 12:13 (NLT)

demons, sickness, and sin. Jesus, the great healer, clearly indicated that sickness is not necessarily caused by sin on the part of the person who is ill. Rather it can result from living in a sinful, fallen world."[71]

God is our Healer. As a child, I believed God could heal. I had heard the stories of Jesus healing the blind man, the lame man, the lepers, and raising people from the dead. God had created humanity; He could heal us. I was able to personally experience God's miraculous healing power in a way that gave me a whole new perspective on Jehovah (Lord) Rapha (Healer). Soon after getting married, I began to suffer debilitating reflux. I missed work, lost sleep, and was in so much pain that I couldn't go twelve hours without taking medicine. After suffering for over a year, my dad prayed for me, and I was miraculously healed. One day, I was taking medication every 12 hours, and the next, I was cured! Amazing! God's healing power is not confined to stories in the Bible.

More recently, my understanding of God's ability to heal has come to include spiritually healing our hearts, memories, and souls. My mom shared her insight on God's ability to heal devastating hurts from our past and emotional pain. When she first shared her perspective on God being able to heal emotional wounds the way He had healed my physical illness, I was skeptical. However, God worked on my prideful heart and illuminated the truth. One night, we were talking about something that happened when I was a teenager. Even though it had been over twenty years, talking about it still hurt. Humbling myself, I asked her to walk me through her healing timeline.[72] As she led me through this process, I was miraculously set free from this emotional pain. The pain is gone, and I can see how God replaced what was destroyed with something only He could give.

> *God's healing* **power is not confined to stories in the Bible.**

As a result of this experience, I now look at healing very differently. I realized that it isn't just our physical bodies that need healing, but our spirits and souls. Jesus came to bind up the broken-hearted and heal all our diseases.[73] My understanding of Jehovah Rapha has gone from reading about it in the scriptures to personally experiencing it. My desire is that you also will experience His healing power.

If you can find another person to pray with you, take some time to pray and ask God to heal you spiritually, physically, and emotionally. Just as God healed Miriam and me, God can heal you.

---

[71] Spangler, pg. 100
[72] For more information on the Healing Timeline- see Appendix
[73] Psalm 147:3, Psalm 103:3

Week 4

FINALLY... THE PROMISED LAND?

After two years in the desert, it was time to explore the land that had been promised to their ancestor Abraham. Numbers 13 and 14 tell the tale of this potentially exciting time. Moses sent men to explore Canaan. They came back to Moses and Aaron and the whole Israelite community at Kadesh in the Desert of Paran. There they reported to them and the entire assembly and showed them the fruit of the land. They gave Moses this account: "We went into the land to which you sent us, and it does flow with milk and honey! Here is its fruit." Unfortunately, the excitement about the land quickly turned into misery as ten of the explorers warned about the people of the land being giants and the difficulty in taking the land.

The people (including Miriam) were distraught in response to the report from the Promised Land. "That night all the people of the community raised their voices and wept aloud. All the Israelites grumbled against Moses and Aaron, and the whole assembly said to them, "If only we had died in Egypt! Or in this desert! Why is the LORD bringing us to this land only to let us fall by the sword? Our wives and children will be taken as plunder. Wouldn't it be better for us to go back to Egypt?" And they said to each other, "We should choose a leader and go back to Egypt."[74]

How did the Israelites let fear keep them from trusting God?

Nearly all the people of the community doubted God's ability to lead them into the land he had promised to her ancestor Abraham. They questioned whether God would take care of their children if they followed Him into a risky situation. They allowed their fears for their families to keep them from fully following God. If we are following God's will, we should fear God and trust our all-powerful Heavenly Father to take care of our families.

Since all the Israelites grumbled against Moses and Aaron, Miriam likely was one of the "non-believers," even though she had personally experienced many miraculous signs. She lived through the Passover. She witnessed God's presence every day in the form of the cloud by day and the fire by night

---

[74] Numbers 14:1-4

and God's power had healed her. She sang praises to the Lord after walking across the Red Sea on dry land. She tasted the sweetness of water that had been bitter. She was reminded of God's provision daily through manna and shoes that didn't wear out.

Despite experiencing God's daily presence and provision, Miriam and the rest of Israel still doubted God! They had the manna every day, the fire by night, and water from rocks. How could they not trust God? It is easy to look at Miriam and the Israelites and judge them for their lack of faith. But don't we have so much more? Jesus Christ has miraculously saved us; we have the indwelling presence and power of the Holy Spirit; we are surrounded the magnificent glory of creation; and we have the Bible, God's Word. We have experienced times when God has revealed Himself to us by healing us, providing for us, and showing how He is our Creator, Healer, Deliverer, and True Love.

As I read about Miriam and the Israelites, I was convicted of the times that I let my fears keep me from following God's will. Fear has kept me from giving generously. I have let my fears decide where we would live. I stayed in a job because of fear rather than trusting God to provide. My fear of rejection has kept me from sharing my true self and the miracle of Christ's love with others. I have allowed fear to keep me from experiencing all of God's blessings for me.

Please take a minute to pray and repent for allowing your fears to keep you from trusting God. Then, if God shows you specific areas that you need to trust Him in, please write them down. Ask God to replace your fear with confidence in Him.

Here's how the story continues, "Then Moses and Aaron fell face down in front of the whole Israelite assembly gathered there. Joshua son of Nun and Caleb son of Jephunneh, who were among those who had explored the land, tore their clothes and said to the entire Israelite assembly, "The land we passed through and explored is exceedingly good. If the LORD is pleased with us, he will lead us into that land, a land flowing with milk and honey, and will give it to us. Only do not rebel against the LORD. And do not be afraid of the people of the land, because we will swallow them up. Their protection is gone, but the LORD is with us. Do not be afraid of them."[75]

Joshua and Caleb encouraged the people to trust God. What did they say that helps you trust God and embrace change?

---

[75] Numbers 14:4-9

THE PROMISED LAND DELAYED

The Israelites' response to Joshua and Caleb was to talk about stoning them. They chose to doubt God and let their fears rule them rather than letting God be Sovereign in their lives. The Israelites' lack of faith had significant consequences for them and their children.

To help you connect this story with your own, answer this question: Can you think of times that friends or family members made one foolish or selfish choice that resulted in financial, relational, or emotional consequences for them and their children? How do you think things could have been different?

Numbers 14:10-35 tells an incredibly sad story of a lost generation. Please read these passages and fill in the blanks.

Please read Numbers 14:11 and fill in the blanks. "The Lord said to Moses, "How long will these people treat me with _____? How long will they refuse to _____, in spite of all the _____ I have performed among them?"

Numbers 14:17-19 "Now may the Lord's _____ be displayed, just as you have declared:18 'The LORD is _____, abounding in _____ and _____ sin and rebellion. Yet he does not leave the guilty _____; he punishes the children for the sin of the fathers to the third and fourth generation.' 19 In accordance with your _____ _____, forgive the sin of these people, just as you have pardoned them from the time they left Egypt until now."

Numbers 14:30-34 _____ one of you will enter the land I swore with uplifted hand to make your home, except Caleb son of Jephunneh and Joshua son of Nun. 31 As for _____ that you said would be taken as plunder, I will bring them in to enjoy the land you have rejected. 32 But you—your bodies will fall in this desert. 33 Your _____ will be shepherds here for forty years, suffering for your unfaithfulness, until the last of your bodies lies in the desert. 34 For _____—one year for each of the forty days you explored the land—you will suffer for your sins and know what it is like to have me against you.'

What does God reveal to Miriam and the Israelites about their attitude and His character and justice in this passage?

How can this help us to trust God?

One of the most significant long-term consequences of sin is a missed blessing. An entire generation died before the descendants of Abraham and Sarah were allowed into the land. The children of the unbelievers had to suffer in the desert as nomads for forty years because their parents were afraid of the Canaanites rather than being afraid of disobeying God.

The Lord warned His people when He gave them the Ten Commandments about the importance of obedience and the consequences of disobedience. For example, God commanded His people, "You shall have no other gods before me.[76]" Exodus 20:5 clearly states the consequences of idol worship. It says, "You shall not bow down to them or worship them; for I, the Lord your God, am a jealous God, punishing the children for the sin of the parents to the third and fourth generation of those who hate me."

At first glance, the consequences from disobedience seem really unfair. God punishes the children for the sins of the fathers to the third or fourth generation. But God can transform the curse into a blessing. Look at how this sentence continues after the comma into Exodus 20:6. It reads "but showing love to a thousand {generations} of those who love me and keep my commandments." God's blessing and love extend to a thousand generations, far beyond the sins of one's parents.

What is practical way we can show that we trust God?

Obedience is simply trusting that God knows best for every part of our lives. We have a greater responsibility to trust God after we have seen His presence and experienced His work in our lives. God longs to bless us and be in a relationship with us, but that requires obedience. When we are obedient, God's best (in relationships, where we live, finances, careers, families, and health) is manifested in our lives. This story carries an important lesson: if you trust God, you and generations to follow will be abundantly blessed, but you and your family will suffer if you disobey God. Miriam soon died after the Israelites gave up their chance to enter the Promised Land. Her journey had come to an end. Numbers 20:1 records her death, "In the first month the whole Israelite community arrived at the Desert of Zin, and they stayed at Kadesh. There Miriam died and was buried."[77]

---

[76] Exodus 20:3
[77] Numbers 20:1

A LIFE FOLLOWING GOD

Miriam lived a full life. We learned about her bravery and resourcefulness as a young girl while babysitting her little brother Moses. We saw how God prepared Moses and her to be leaders. Though she lived most of her life in slavery, God used her to lead women after the Israelites escaped from the Egyptians.

Miriam's parents named her as a sign of the bitterness in their lives, but just as God healed the waters of Marah and made them sweet, God transformed the slavery in Miriam's life into freedom. Though the Israelites didn't have GPS, God led them through the desert. He knew their weaknesses and wanted them to succeed; He guided them along the longer way, but that detour kept them from being attacked. While it may seem risky to trust God, in reality, it is the safest and most logical thing to do. During their journey, God provided manna for Miriam and all the people.

Though Miriam was a prophetess and a leader, she wasn't perfect. Her story reminds us not to complain, criticize, or gossip. Miriam learned the hard way that criticizing and gossiping led to misery. Miriam had elevated herself by judging and talking badly about her brother and wife, so God humbled her. During this episode of bad skin, Miriam's brother, Moses, showed us how to respond through prayer and forgiveness when someone gossips or criticizes us. God is our healer, and just as he healed Miriam from leprosy, He can heal the wounds in our body, mind, and soul.

Miriam's life illustrated the blessings of obedience when she asked her Egyptian oppressors for gold, jewels, and provisions for their journey. While it was risky for them to ask their neighbors for these things, the reward was great because the blessings of obedience always dwarf the risks of following God. Whenever God calls us to do something, we need to remember that God has gone before us and has prepared the way to bless our obedience.

Miriam's life also taught us how disbelief and disobedience could lead to devastating consequences. One of the most significant long-term consequences of diverging from God's plan is a missed blessing. An entire generation died before the descendants of Abraham and Sarah were allowed into the Promised Land. The children of the unbelievers suffered in the desert as nomads for forty years because their parents were more afraid of the Canaanites than the consequences of disobeying God. As we embrace change, we need to leave fear in the desert and trust our All-Powerful God because He is our Deliverer, Provider, Light, and Healer.

HOW HAVE YOU LEARNED TO TRUST GOD THROUGH STUDYING MIRIAM?

CHAPTER IV

Naomi

MOTHER-IN-LAW

FRIEND

Lived about 1,100 BC

For the Lord is good and His love endures
forever; His faithfulness continues through
all generations.
Psalm 100:5

Week 1

Naomi

I have a confession. I love romance stories and happy endings. In my early teens, I went through a stage where I read hundreds of fairy tales. As I grew older, I became enthralled by the drama of Regency romance novels; stories that take you through the trials of true love and end when the hero kisses the heroine. At the movies, I prefer romantic comedies. The greatest attraction of these stories is their predictability. Before I pick up the book or buy my popcorn, I know how the story will end. With a happy ending guaranteed, I can enjoy the twists and turns of the plot.

The Book of Ruth has the makings of an ancient romance novel. Ruth is the heroine, a beautiful, hardworking, and kind widow. Naomi, her mother-in-law, is a supporting character, comparable to Cinderella's fairy godmother. Boaz is the handsome, rich, older man who protected and took care of Ruth. During barley harvest season, Ruth and Boaz fell in love. Yet, in a dramatic twist of fate, just as Boaz is about to marry Ruth, they find out that another relative has the legal right to buy Ruth's land by marrying her. For a brief while, all appears to be lost. But just before the book ends, Boaz and Ruth are joined together in wedded bliss, have a wonderful baby boy, and live happily ever after (okay, I added the "happily ever after" part, but it fits.)

In the past, when I read the Book of Ruth, I would gloss over much of Naomi's role in this story and focus on Ruth and Boaz's romance. However, after working on this study, I have grown to appreciate Naomi as a wife, mother-in-law, and grandmother who lived her faith in such a genuine way that her daughter-in-law chose to follow the Lord. Naomi's life has love, drama, and a happy ending for all of us.

NAOMI'S BACKGROUND

Naomi's story starts in a harsh and bitter time in Israel's history. About 300 years had passed since Miriam's brother Moses led the people out of Egypt. After the people settled in their new homes, they began a vicious cycle of idolatry, defeat, repentance, new leadership, and peace. "They forsook the LORD, the God of their fathers, who had brought them out of Egypt. They followed and worshiped various gods of the peoples around them. They provoked the LORD to anger."[78] In response to their

---

[78] Judges 2:12

idolatry, God would allow the nations around the Israelites to attack and defeat them. This conflict would lead to famine, death, and persecution. Then, the people of Israel would repent and cry out to God for help. So, God would appoint leaders called "Judges" to lead the people of Israel in battle and back to God. Unfortunately, the Israelites would get complacent after victory. They would go back to worshiping the gods of the nations around them, and the cycle would start again.

The Book of Ruth opens with a lot of information about Naomi and her family. Please write out Ruth 1:1-2.

As we learned from these first two verses, Naomi is from Bethlehem; she is married and has two sons. For fun, let's try and figure out Naomi's age. Her children provide a good clue. She had two sons, who were young enough to travel with her and her husband to Moab. They weren't old enough to stay in Bethlehem by themselves, and they weren't old enough to be already married. Since we can guess her sons were no older than teens, so she probably was in her 30s when she left Bethlehem.

Naomi's name means pleasant. Times may have been good when Naomi was born, but as she grew older during the reign of the Judges, life became challenging. She lived through desperate times, including famine and spiritual depravity. The biblical book of Judges records this time in history. Ruth 1:1 begins with the phrase, "When the Judges Ruled." We don't know for sure when Naomi and her family left their home and moved to Moab so they could avoid the famine. However, it was likely during a time such as the one described in Judges 6:1-5 when God allowed raiders to invade the country, destroy the Israelite's crops, and steal all their sheep, cattle, and donkeys because of the Israelites' idolatry.

The time of Judges was a time of rampant idolatry. Judges 10:6-7 explains a vicious cycle of idolatry and suffering, "Again the Israelites did evil in the eyes of the LORD. They served the Baals and the Ashtoreths, and the gods of Aram, the gods of Sidon, the gods of Moab, the gods of the Ammonites and the gods of the Philistines. And because the Israelites forsook the LORD and no longer served him, he became angry with them. He sold them into the hands of the Philistines and the Ammonites."

It is easy to read about the Israelites' idolatry and think, "That's not a problem for me." Worshipping idols is as foreign to me as sleeping in a grass hut and eating grubs. In America, we are not surrounded by shrines, altars, and temples to false gods that Christians face every day in other parts of the world. However, our culture can entice us into a form of idolatry that is just as deceptive and dangerous.

The Israelites thought worshiping idols would give them the things they wanted like security, children, happiness, health, and success. What are some modern pursuits that could become a form of idolatry?

Just as the Israelites looked for their security and identity in the culture around them, we are focused on material things and relationships for significance and meaning. It is very tempting to look for our security in the things of this world, such as money, cars, houses, or clothes. We have internalized the perspectives that greed and wanting more are typical, and personal power is something to be attained. We look for our identity in roles and relationships, such as being a professional woman, a wife, a mother, and a friend, seeking others to define us and help us feel loved and secure. These are all temporal. Instead, as God's chosen beloved child, our value and confidence should come from our security and identity in Him.

Our primary relationship and service must be to God. In Matthew 6:24, Jesus said, "No one can serve two masters. Either he will hate the one and love the other, or he will be devoted to the one and despise the other. You cannot serve both God and Money." Money is not bad, and neither are jobs, kids,

Our security **and identity as God's chosen beloved child is where our value and confidence should come from.**

clothes, food, or houses, but we cannot serve the things of this world without committing idolatry.

Though Naomi lived in Israel during a time of rampant idolatry and later moved to a place that was even more wicked and perverse, she did not let the culture diminish her belief and trust in God. She knew that God was her Creator and the Lord Almighty. She believed that the Lord who provided for the Israelites when they left Egypt, healed Miriam and Sarah, created her was worthy of worship in good and bad times.

When I am struggling in this area by focusing on things our culture defines as important, God brings to mind several verses from Matthew 6. Please read Matthew 6:25-33 and write out Matthew 6:31-33.

I love these verses. They are so simple yet powerful and practical. Worry can occupy our minds so much that it replaces God in our lives. I think it is interesting in Matthew 6:31, Jesus tells us not to worry about what we will eat, what we will drink, or what we will wear. Aren't these things that occupy a woman's mind, whether we are in extreme poverty and do not have enough for our children to eat or we are dieting and need to lose weight!

The cure for worry and our cultural idolatry is to seek first the things of God: His kingdom and His righteousness, which is a deeper relationship with Him. God desires our righteousness because He wants a relationship with us. The wickedness of idolatry is the opposite of righteousness.[79] Worshiping any god plus God meant that they were rejecting the LORD. Imagine if your husband told you he loved you and another woman. If he asked, "What's the big deal with a little something, something on the side? I still love you." You would still feel rejected by your husband even though he said he loved you.

Similarly, idolatry hurts our relationship with God. When the people of Israel took part in the culture of the people around them and worshiped the gods of the land, the Baals and Ashtoreths, they were no longer righteous (in a right relationship with God) because they had damaged their relationship with God. They had decided to love God *and* other gods. As a result, they had rejected God.

When we focus on God by making it our priority to seek His kingdom and His righteousness, then all the things which often turn into idols (food, clothes, homes, and the other things of this world) will be given to us as well.

Hold on to this truth: The God who made you and knitted you together in your mother's womb, who sacrificed His Son so that you would have eternal life, can handle your finances, your pain, your relationships, your fears, and worries. Rather than trying to do it all on your own, trust Him.

Take a minute to pray and ask God to show you areas in your life where you've focused your attention on material things and relationships other than God. Pray that God would help you focus your attention on Him and restore your relationship with Him and help you trust Him.

BAD TIMES GET WORSE

The famine and ongoing attacks by raiders made life in Bethlehem miserable. Naomi's husband hoped to make things better by moving to Moab, a neighboring country on the eastern side of the Dead Sea. But unfortunately, things became even worse.

While Moab was only 50 miles away from Bethlehem (ancient Moab is located in modern-day Jordan), it was worlds away in culture and beliefs. The people in Moab were descendants of an incestuous relationship between Abraham and Sarah's nephew Lot and his daughter after they escaped the destruction of Sodom and Gomorrah.[80]

The Moabites worshipped a god named Chemosh. The worship of Chemosh likely required child sacrifice.[81] The Moabites also participated in the worship of Baal-Peor, a god worshipped for providing fertility. During the years of wandering after the Exodus, the Israelite men worshipped Baal-Peor by

---

[79] 1 Corinthians 6:14-16
[80] Genesis 19:30-38
[81] 2 Kings 3:27

having sexual relations with the Moabite women, eating sacrificed food with them, and bowing down to Baal Peor.[82] Moab was an ungodly place. I imagine it was scary for Naomi to move her young family to this foreign land.

Imagine moving your family to a new land like Naomi. What would be your biggest concerns?

Please read the following passage from Ruth 1:3-5 and answer the questions.
Ruth 1:3-5 "Now Elimelech, Naomi's husband, died, and she was left with her two sons. They married Moabite women, one named Orpah and the other Ruth. After they had lived there about ten years, both Mahlon and Kilion also died, and Naomi was left without her two sons and her husband."

What happened to Naomi's husband?

What happened to Naomi's sons?

Naomi's reality in Moab was much worse than she could have imagined when she left Bethlehem. As women, our relationships define our view of ourselves. Naomi's identity was devastated in ten short years. First, she lost her husband, and then both of her sons died. How can you be a mother when both of your children have died? How can you be a wife when your husband has died? Death and divorce create times of deep mourning for the person or relationship that was lost and the survivor's former identity. Several of my friends have lost their fathers recently. As they have deeply mourned their father, they have also mourned their lost identity as a Daddy's girl.

* Have you ever felt as if you have lost who you were? How did that change your relationship with other people and God?

Our roles and relationships as women give us meaning and identity, yet they are temporary because children grow up, parents die, and friends move away. While our relationships are important to help us fulfill the greatest commandment, to love God and love others, they are not meant to be our identity.

---

[82] Numbers 25:3

Our identity must be in Christ, who does not change like the shifting shadows; who never leaves or forsakes us; who laid down His life for us and has defeated sickness and death.

If our identity depends on our relationships with our spouse, children, or friends, we will let their happiness and joy determine how we live our lives rather than allowing the Lord to guide us. We will compromise what God has called us to do for the short-term benefit of their happiness.

Our passionate desire for relationships with people must be superseded by our passion for a relationship with Christ. Earlier in this chapter, we read Matthew 6:28, "Seek first the kingdom of heaven and His righteousness and all these things will be given to you." Righteousness means a right relationship. Here's my paraphrase, "Seek first a right relationship with God and all the other things will be given to you."

Putting Christ first is simply a trust issue. It requires letting go of valuing ourselves by the relationships we have. We have to let go of defining our success by other people's happiness. It requires believing that God has infinite love and infinite resources to take care of our loved ones. If you put God first in your life, even before the people you love the most, God will bless you and enable you to bless them more than you on your own with all your resources. He made all of us and loves us more than we could ever comprehend.

> **Our passionate desire for relationships with people must be superseded by our passion for a relationship with Christ.**

Putting God first will result in better relationships and lasting blessings for generations. Naomi's faithfulness and belief in God resulted in blessing her daughter-in-law Ruth and generations to come through her descendants, King David and Jesus Christ.

As you wrap up this week's lesson, pray and ask God to help you put Him first. Repent of places of idolatry in your life and ask God to fill you with His presence. Praise Him because He is our Creator, God Almighty, our Lord, our Healer, our Light in the desert, our True Love, and our Peace.

Week 2

GOING HOME

When a review starts with "Spoiler Alert," I always continue reading. Knowing how a story or movie will end makes me so happy. As a teenager, I read Agatha Christie mysteries, and I couldn't stand the suspense, so I would skip to the end to find out "who-dun-it" and then read the book to see if I could find out the clues. When the Book of Ruth was written, everyone already knew the ending. So, the author's goal was to show God's sovereign hand and blessing during hard times so that readers would trust God's kindness and love in their daily lives. Naomi's story has a happy ending, but things didn't get better right away. After the death of Naomi's two sons, she decided to go home to Bethlehem back to her home, her people, and her God.

Please read Ruth 1:6-11 and answer the following questions.
Where did Naomi plan to go?

What did Naomi say to her daughters-in-law in verses 8- 9?

What does this say about Naomi's view of God?

How did her daughters-in-law respond?

Naomi decided to return home to Bethlehem because she heard that the LORD had provided food for His people. She told her daughters-in-law to return to their mother's homes. My friend Joyce, who has been a mother-in-law for over 50 years, shared with me her perception of Naomi. As she read the story of Naomi and Ruth, she was amazed by Naomi's love for both of her daughters-in-law. Naomi gave her daughters-in-law the freedom to choose if they wanted to go with her or leave.

Nancy, a mom of adult children commented on the contrast between helicopter parenting today and Naomi's ability to let the two young women chose their own path. She wrote, "I am convicted to try and be more like Naomi in allowing my adult children the freedom to manage their own lives... The problem (of letting go) comes when we are not ready for God's next step for *our* lives. If our lives have been focused around Christ instead of our children, then the freedom that comes with the empty nest opens up all sorts of opportunities timewise for us to serve the body of Christ, in whatever way our talents, experiences, and convictions lead us."

Trusting God and letting go can only happen if we fully rely on God, His character, and His amazing love for us and our children. Naomi understood the love and mercy of the LORD and prayed for Him to show His kindness to her daughters-in-law. In this passage, Naomi shows that she knew the LORD (Jehovah, Master) had provided the food for His people in Judah just as He had provided for the Israelites in the desert.

> **Trusting God and letting go can only happen if we truly know God, His character and His amazing love for each of us and our children.**

Though Naomi had been living in the foreign land of Moab for over ten years; she hadn't forgotten the LORD's goodness and kindness, and she even taught her daughters-in-law about Him. Naomi's blessing, "May the LORD show kindness to you, as you have shown to your dead and to me. May the LORD grant that each of you will find rest in the home of another husband," gives us insight into her understanding of how the LORD could bless these young widows.

First, Naomi prayed that the LORD would show "kindness" to them. The Hebrew word for kindness is "חֶסֶד" *chesed*, typically translated as mercy, kindness, unfailing love, and loving-kindness. Foundational to this word is an understanding of the LORD's love. Naomi knew and understood her Lord Master; He was loving, kind, and merciful. The idea of God's mercy and kindness is found throughout the Bible. I looked up the word "*chesed*".[83] This word is used over 200 times, and the majority of the time, it refers to God's love and mercy on His people despite their sinfulness. In the NIV, *chesed* is frequently translated as "unfailing love."

Please look up and write down the following verses.
Exodus 15:13

Psalm 23:6

Psalm 25:7

---

[83] http://www.blueletterbible.org/lang/lexicon/lexicon.cfm?Strongs=H2617&t=KJV

Psalm 100:5

Hopefully, the previous verses give you a taste of the steadfast, unfailing love that God has for you. In Exodus, after the escape from Pharaoh's army, Moses praises God for His unfailing love. In the Psalms, King David writes that God's love will follow him all the days of his life, he asks God to look at his sins through the eyes of love, and he praises God because His love endures forever. Our LORD Master loves us despite our sins and the times when we choose our will over His will. He loves us because it is His nature to love.

Our view of God must be based on the reality of God as manifested throughout the Bible. Too often, we project our image of God based on flawed human relationships or other people's faulty understanding rather than the Word of God. Several people have shared their view that the God of the Old Testament is a harsh, punitive Master. This is a distorted view of a loving God. Without a doubt, God is just; but He is also always loving and kind. Our sin doesn't change His unfailing love because it is His nature. God hates sin, but He loves His people even though they sin.

God loves us because God is love.[84] Since Creation, God has not changed. Numbers 23:19 gives us great insight into the unchanging nature of our God. It says, "God is not a man that he should lie. He is not a human, that he should change his mind. Has he ever spoken and failed to act? Has he ever promised and not carried it through?" *God's love for us doesn't change based on our actions.* He created us for a relationship, he is our Lord, and He loves us with unfailing love.

Naomi knew that she would not be able to have other children, so she prayed for the LORD to grant Ruth and Orpah rest in a home with a husband of their own. The word "home" in verse 9, also means household and includes both husband and children. As a widow, Naomi understood their desire for a husband and a family. Even while grappling with grief over her sons' deaths, God empowered Naomi to minister to these young women in the loss of their husbands. She knew that God could bless them even though their current situation seemed hopeless. In the same way, God can use you to bless others even when you are going through difficult and heartbreaking times.

Please take a minute to pray and ask God to show you how you could help someone going through a difficult time. Then, write down their name and the specific ways that God brought to your mind to help them.

---

[84] 1st John 4:8

Naomi's gift to these young women was a prayer that included a valuable blessing. Naomi knew that the LORD could provide a peaceful home. The word "rest" in the Bible connotes a place of security, protection, and no strife. Our homes can be and should be a place of rest for ourselves, our husbands, and our children. An oasis provides rest, refreshment, and a break from the harsh land in the desert. Likewise, your home can be an oasis for your family and all who come to your door.

If you, your husband, or your kids say that your home is not a place of rest, pray as Naomi did and ask God to make your home a place of rest and blessing. We can claim the promise of Isaiah 32:18 for our homes and families, "My people will live in peaceful dwelling places, in secure homes, in undisturbed places of rest."

We've covered a lot of ground; please pause for a moment to pray and ask God to help you see His unfailing love for you, His desire to bless you with the desires of your heart, and His promise of a peaceful home.

GOD'S HAND

We will learn more about Naomi's view of herself and God when she returns to Bethlehem from Moab. Please read Ruth 1:12-13 and answer the following questions.

How did Naomi describe herself in this passage?

How does Naomi view the LORD?

Do you think the Lord's hand can be against someone?

In verse 12, Naomi calls herself "old." Interestingly, she is probably the youngest of the women in this study! If she was in her thirties when she left Bethlehem, her sons had to be young enough to travel with their parents, yet they were old enough to marry ten years later. As I calculate it, she was probably in her late thirties to early forties when she told her daughters-in-law that she was old.

This shows that "old" is a state of mind as much as an actual age. Remember Princess Sarah called her husband Abraham "old" at 99. Miriam was never called "old," and she was in her mid-80s when she led the women of Israel in praise on the banks of the Red Sea. Though Naomi was chronologically young, she felt old. Calling herself "old" was another way of saying she felt as if her life was nearly over. She experienced extreme poverty during a famine; plus, her two sons and husband had died. The reality of her situation left a bad taste in her mouth, it was bitter, and Naomi felt old.

Naomi knew about the loving-kindness of God, prayed for God to bless her daughters-in-law, and shared the kindness of the Lord with them. But in her heart, she felt as if the LORD's hand was against her, fighting, and punishing her.

Can you relate to Naomi? Have there been times that you knew that God loves you, but your situation left you felling hopeless and overwhelmed by the misery of your situation?

Naomi had lost both of her sons, she was in mourning, and she may have been depressed. She felt as if the Lord's hand was against her, but the Lord may not have been punishing her. Without a doubt there are times when the Lord's hand is against His people because of their sin and idolatry.[85] However, not all hard times are the result of sin or idolatry. There are times when our physical suffering results from spiritual conflict, such as Job experienced. Other times, God will also use affliction to refine us[86] and to open others' eyes to His glory and power.[87]

Occasionally, what feels like God's hand being against us is actually God's hand moving us in the direction that He wants us to go. For example, God went to extreme lengths to save the jailer and his family in Acts.[88] Without a doubt, God's hand was at work to bring Ruth, who was King David's great-grandmother, to Bethlehem, where her descendant Jesus Christ would be born 1,000 years later.

One of the most important lessons we can learn from Naomi is to trust God and believe His Word even when our circumstances make us feel as if God is against us.

Naomi had no idea of God's plan to use famine, death, and hardship in her life for His eternal glory. As a result, Naomi felt as if God was against her because she was surrounded by unrelenting heartbreak and suffering. In the same way, our feelings have immense power over us. Though we may know in our minds that God is good, kind, and loving, we may not feel it during pain and suffering.

Naomi acted on what she knew about God rather than her feelings. Her faith in God's character despite her circumstances allowed her to trust God and bless her daughters-in-law. Naomi prayed for Ruth and Orpah to experience rest because she knew God could provide that for them, even though she felt God was against her. We can learn from Naomi to trust God and believe His Word even when our circumstances make us feel like God is against us.

---

[85] Judges 2:15
[86] Isaiah 48:10
[87] John 11:4
[88] Acts 16:25-40

God's steadfast and unchanging Word is a counterbalance for our feelings which tend to ebb and flow with our circumstances, finances, and even day of the month. Studying the Bible allows us to know God's character, know His power, and know His love.

* Psalm 119:105 says, "Your word is a lamp to my feet and a light for my path." Memorizing scriptures is one of the most important things we can do to prepare for times when we do not feel God's presence or blessing. Look back through this chapter to find a scripture that you would like to memorize. Write it here and on a 3x5 card to carry with you as you learn it.

CHOOSING YOUR GOD

A turning point in Naomi's story begins in Ruth 1:14-18; please read it and fill in the blanks.

At this they wept again. Then Orpah _____ her mother-in-law good-bye but Ruth _____ to her.

"Look," said Naomi, "your sister-in-law is going back to _____and _____ Go back with her."

But Ruth replied, "Don't urge me to leave you or to turn back from you. Where you go I will go, and where you stay I will stay. _____ _____. Where you die I will die, and there I will be buried. May the _____ deal with me, be it ever so severely, if anything but death separates you and me." 18 When Naomi realized that Ruth was determined to go with her, she stopped urging her.

When Ruth says, "Your people will be my people and your God, my God," She is choosing to leave the idols and false gods of Moab and follow the God of the Israelites. This is one of the most quoted passages in the Bible; it is used in weddings and on friendship necklaces, yet it's from a daughter-in-law to a mother-in-law, a relationship that people don't automatically assume has much love.

> *Would your words,* deeds and attitude bring others to Christ if people saw your life 24/7?

Naomi's love for these young women is remarkable. When her sons got married, their wives Ruth and Orpah likely moved into Naomi's home because it was technically her sons' house after her husband died. Naomi built relationships with these two women in a tiny house and a challenging situation by allowing them the space and respect they needed. Imagine sharing the home you worked on for years to make beautiful with two other women who now thought it was their house!

During their time together, these three women had a chance to get to know each other and share their beliefs. Naomi's love for her daughters-in-law allowed her to give them the freedom to choose what they wanted to do with their lives, whether they wanted to return to their families or go with her to Bethlehem. This choice may appear to be a decision for Ruth and Orpah to return to their families; it was more significantly a choice to leave Moab's false gods and follow the Lord.

Why do you think Ruth was able to make this choice? How had she learned about God?

Naomi taught Ruth and Orpah about God who created the earth and all that was in it, including her during her everyday life of cooking, cleaning, and getting water; and after the death of her two sons, she taught them about the hope she had in God. Even after the devastating loss of her husband and sons, Naomi had something that Ruth wanted: her love and understanding of God. Ruth knew that she wanted Naomi's God to be her God. If someone lived with you 24/7, would your words, deeds, and attitude bring them to Christ?

Sharing what we know and understand about God with others is an important part of growing in our personal understanding of God. Pray and ask God to bring to mind a friend or child that you can share the Gospel.

A NAME CHANGE
Please read Ruth 1:19- 22 below and answer the questions that follow.

"So the two women went on until they came to Bethlehem. When they arrived in Bethlehem, the whole town was stirred because of them, and the women exclaimed, "Can this be Naomi?"

"Don't call me Naomi," she told them. "Call me Mara, because the Almighty has made my life very bitter. I went away full, but the LORD has brought me back empty. Why call me Naomi? The LORD has afflicted me; the Almighty has brought misfortune upon me."

"So Naomi returned from Moab accompanied by Ruth the Moabitess, her daughter-in-law, arriving in Bethlehem as the barley harvest was beginning."

Why did Naomi ask the people to call her Mara?

Naomi used two names for God in this passage: Almighty and LORD. Based on what we've learned in the previous chapters, what do these words mean?

Why do you think she used both names?

What had the Lord done to Naomi?

What did she say the Almighty did to her?

Naomi asked the people of the town to call her "Mara" because the Almighty had made her life bitter. The footnote in my Bible for Ruth 1:20 explains that Mara means "bitter" and Naomi means "pleasantness." The word "bitter" in the Old Testament often refers to difficult situations like the time when the Israelites were enslaved in Egypt.

During the Passover celebration, the Israelites were to eat "bitter" herbs to symbolize the miserable times from which God had delivered them. Bitter in the Old Testament describes bitter water and bitter herbs. This is different from "bitterness" in the New Testament, which has to do with an emotion closely related to anger and wrath. Just as bitter foods leave a bad taste in your mouth, Naomi's life left a bad taste in her mouth. Naomi wasn't resentful or angry at God; she was just stating her reality. She didn't like how her life had turned out.

Naomi understood that the LORD (Jehovah) was her Master. The LORD was responsible for her travels and for her work. She knew that the Lord brought her back from Moab; like when I worked for a bank, my boss would send me on business trips.

God is El Shadday, **Almighty God, all powerful. His power and might trump all other forces, good and evil. Everything is under His dominion.**

Naomi also knew that God was Almighty (El Shadday). El Shadday was all-powerful and sovereign. By His power, both good things and "yucky" things happened.

The sovereignty of God to bring blessing and hard times raises difficult questions. If God is good and loving, how could He bring misfortune and affliction to Naomi?

Naomi said, "The Almighty (Shadday) has made my life very bitter and that the Almighty (El Shadday) has brought misfortune upon me." God is El Shadday, Almighty God, all-powerful. His power and might trump all other forces, good and evil. Everything is under His dominion.

Ann Spangler asks the following questions in her book *Praying the Names of God*, "What if God were good but weak? Beautiful but powerless? He might want to bless but would be unable to. Wouldn't this God of good intentions be a bit pathetic?"

A God who can be moved by our strength, one who doesn't have power, isn't Almighty. Naomi had spent over ten years living in Moab, a land of false, fickle, and powerless gods. Even in the midst of her suffering, she knew that the Almighty, "Shadday," was powerful. Like a mountain that could not be moved, there was nothing stronger than the Almighty.

God was not only powerful; He was her LORD and Master. Though Naomi left Bethlehem in the midst of a famine, her life was full. After famine ended, Naomi surveyed her situation and said, "The LORD has brought me back empty." This is such an interesting contrast; during the famine, she was full, but after the famine was over, she was empty. Even though we often focus on external material things, our outward environment doesn't determine how we feel whether good or bad. Sometimes even when we are in the middle of the LORD's will, we will feel empty.

> **A God who can be moved by our strength, one who doesn't have power and isn't Almighty.**

Naomi said, "The LORD has afflicted me." She was stating the facts of her reality. Her life was very hard. She knew that the LORD, her Master, had put her in situations others would see as misfortune or disaster. Acknowledging her miserable situation created an opening for her neighbors and Ruth to minister to her.

When we don't share our hard times with others, we deprive them of the privilege of walking with us, helping us and encouraging us. We also miss the opportunity to bless them. I have two friends who both had children who struggled with life-changing illnesses. Even as they shared with me the challenges of hospital visits, sleepless nights, and many tears, I was blessed that both of my friends were able to see dealing with this terrible affliction as a part of their ministry and calling from the LORD.

Focusing on the power of the Almighty rather than whatever hardship or grief you are facing will help you through the hardest situations. The Book of Job provides an eye-opening example of this. After intense suffering, physical pain, and unspeakable loss, God speaks to Job. Though readers know the story behind Job's suffering, God doesn't explain the reason for the hardships to Job. Instead, God refocused Job's attention from himself and his heartbreak to God's awesome power that created the stars, the oceans, and the vast diversity of creation.

When we focus our attention on the Almighty as Naomi and Job did, we can see the truth of God's power over any situation and His absolute love for us despite our circumstances. I have learned to ask Christ to reveal himself in my life challenges. Being able to picture Christ amid the stormy times in my life, see his presence during hard times in my past, and glimpse how he has protected me has been so valuable and has giving me stability in the midst of a storm.

If you are in time of affliction or feel as if your life is "yucky," pray and ask God to show you His sovereignty and might. Paul articulates the absolute power of our Almighty God in Romans 8:38-39, "For I am convinced that neither death nor life, neither angels nor demons, neither the present nor the future, nor any powers, neither height nor depth, nor anything else in all creation, will be able to separate us from the love of God that is in Christ Jesus our Lord." He is all powerful, and just as He answered Job in his affliction and suffering, He will answer you and show you His power and might.

Week 3

THE BLESSING OF MARGIN

As I was writing this book, I set up the pages with margins of white space at the top, bottom, and sides. The top margin contains the title, and the bottom includes the page number. The inside margin has to be large enough that the text isn't caught in the binding. And the outside margin is even wider, so there is a space for notes. Margins and white space on a page give your eyes a rest and allow you to focus on the words. Similarly, God designed a system of margin to give us rest for our benefit and to bless others.

Naomi's story continues in the second chapter of the Book of Ruth. Though Naomi returned to Bethlehem "empty," God had a plan to fill her up, provide for her and Ruth, and ultimately fulfill His eternal plan to bless future generations. After talking with Naomi, Ruth went into the fields to harvest the barley that the regular workers didn't gather. While she was working, she caught the attention of Boaz, the owner of the field. Boaz made sure that she had a safe place to work and even instructed his workers to leave a little extra on the field so that Ruth would have more to bring home with her.

Boaz's generosity to Ruth was based on a Levitical law that instructed the landowners to leave the edges of their fields and vineyards for the poor.

Please read Leviticus 19:9-10 and fill in the blanks-
"When you reap the harvest of your land, do _____reap to the _____ of your field or gather the gleanings of your harvest. Do _____ go over your vineyard a second time or pick up the grapes that have fallen. Leave them for the _____. I am the LORD your God."

Why do you think that God commanded His people to not reap the very edges, the margins of their fields?

God instituted the Law (not for our salvation) but for our blessing. In the New Testament, Jesus summed up the Law and the Prophets to do to others what you would have them do to you.[1] God called the farmers and workers to leave a margin on the edges of the field to provide food for the poor. Following God's ways provides a blessing to the giver and the recipient not only were the poor blessed but for the workers leaving a margin was a more efficient way to harvest because they did not have to pick up every dropped husk of barley or grape.

Ruth's gleaning in Boaz's field is a sign of the margin in Boaz's life being a blessing to others. God instituted the Sabbath to provide a margin of our time; the tithe is a margin in our finances; and limits on the harvest created a way to help those who were poor without giving them a handout.

God has called us to have margin in our lives through these areas to bless us and to bless others. Just as Boaz was able to bless Ruth and Naomi through the margin on the edge of his field, we can carve out places of margin in our lives to bless others. When we have margin in our lives, we can give to others, and we are more effective and efficient with what we have left.

What areas of margin in your life can you use to help others?

I have tried to create margin by making a "tithe" by donating items from my food pantry, closet, toy chest, and other areas. I also try to create times of margin in my schedule. This helps me be more efficient so my time doesn't get wasted on meaningless activities, and I can be more flexible so that I can embrace times of change.

If we don't use the margin in our lives to bless others, our excess will become stale and useless, and our activities will become self-centered and less effective. If Boaz had not opened his fields to the poor and the foreigner, the grain would have rotted, and the workers would have been much less efficient trying to pick up every tiny grain that fell to the ground.

Too much food spoils, clothes go out of style, toys create clutter, and too much stuff can keep us from truly enjoying all the good things that God has given us. When it comes to managing our time and resources, God knew our tendency to push limits, maximize our productivity, obsess about ourselves, and focus on what we want. God created times of rest to enjoy the land and His blessing because we need to have room to breathe and margin in our lives.

If you feel as if you have absolutely no margin in your life, pray and ask God to help you see the places of margin in your life. Ask Him to reveal which grains of barley you should not pick up because it is a waste of time and energy and what you should release.

A KINSMAN-REDEEMER

When Ruth returned home, she had gathered about 30 pounds of barley! Naomi was amazed and asked where Ruth had been gleaning. When Ruth explained it was Boaz's field, Naomi was amazed and asked where Ruth had been harvesting. When Ruth said Boaz' field, Naomi exclaimed, *"The LORD bless him!" Naomi said to her daughter-in-law. "He has not stopped showing his kindness to the living and the dead." She added, "That man is our close relative; he is one of our kinsman-redeemers."*[89] It was as if a light bulb went off in her head as she realized Boaz, as kinsman redeemer, might be an answer to her prayer for Ruth to find rest in a home of her own.

In Christ, we **are all brothers and sisters of the promise. Therefore, we are the same race since we are all members of one family and citizens of God's kingdom.**

The kinsman-redeemer, "ga'al" (גָּאַל), also called guardian-redeemer, was a crucial role created by God to protect tribe members and the family's inheritance. [90] They were responsible to buy back family land if a family member sold it to pay debts. The kinsman-redeemer made sure that God's people and tribes' inheritance of land were protected, and they were responsible to buy back the land if a family member sold it to pay debts.[91] His responsibilities included buying a fellow Israelite out of slavery[92] and being the "avenger of blood" to make sure that justice was carried out if a family member was murdered.[93] Of particular importance to Naomi was his responsibility to carry on the family name by marrying a childless widow[94] Widows had the right to marry a close relative of her husband under the law of Levirate marriage so that her husband's name would not die out and so that the inheritance would remain in the family. [95]

Though Naomi knew that Boaz, as a kinsman-redeemer, was responsible for carrying on the family name by marrying a childless widow, I found it interesting that after she exclaimed, "He is one of our kinsman-redeemers," she didn't explain the concept to Ruth. And she didn't push Ruth into a relationship with Boaz as her kinsman-redeemer either.

---

[89] Ruth 2:20
[90] Guzik, David. "Study Guide for Ruth 3." Enduring Word. Blue Letter Bible. 7 Jul 2006. 2010. 3 Nov 2010. <http:// www.blueletterbible.org/commentaries/comm_view.cfm? AuthorID=2&contentID=7552&commInfo=31&topic=Ruth >
[91] Leviticus 25:25
[92] Leviticus 25:48
[93] Numbers 35:19
[94] Deuteronomy 25:5-10
[95] Deuteronomy 25:5-10

Naomi had been out of Bethlehem for over a decade, people change, and character shows over time. It seems likely to me that she wanted to check Boaz out and find out what kind of a man he had become. As a widow, she knew that marriage takes a lot of hard work. I am sure she wanted to discover if he was a Godly man, understand why he was not married, and give Ruth and Boaz a chance to get to know each other while they worked together.

During harvest season, Naomi learned about Boaz from the other women in the town, plus she was able to hear Ruth's opinion of Boaz during the three months they worked together. It is likely her friends told her about Boaz's family history. His mother was Rahab.[96] Rahab was a significant figure in the Israelites' miraculous invasion of Jericho (which took place soon after Miriam's brother, Moses, died), but she was also a Canaanite prostitute.

After Moses died, Joshua became the leader of Israel. He sent two spies into Jericho, who stayed at Rahab's home. Despite her occupation and upbringing, Rahab believed in the God of Israel. In fact, she is commended in Hebrews 11:31, "By faith the prostitute Rahab, because she welcomed the spies, was not killed with those who were disobedient." She confirmed to the spies that the Lord had given them the city of Jericho and said, "I know that the LORD has given you this land and that a great fear of you has fallen on us, so that all who live in this country are melting in fear because of you…. When we heard of it, our hearts melted in fear and everyone's courage failed because of you, for the LORD your God is God in heaven above and on the earth below."

Though Rahab believed in God, her background created a challenging situation for Boaz as he was growing up. Imagine being in a very small town with a mother who was a foreigner (hard enough) and a former prostitute. Kids pick on people who are not like them and look different. Boaz probably had a different skin color or hair color than the other Israelite children. His great-grandson David is described as ruddy and red when most of the Israelite children had black or dark brown hair. Though Boaz grew up to be a kind boss and a godly man, his younger years were likely miserable.

Boaz is a great encouragement to all of us who were embarrassed by our parents, our heritage, or mocked because we didn't look like everyone else. We can take comfort in the thought that though people look at the outward appearance, God looks at the heart. He made us and designed us with a special purpose that uses each of our unique attributes and our life history for His glory.

Another challenge that Boaz faced because he was half-Canaanite: no good Jewish father would allow their daughter to marry him because marriage to a Canaanite was forbidden in the Law. Deuteronomy 7:3-4 contains regulations regarding marriage to Canaanites, "Do not intermarry with them. Do not give your daughters to their sons or take their daughters for your sons, for they will turn your children away from following me to serve other gods, and the LORD's anger will burn against you

---

[96] Matthew 1:5

and will quickly destroy you." Of course, no parent wants the LORD's anger to burn against them and destroy them, so they did not allow their daughters to marry Boaz.

Because of their fear of God's wrath and anger, these parents missed God's heart. God's desire for His people is to be set apart, holy. He commanded them not to marry people from other nations because He did not want them to worship the gods of the other countries. As Deuteronomy 7 explains, God's concern is that their children will turn away from following him. The New Testament clarifies this concept when Paul writes in Galatians 3:26-29 that "in Christ, there is neither Jew nor Gentile. In Christ, we are all brothers and sisters of the promise. Therefore, we are the same race since we are all members of one family and citizens of God's kingdom. The problem isn't race, skin color, or language; the problem is our hearts.

God used Boaz's half-Canaanite status to "save" him for Ruth. Can you remember times in your life when God used what seemed like a negative trait or experience ultimately to bless you and others? Thank Him for His love and pro-vision.

Week 4

SHARING A BLESSING

Our family had a wonderful opportunity to go to Tijuana, Mexico, on a family mission trip. Some people might not think taking a 15-year-old and an 11-year-old to the Red-Light District just across the border from San Diego would be an appropriate place for them, but we felt called to go. So, we went.

My husband's cousin Amanda and her husband have spent the last five years working with the kids and their parents who live in the dangerous area along the US border. Drugs and prostitution are rampant. Violent cartels control streets around the playground our cousins use for their Zone Kids meetings. (After we left Mexico, human remains were found buried in the park!) Each Zone Kids meeting is like Vacation Bible School with games, music, and a Bible lesson. Over the years, trust has grown, so my kids safely played soccer and basketball with the local kids.

Amanda asked me to share a message with a few of the kids' moms. I struggled with what to say; God's word is not limited by language, economic status, or past life choices, but I didn't want to come across as oblivious to their hardships and suffering. I wanted to share hope and love with them in a real and tangible way. I decided to share what I had learned about the power of spoken blessing with the ladies.

A couple of weeks before our trip, I learned about the power of blessing from Sally Meredith, author of *"Ruth: The Story is in the Names"*. Sally highlighted the pattern of blessing throughout the Book of Ruth. Blessings have power because they communicate what God is currently doing in someone's life and provide insight into future gifts from God.

God will allow us to choose if we want to receive the blessings that he has planned for us.

Naomi's blessing for Ruth and Orpah was that the Lord would deal kindly with them and give them rest in a house of their own.[97] In their grief, Ruth and Orpah may not have considered remarrying until Naomi prayed for them. Spoken blessings can open our eyes to what God has in the future for us and others; sometimes when I pray for others, God gives me words and supernatural insight beyond what I know about them.

Naomi's blessing before she leaving Moab takes on new meaning in Ruth 3 which begins with a question from Naomi to Ruth, "My daughter, shall I not seek security (home) for you that it may be well with you?" The Hebrew word for "security" or "home" in this verse is the same word for "rest" in Ruth 1:9 when Naomi prayed that her daughters-in-law would find rest and security in the home of a new husband.

Naomi's desire was for Ruth to be blessed with a peaceful home and a family, but she still gave Ruth the choice whether she would follow Naomi's plan. God will allow us to choose if we want to receive the blessings that he has planned for us. Forcing a gift on someone can take away the joy of receiving the gift. Ruth had a choice; would she trust Naomi's plan or resist it.

*Please read all of Ruth 3 to find out how Naomi's plan to seek a home for Ruth goes. Why do you think Ruth went along with Naomi's plan? Would you have?

Ruth agreed to do as Naomi advised because she knew that Naomi loved her, and she trusted Naomi's wisdom and perspective. When Boaz woke up in the middle of the night after a long day winnowing barley, he was frightened to find Ruth at his feet. However, after he realized her intention, he was blessed by Ruth's kindness because that she had chosen him to be her kinsman-redeemer. Marriage was a dream that Boaz had long given up. But God's plans are not limited by time or age.

When Ruth returned home the following morning, she brought Naomi six measures of barley from Boaz. With this gift, Boaz signaled to Naomi that he would take care of Ruth and her. Since

---

[97] Ruth 1:8-9

Naomi was also a childless widow, he was acknowledging that she was giving up her right to claim Boaz as her kinsman-redeemer and was deferring to Ruth.

Naomi encouraged Ruth to have patience, "for the man will not rest until the matter is settled today."[98] I love Naomi's perspective on Boaz. She knew that the right guy would jump through hoops for his prospective wife. He will keep the relationship pure; he will maintain good relationships with the in-laws, and he will not wait too long to get married! Too many women settle with hooking up and acting married rather than following God's plan and getting married!

Just when it seems that everything is going hunky-dory and that Ruth and Boaz will live happily after, another man appears in the picture who has a right to marry Ruth. Oh no! What happens next?

Please read Ruth chapter 4 to find out the rest of the story and then answer these questions. Where did Boaz meet the other kinsman-redeemer?

Who was selling the land vs. 3?

What did the buyer acquire with the land vs. 5?

What did Boaz do vs. 9-10?

What blessings were given by the elders to Ruth and Boaz?

How did the LORD bless Ruth vs. 13?

What blessings were given to Naomi vs. 14-15?

Who was Ruth's great grandson?

---

[98] Ruth 3:18

Boaz went to the city gate to redeem the land and Ruth. He was determined to marry her. They were both blessed by the leaders. Soon Ruth gave birth to a son named Obed, who was the great grandfather of King David. King David was the ancestor of Jesus, God's perfect plan for our redemption.

Multiple blessings were given to Ruth, Boaz and Naomi. The women of the Bethlehem said to Naomi "Praise be to the LORD, who this day has not left you without a guardian-redeemer. May he become famous throughout Israel! He will renew your life and sustain you in your old age. For your daughter-in-law, who loves you and who is better to you than seven sons, has given him birth." This blessing is one of many throughout the book of Ruth.

THE POWER OF BLESSING

Just as Naomi's friends in Bethlehem blessed her, we can bless our husbands, children, and friends. After doing further research on blessing, I have realized the power of blessing to undo the harm caused by poor choices, hurtful words, and family history. Blessings can unleash the work of the Holy Spirit in someone's life to empower them to be what God wants them to be and enable them to see God's hand at work in their life. Once you start looking for blessings in the Bible, it will transform your interactions with others and your view of God. (My book *Seeing Value A Biblical Perspective on Intrinsic Value* is an in-depth look at biblical blessings and curses.)

Blessings have **the power to undo harm caused by poor choices, hurtful words, and family history.**

When the time came for me to share with the Zone Kids' moms, I knew teaching them about the power of blessing could have immediate benefits in their lives. They could bless their kids and each other. So we started with the priestly blessing found in Numbers 6:22-27.

Please look up Numbers 6:22-27 and fill in the missing words.

The _____ said to Moses,

"Tell Aaron and his sons, 'This is how you are to _____ the Israelites.

_____to them:

"The _____ _____ you and _____ you;

the _____ make his _____ shine on you and be _____ to you;

the _____ turn his _____- toward you and give you _____."'"

"So they will put my name on the Israelites, and I will bless them."

If you look back over the words you just filled in the blank, you may notice some similarities. First, this was a command by the LORD to Moses. As we learned in the First Chapter about Eve, think of "relationship" and "boss" whenever you see the word LORD. The Lord had a relationship with Moses, and when he asked Moses to do something, it wasn't a suggestion.

The power of this blessing comes from the LORD, the Ruler, and Master of All; He has infinite resources. Nothing is too hard for him. He commanded Moses to tell Aaron to speak a blessing on His people because God wants our words to be conduits of His love and goodness.

An important word in this passage is "Keep." Write a one-word definition of "keep" _____

My one-word definition of "keep" would be "hold." But in this passage, the word "keep" means a safe place. For example, the "keep" was the most secure part of a castle in ancient times. The moms in Tijuana picked this up quickly because the Spanish translation is "te guarde." They quickly understood that this was a prayer for God's protection and security. I explained that we are to pray for God to guard us, our kids, our husbands, and our belongings.

The word "face" is repeated twice in this prayer. Often words in Hebrew had multiple meanings. This word can also mean someone's presence or their wholeness of being. In this prayer, we are asking God to bless us with his presence and the fullness of his power in our lives, so we see the Lord's face and feel His presence. A synonym for the word "shine" would be "illuminate." When something shines, it is illuminated, and we can see it. God wants us to see him and understand his gracious blessings.

Often people describe grace as God's unmerited favor. Through grace, we are saved; it is a gift from God.[99] Here's another way to think about the word "gracious" in this passage; grace protects us and others from our past mistakes. God's grace provides healing, help, refuge, safety, rescue, and being uplifted. Not because we deserve it; in fact, our mistakes and those of the people around are the reason we need grace; we are in a situation that we couldn't get ourselves out of on our own.

My favorite word in this blessing is "Peace." *Shalom* is the Hebrew word for "Peace." It has a deeper and richer meaning than simply the absence of strife and conflict. Peace is not a boring place where everyone sits around being nice and twiddling their thumbs. *Shalom* is perfection; it is life as God designed it to be, the best life. Abundant Life.

Take a minute to write out Numbers 6:23-27 in the margin using your own words based on the meanings of the words in the passage. Pray this as a blessing for yourself and your loved ones.

After explaining the meaning of this blessing in Numbers, I looked at the women at the playground in Tijuana. Peace in a city torn by drugs and trafficking seemed impossible. One of the women was a widow trying to survive and raise two small kids. Safety? No conflict? Abundant Life? How? I could see

---

[99] Ephesians 2:8

on their faces, it sounded nice, yet they knew reality on the streets surrounding the park. So, I paused and said, "This wasn't just a prayer for the priest and the Israelites. We can ask God to bless each other."

In halting Spanish, I put my hand on the shoulder of the young mom next to me, and I read this blessing:

'El Señor te bendiga y te guarde;

el Señor haga resplandecer su rostro sobre ti,

y tenga de ti misericordia;

el Señor alce sobre ti su rostro, y te dé paz.'"

The young woman on my right put her hand on the woman next to her and blessed her. The blessing traveled around our little circle and came back to me. Whenever we bless someone else, we will be blessed. In Jerusalem, twice a year, during Sukkot and the Passover, a descendant of Aaron reads this blessing over the crowd; as he recites each line, all the people gathered repeat it back to him. I encouraged each of the women in the circle to go home and bless their family and friends. Speaking words of blessing can change their lives and their family.

Cousin Amanda wrapped up our time together by sharing with the women a bit of the kids' lesson about how important our thoughts are. She shared that sometimes she gets frustrated with her husband and tries stop negative thoughts from taking over her mind by taking them captive.[100] The other women in the circle agreed and shared stories of frustration with kids and other people in their lives. I felt like God prompted me to add one crucial point to our discussion about blessings: *Blessings aren't just for our loved ones. They are also for the people who hurt us and frustrate us the most.*

Please write out Luke 6:28-

Why do you think Jesus commanded his followers to do this?

I am confident that the people listening to Jesus frequently blessed their loved ones. Even now, Orthodox Jews say 100 blessings a day. But Jesus' admonition to bless our enemies was quite remarkable. By praying for God to bless the people who have hurt us, upset us, cursed us, and disrespected us, whether they are a boss, co-worker, teacher, family member, or friend, we are freeing God to work all of our lives, including our enemies.

Just as the blessing went around the circle and came back to me, God will bring an amazing blessing back to you when you bless your enemies. A friend of mine tried this with her husband, who

---

[100] 2 Corinthians 10:5

had been abusive. After praying for God to bless him, God blessed him in his work and their marriage. My friend's husband didn't deserve the blessing. She had grounds for separation, but she stayed and prayed for him, so God blessed her.

A couple of notes: If you or a friend are in an abusive relationship, pray and then contact the National Domestic Abuse Hotline at 800-799-7233. God's blessings only include behaviors and things that would be acceptable in heaven. There is no abuse, lying, stealing, addiction, murder, adultery, or sin of any kind in heaven. When you pray for God to bless your enemies, you are praying for their behavior and attitude to be holy and good like Christ. Pray for God's will to be done in their life as it is in heaven.

If God brought the names of loved ones and enemies to mind, take a minute to pray for God's blessing on them. Write it down and share it with them, if it is safe, so they will have physical reminder of the blessing in the future.

REDEMPTION

Sportswriters love to use the word "redemption" when they tell stories of victories and justice in impossible situations. Naomi's story is a true story of redemption. When Naomi returned to Bethlehem, she was a widow and an empty woman. Since both of her sons had died, it was as if she had never had children and was barren. Even after giving up her property and right to marriage, God blessed her with a precious grandson to fill her empty arms and a kinsman-redeemer to take care of her.

*Please read Isaiah 54:1-8 and write down your thoughts. Please take some time to meditate on this passage and how it would relate to your life.

God is our Redeemer. He wants to bless us with our heart's desires. He knows our cry for a home of our own, a place of security and peace, our barren heart's passion for children, our widowed heart's desire for love, our captive heart's longing for freedom, and our single heart's cry for a husband. Like Boaz, He will not rest until He has answered our heart's cry.

Please write out Psalm 19:14 and Isaiah 44:6 below and underline the names of God.
Psalm 19:14

Isaiah 44:6

God is our LORD (Jehovah), our Rock, our Redeemer (ga'al), the King, LORD Almighty (LORD of HOSTS Jehovah' tsaba), the first and last, only True God (Elohim).

Boaz was Ruth and Naomi's kinsman-redeemer. Can you think of ways that Jesus acts as our Kinsman-redeemer? (Feel free to look back to page 108 to review the responsibility of the kinsman-redeemer.)

God redeemed us in person through Jesus Christ. He is our kinsman-redeemer who has set us free from the yoke of slavery. Though we were enslaved by sin and death, he has set us free and paid the price for our ransom that we could never pay. "For you know that it was not with perishable things such as silver or gold that you were redeemed from the empty way of life handed down to you from your ancestors, but with the precious blood of Christ, a lamb without blemish or defect."[101] Jesus paid the price for your sin and has set you free from the chains of your past choices, your parents' sins, and other people's destructive behaviors. You are Free![102]

If you feel there are areas in your life where you are still in bondage, pray and repent for staying in a place of slavery and bondage and discounting the power of His blood and the price He paid for you. Then ask Jesus to show you the Truth; and claim these blessings:

He has set you free, redeemed you, and paid the price for your sin.

You are a precious Bride redeemed and valued by her Beloved.

You have a magnificent home waiting for you in heaven.

You are no longer a slave.

You are protected and guarded as a child of the King.

You are an heir to a priceless inheritance.

Your debts have been paid. Jesus' blood covers it all.

Thank Him for His sacrifice, His precious blood, and His amazing love that washes away all of our sins so that we can have a right relationship with him. He is your kinsman-redeemer.

HOW HAVE YOU LEARNED TO TRUST GOD THROUGH STUDYING NAOMI?

---

[101] 1 Peter 1-:18- 19
[102] Galatians 5:1

CHAPTER V

Shunammite Woman

GRACIOUS HOSTESS

FAITHFUL TO GOD'S WORD

Lived about 840 BC

If you, then, though you are evil, know how
to give good gifts to your children, how much
more will your Father in heaven give good gifts
to those who ask him!
Matthew 7:11

Week 1

Shunammite Woman

Being a guest in someone's home is a blessing and a privilege. It means they not only trust you not to steal their, to see them without makeup, and all the imperfections of real life. Not too long ago, I had the opportunity to be a house guest of my friend Kathryn. Though my family and I showed up on her doorstep with only a few days' notice, she overwhelmed us with her generous hospitality. Kathryn's hospitality began before we even arrived. When I called to let her know about our upcoming trip, she kindly offered us a place to stay and asked me for my family's breakfast preferences. She bought three kinds of milk, two kinds of cereal, and everything else we needed for a one-night stay! She put my husband and me up in a beautiful suite that was so comfortable that I asked her about the mattress manufacturer.

The following day, she put her two miniature dachshunds in another room so my boys wouldn't be scared. Then when I couldn't find my saline solution, she gave me hers; technically, I think she loaned it to me, since I packed it in my suitcase and I didn't realize I had taken it until we were an hour away. She told me I could keep it when I called to apologize for taking it, reinforcing the importance of having people as houseguests that you trust not to steal from you!

Her gracious hospitality meant we didn't have to drive another two hours to our destination after a five-hour flight across the country. It was a relaxing respite after a long day of traveling and allowed us to catch up with her husband and her in a low-stress environment. Our visit was so delightful, warm, and welcoming that I am already trying to figure out how we can visit again and stay longer, maybe even move in. Did I mention that she had a really comfortable guest suite?

In this chapter, we will get to know another gracious hostess, the Shunammite woman, named after her hometown of Shunem, a small town where she lived. For short, we'll call her "Shuna." It sounds a little like "Shana," which means "God's Grace," and is an appropriate name for a gracious hostess who used the gifts and resources that God had given her to bless others.

SHUNA'S BACKGROUND

Shuna lived about 250 years after Naomi held baby Obed on her lap. Obed's birth provides a connection between the tumultuous times of the Judges during Naomi's life and the transition into the era of the Kings. Naomi's great, great, grandson was King David, the second King of Israel. King David ruled Israel for 40 years and his son, Solomon, ruled Israel for another 40 years. Solomon's reign was a time of peace and prosperity even though his many wives and concubines from other nations led him and the country away from the Lord.[103]

After Solomon's death, the nation of Israel split into two kingdoms, the Northern Kingdom of Israel and the Southern Kingdom of Judah. Only two of the twelve tribes of Israel, Judah, and Benjamin, continued to follow Solomon's son, King Rehoboam. The two tribes were called Judah. The other ten tribes rebelled against Rehoboam as king and appointed a soldier named Jeroboam as their king. These ten tribes retained the name of Israel. Many of the kings after David, especially in Israel, did evil in the sight of the Lord. They worshipped idols and were very wicked.

God responded to the wickedness of His people by sending prophets to call the leaders and people of Israel and Judah back to Him. A prophet is a spokesperson for God. The word "prophet" comes from two Greek words, "pro" which means "before, in front of, or in place of" and "fayme" which means "to speak." A prophet, therefore, is someone who speaks in place of someone else. During the reign of King Joram, God anointed Elisha as a prophet to communicate God's word to the king and his people. The Spirit of the Lord was on Elisha, which resulted in both prophetic words and miracles.

The book of 2 Kings contains many exciting stories about Elisha. Some are almost funny, like when a band of young men made fun of Elisha for being bald, he called on the name of the Lord, and two bears mauled the young men.[104] Other stories provide a foretaste of the miracles of Jesus. For instance, Elisha fed 100 men with only 20 loaves of barley bread, and they had some left over.[105] Elisha also helped a soldier be healed from leprosy.[106]

As a prophet, Elisha traveled extensively throughout the land of Israel. He frequently passed through the small town of Shunem on his travels to Samaria, the capital of Israel. Whether he was fishing in the Jordan River or traveling along the coast of the Mediterranean Sea, during his travels, he would stop by Shunem, a small town where Shuna, the Shunammite woman, lived.

Let's read 2 Kings 4:8-10 in the Amplified Version to get a picture of Shuna. "One day Elisha went on to Shunem, where a rich and influential woman lived, who insisted on his eating a meal. Afterward, whenever he passed by, he stopped there for a meal. And she said to her husband, 'Behold now, I perceive that this is a holy man of God who passes by continually. Let us make a small chamber on the [housetop] and put there for him a bed, a table, a chair, and a lamp. Then whenever he comes to us, he can go [up the outside stairs and rest] here.'"

---

[103] 1 Kings 11:4,11
[104] 2 Kings 2:23-25
[105] 2 Kings 4:42-44
[106] 2 Kings 5

Please write some facts and your impression of this woman, based on the previous verses.

Even though we only have a few sentences to learn about this woman, several things jump out to me:

She was a woman of resources and influence.

She was generous and thoughtful.

She had discernment because she perceived Elisha was a holy man of God.

She was persuasive. She insisted that Elisha eat with them, and she convinced her husband to
 build and furnish a room for Elisha.

She was also blessed with the gift of hospitality. In my imagination, I would love to be like Shuna, a gracious thoughtful hostess; however, in real life, I struggle with feeling less than adequate in all these areas. God led me to an inspiring verse on this subject to encourage me in my struggle.

Please write down Romans 12:13.

* This passage says to "practice hospitality" (NIV) or "seek to show hospitality." (ESV) What are some ways that you practice hospitality?

Romans 12:13 in the NIV translation encourages us to "practice hospitality." This was such a freeing verse to me; I realized I don't have to be the best hostess, but I do have to practice. Hospitality is something you can get better at with practice, just like playing baseball or the piano. I may not be an expert, but just as people understand errors at a t-ball game or a piano recital, I realized that people will understand and appreciate my effort if I do my best when I practice hospitality. I have come to terms with the reality that I may never achieve Martha Stewart's perfection, but my goal is to get better every time I practice hospitality.

Reading about Shuna can make us think, "Of course she was hospitable; she had the money and influence to get things done. I don't have any money, and I can't even influence my kids to pick up their clothes!" Stop focusing on what you don't have and focus on all God has given you. Appreciate that God has blessed each of us with a mix of physical, emotional, and mental resources we can use to bless others.

I learned this lesson firsthand when I was in college. My friend Betts invited ten girls and guys to spend the weekend at her family farm in the mountains of NC. We traveled through winding roads and tiny towns before arriving at Betts' house. Her parents graciously welcomed us, fed us a great spaghetti meal, and entertained us with her dad's bluegrass playing accompanied by blue tick hound. It was such a wonderful, delightful, and refreshing experience that it continues to inspire me over 20 years later.

Betts's heart for hospitality did not let her small house with only one bathroom, four bedrooms (for 14 people, including her family), and no "formal areas" keep her from inviting all of us. I realized that hospitality is not about what you have but about your heart. Betts' heart was to share her home with a group of friends who were far from our families.

Romans 12:13 tells us to share with those in need; when we share what God has blessed us with, we are being obedient to practice hospitality, and we become a conduit that allows God's love to flow from us to others.

God has gifted each of us differently. The resources that God has given you may not be material things like a large house or lots of money, but without a doubt, He has gifted you with unique physical, mental, and emotional resources. Focus on what you love and value; then share it with others.

Stop focusing on what you don't have and focus on all that God has blessed you with.

Even little kids realize they can't do everything, and they love doing some things more than others. One day, I started my kindergarten Sunday School lesson by asking the kids what they were good at doing. Some said swimming, others said bike riding, three were good at coloring, and one little boy was good at fighting (maybe he will be a military officer.).

I told them, "I am good at reading." The little boy sitting next to me said, "Oh, I am not good at reading." Even at age five, these kids knew they could do some things very well, but they weren't good at everything. God had given them physical resources that allowed them to fight, color, bike, and swim. In the same way, God has given you physical, emotional, and mental resources that will enable you to influence people for His kingdom and His Glory. You have an opportunity to use the resources God has given you to bless everyone you are around.

Can you think of some of the resources and abilities that God has given you? As you ponder this question, don't focus on what you can't do; instead, think about what you can do. Think about what you love in your life and write it all down.

Then, thank God for them. One more thought, you aren't bragging if you are giving the glory to God, the giver of all good things, for the things He has given you.

Week 2

DISCOVERING YOUR GIFTS

This lesson is remarkably short because I really want you to spend some time thinking and praying about the following questions and to take the spiritual gifts test at the end of the questions. If it was hard for you to come up with a list of some of the gifts and abilities God has given you in last week's lesson- don't lose hope, help is on the way. My sister attends North Point Church in Atlanta and told me about this great interactive tool that they put together called the Dream Job to help their members get a picture of the resources and gifts that God has given them. The online spiritual gifts test can be found at https://northpointministries.org/dream-job-gifts-assessment.

North Point Church also put together questions for a sermon series called Game Plan to help people discover their giftedness. **Here are some questions from their online tool to help you get started.**
1. What gets your heart beating fast?

2. What do you stay up at night thinking about?

3. What makes you cry?

4. What breaks your heart?

5. What do you think is your passion?

6. If time, money, or education were not an issue, what would you do?

7. What are some unique experiences that have happened in your life?

8. What have been "defining moments" or spiritual markers along the way?

*9. What are your spiritual gifts? Take the test at https://northpointministries.org/dream-job-gifts-assessment. Please list them here.

God has gifted each of us with experiences, personality traits, passions, and abilities to carry out His plans and mission in this world. Just as God gave Shuna financial resources, the gift of hospitality, and a persuasive personality that she used to provide food and a place to stay for Elisha, God has equipped you for the mission that He has for you. When you use the gifts and resources that God has given you for His glory, you will expand your view of God and better understand His great love, His unlimited resources, and His abilities. It's amazing.

Week 3

VALUING GIFTS YOU HAVE AND DON'T HAVE

When I was a kid, I loved to take personality quizzes in magazines. I took many silly ones like "Find out if you are an organized person or a messy person?" or "What is your perfume personality?" I still like taking quizzes, so the spiritual gifts assessment was eye-opening and humbling at the same time. It is important to read your scores on the spiritual gifts assessment as a guide. The assessment is a tool to help us see how God has given each of us unique gifts, talents, and life experiences to empower us on His Mission to go unto all the world, teaching and preaching the good news of Jesus Christ. It isn't a way to judge how spiritual you are, just like the "perfume personality" test was not a comprehensive measure of your personality.

As I pondered my scores and talked to friends who had taken the test, I realized that God had given us different amounts of spiritual gifts, just as the master in the parable of the talents (Matthew 25:14-28) did not give equal amounts of money to his servants. Similarly, when we practice using any of our gifts, whether hospitality, prophecy, mercy, administration, or discerning spirits, God will multiply our resources; we will be blessed like the wise servants who increased the talents given to them by the master.

As we grow in our relationship with Jesus Christ and use our gifts, they will increase when we invest them in God's kingdom. God has given each of us gifts so that we can bring Him glory. However, it must break His heart when we use the resources and talents entrusted to us to seek glory for ourselves rather than for Him.

People with similar spiritual gifts will often gravitate to each other because they can encourage and support each other. However, different spiritual giftings can lead to conflict when we don't value or understand another person's gifts. I've seen this in churches where one values Missions and Speaking in Tongues and another church values Helps and Mercy. All of the spiritual gifts are valuable. We shouldn't think that people who have the gift of teaching or giving are more spiritual or more important than those who have gifts of mercy or prophecy. Since we are all part of one body, just as the eye is not more spiritual than the foot, one gift is not more important to the body of Christ than another. All are necessary and given by God for His glory and to bless others.

All spiritual gifts have a purpose in the kingdom of God. None of the spiritual gifts are better than the others. In marriage, conflict can occur when only one spouse has a gift hospitality or giving and the other has the gift of prophecy or service. One of my friends was extraordinarily generous, but her husband didn't support giving to the church at the same level. My advice was to respect her husband's wishes. Second, I told her to mentally dedicate the money she would have given to God and pray that God would allow her to give in other ways. One of the doors that God opened for her was to support a little boy in Cambodia through Compassion International. Her generosity changed that little boy's life because she was patient and willing to find a way to give that was supported by her husband. God is faithful, and if we genuinely want to be used by Him to bless others with the abilities, He has given us, He will provide amazing opportunities specifically tailored to our hearts and giftedness.

> *When we practice* using any of our gifts - whether hospitality, prophecy, mercy, administration, or discerning of spirits, God will multiply the resources we have.

*How do you use your gifts and resources for the glory of God?

How can you expand your reach to share with those in need, both physical need and spiritual need?

Are there spiritual gifts that you wish you had?

Though God does not give gifts equally, He is abundantly generous and will provide a measure of every spiritual gift if we ask for it. As James 1:5 says, "If any of you lacks wisdom, you should ask God, who gives generously to all without finding fault, and it will be given to you."

I don't naturally have a discerning spirit, and as a result, I am oblivious to much going on around me. After reading this scripture, I realized that I could ask God for discernment just as Solomon asked God for wisdom. In the years since I asked God for discernment, God has heightened my sense of discernment into a tool that can be used for His glory. One of the most significant benefits of using our gifts to glorify God is that we expand our view of God's attributes as we expand our use of gifts from him. If there are spiritual gifts that you desire, ask God for them. God wants to shower His love on us, bless us, and give us good gifts, just as parents want to bless their children.

Please read Matthew 7:7-11 and write out verse 11

Every one of God's gifts is good, but that doesn't always mean we will appreciate what He has given us. Sometimes we resist the gifts He wants to entrust us, or we don't use the gifts He has given us. This reminds me of how my kids view Christmas socks. One of my family Christmas traditions is to put socks in my kids' stockings. I love the irony, and inevitably my kids need new socks. However, they don't appreciate the socks. So, after they open their stockings on Christmas morning, the socks get thrown in the "gifts I don't care about" pile. In the same way, there are spiritual gifts that we "throw away." These are gifts that we are uncomfortable with or don't understand.

As I took the spiritual gifts assessment, I was convicted that the reason I had such low scores in some areas wasn't because the Holy Spirit hadn't tried to give me the gift but instead because I had

An important facet of trusting God means we trust that God gives good gifts; gifts to bless us and to bless others.

resisted receiving the gift. Pay attention to this point: God gives different amounts of gifts and abilities, but he gives something to everyone. Just as in the parable of the talents, one servant was given five talents, one given three talents, and one was only given one, but the master gave *all* three servants a talent. Often God has already given us a gift, such as prophecy, speaking in tongues, or healing, but we have resisted receiving the gift.

One of my lowest scores was in mercy. As I was sharing this with a friend, she said, "You weren't surprised, were you?" I guess I don't come across as a very merciful person. She shared with me that people with the mercy gift let their heart be broken by other peoples' miserable situations. After talking with her, I realized that I would distance myself from sad things. I would turn off the TV, find something else to focus on, or assume it wasn't that bad. I would limit my exposure to things that would require mercy. Since I was not comfortable with misery and sad situations; I was avoiding God's mercy in those situations and limiting the gift of mercy in my life.

I have been a Christian for over thirty years; though I am not an old woman, I am certainly a middle-aged woman of God. As the Holy Spirit has been working in my life these past 30 years, molding me and making me more like Christ, it makes sense that I would exhibit more and more of the gifts of the Spirit in my life.

While I may never have as much mercy as someone for whom it is a primary gift, our Lord is full of compassion; shouldn't I have at least a little? I realized that my resistance to this gift showed a lack of faith and trust in God. Resistance to God's gifts can come from a fear of the unknown, concern about other people's opinions, or a need for control.

The parable of the talents teaches us, if we do not use the gifts that God has given us, we run the risk of the gift being taken away, just as the one who had only one talent lost even what little he had.[107]

---

[107] Matthew 25:14-30

An important facet of trusting God starts with believing that God gives good gifts; gifts to bless us and to bless others. I pray that you and I will embrace His blessings for us by embracing all of His gifts.

Take a minute to look at your spiritual gifts test and focus on your lowest scores. Ask God to reveal to you the areas where you need to ask for more of the gift in your life and areas where you need to repent of fear and ungratefulness for resisting the good gifts that God has for you. God has wonderful plans to bless you and bless others through you. Embrace the spiritual gifts He has for you.

THE BLESSING OF USING OUR GIFTS FOR GOD'S GLORY

When we use our gifts for God's glory, the people around us benefit, and we will be blessed. Shuna's story shows how this principle works. In response to Shuna's gift of hospitality, Elisha wanted to bless her, and God had a miracle in store for her.

Please read 2 Kings 4:11-17 and answer the following questions. Shuna was a woman who seemed to have everything. What was the one thing she did not have?

What was Elisha's prophecy for her?

What was her response?

Shuna's heartfelt cry after being After being told she would have a baby, Shuna's heartfelt cry was, "Please, man of God, don't mislead your servant!" It was as if she was saying, "Don't kid me." Her plea gives us a window into her heart and the hopes she had given up. Though she had come to terms with her life and was using the gifts and resources God had given her, Elisha's prophecy hit a nerve because she knew her dream of being a mother was impossible since her husband was old.

The conversation between Elisha and his servant is truly a lesson in different spiritual gifts. Elisha's servant said, "She doesn't have a son and her husband is old." What was apparent to him, Elisha completely missed. I am somewhat like Elisha; I assume people have what they want, and when I am looking for a Christmas or birthday gift, I often don't notice the obvious things they need. God had given Elisha's servant mercy and discernment, and Elisha had faith and the gift of prophecy; these were complimentary gifts that God used together to bless Shuna.

On the outside, Shuna seemed to have it all together. She busied herself in the town and at home and found contentment in using the gifts that God had given her. She was able to host Elisha and be a part of his ministry through her generosity and hospitality. Things looked pretty good. But God used Elisha's servant to see past the exterior to her heart. She may have given up or lost hope in her dreams of having a son. Though her need was not apparent to Elisha, once he realized it, he prophesied that she would have a son in a year, and she did! God desires to give us good gifts, and He can see what we truly need.

When we pray for others, God allows us to see His hand at work in other people's lives just as He is at work in our lives.

This passage reminds me of the importance of praying for each other. God cares about the things that we care about. No matter is too big, too small, too personal, or too trivial for God. Prayer does not waste God's time. Prayer allows us to see God at work in our lives and in the lives of others. God does amazing things when we join in unity with others through prayer. I am positive that Shuna had cried out to God over many years for a child. Yet it was only after Gehazi noticed her need and Elisha prayed that she was given a son. When we pray for others, God allows us to see His hand at work in other people's lives just as He is at work in our lives.

Please take some time to pray and ask God to show you how to intercede for the people around you. Pray for their healing, discernment, salvation, and answers to unanswered prayers. God could use your prayers as a catalyst for His power, just as He used Elisha.

Week 4

LIFE COMES FROM THE LORD

Though I am usually a laid-back mom, a sick child can send me spinning into motion. My first response is, "How can I fix it." Recently, when my son had a high fever, I went into triage mode; I opened the medicine cabinet and started frantically sorting through my collection of cures and remedies to find the exact solution needed for his ailment. As I looked for the right medicine to fix my son's problem, he looked at me and said, "Mom, shouldn't we pray?" Wow, I was humbled and taken aback. He was right; I was so focused on finding the solution in my medicine cabinet that I didn't even think to call on the Master Physician, God our Healer, until I had after I had done all that I could on my own. In this part of Shuna's story, she lives out her faith by trusting that since the Lord lives, He will heal her son and take care of her family.

Please continue reading Shuna's story in 2 Kings 4:18-36
What happened to Shuna's son?

What was Shuna's response? Why do you think she did this?

What did Shuna say to Elisha in verse 30?

What did Elisha do when he got to the woman's house?

What was Shuna's view of God? How did it influence her actions?

Shuna's precious son came home from working in the fields with his father and died in her arms. She was distraught and went to get Elisha because she was confident that God would be able to fix this problem.

She said to Elisha in 2 Kings 4:30, "As surely as the Lord lives and as you live, I will not leave you." Shuna's remarkable faith allowed her to trust that the Lord lives, and just as God had brought life to her womb, He could bring life to her son.

Shuna had to ask Elisha to pray for her rather than praying on her own because God's Spirit rested on specific people for specific times in the Old Testament. Prophets shared God's Word with His people. Priests served as intermediaries between the people and their LORD God.

As New Testament believers, we have been given direct access to the throne of God through Jesus Christ. As Hebrews 4:15-16 says, "For we do not have a high priest who is unable to empathize with our weaknesses, but we have one who has been tempted in every way, just as we are-yet he did not sin. Let us then approach God's throne of grace with confidence, so that we may receive mercy and find grace to help us in our time of need. We have also been blessed with the Holy Spirit who prays and intercedes for us."

As surely as the Lord lives, He is able to heal, deliver, and restore.

Just as Elisha interceded for Shuna's son, Romans 8:26 explains how the Holy Spirit intercedes for us, "In the same way, the Spirit helps us in our weakness. We do not know what we ought to pray for, but the Spirit himself intercedes for us through wordless groans. And he who searches our hearts knows the mind of the Spirit because the Spirit intercedes for God's people in accordance with the will of God." Nothing is impossible for God, and as surely as the Lord lives, He can heal, deliver, and restore.

WALKING BY FAITH

Over seven years passed between Shuna's son's miraculous recovery and the next time she is mentioned in 2 Kings. Unfortunately, during these seven years, a devasting famine occurred in the land of Israel. **Shuna's story picks up in 2 Kings 8:1-6. Please read these passages and answer the following questions. What did Elisha told the Shuna before the famine started?**

What did she do in response?

* If God warned you about something bad happening, what would you do?

When she got back to Israel, what did she have to do to get back her home and land?

Why do you think she had to go to see the king?

Who was talking to the king at the exact time that she arrived in Samaria?

What was the king's response to her request?

Do you think Gehazi's talking with the king at the exact time she arrived helped influence the king?

Shuna believed in God's word completely and went away for seven years to avoid the famine. Imagine if she had only moved away for five years or three years. She and her son would have needlessly suffered because she had not fully believed God's Word.

So often, when we step out in faith, we only go halfway, or we hold back some of our heart or resources from God. When we do that, we miss out on the fullness of His blessing, and we risk the consequences that God was trying to protect us from.

When the famine was over, Shuna returned home. God miraculously timed her arrival and appeal at the exact time when Gehazi was talking to the king about her and her son. By this time, Shuna was probably a widow since her husband didn't appeal to the king. After hearing her story, the king assigned an official to her case and said, "Give back everything that belonged to her, including all the income from her land from the day she left the country until now." Through God's perfect provision, Gehazi was in the court to speak for her, and the king assigned an official to make sure that she received what was rightfully hers.

*Can you look back on situations in your life when a one-second difference, a one-day delay, or a week-long wait made a significant difference in the trajectory of your life?

I can think of accidents avoided, friendships that were fostered, dates I didn't go on, and jobs I didn't consider because of timing. God spared Shuna from the famine, and He also restored her house and lands and gave her all the income that she left behind when she was obedient to God. God has unbelievable blessings in store for us when we are obedient to follow His Word. Any short-term suffering (like leaving our home during a famine) is intended to protect us and leads to even greater blessings.

God has unbelievable blessings in store for us when we are obedient to follow His Word.

Shuna was a woman who put her faith into action. She used the gifts and resources that God had given her to bless Elisha. She was miraculously blessed after she used her resources and spiritual gifts to bless others. She was a woman of faith who knew that the God who created her son could heal him and give him life. Later, when warned about a famine, she trusted the Word of the Lord that was given to her by Elisha.

Too often, we don't walk in faith because we focus on the bad of leaving rather than the good of going. One of the greatest lessons that we can learn from Shuna is to believe God's Word and act on it.

We can trust God because: He loves us. He wants the best life for us.

He knows the future. He will protect us if we obey him.

He created us for a purpose. He will provide for our needs and our family's needs.

Like Shuna, we can confidently put our faith into action by following His plan

and acting on his word and then reap the rewards of obedience.

HOW HAVE YOU LEARNED TO TRUST GOD THROUGH STUDYING SHUNA?

CHAPTER VI

"How Not To Handle Change" Grandmother

Controlling and Manipulative

Lived to year 837 BC

Walk with the wise and become wise,
for a companion of fools suffers harm.
Proverbs 13:20

Week 1

Athaliah

How do you learn best? Do you learn best from people who do things the right way, who will show you the right path, or do you learn best from watching other people's mistakes and poor choices? While I tend to gravitate towards learning from people who make good choices and do the right thing, I've learned significant lessons from watching people who made terrible choices. I look at their lives and think, "I don't want to be like that," so I avoid the circumstances and choices that led to their downfall.

Athaliah's story is one of those "what not to do" lessons. It is a warning that resisting change by holding on to the past and clinging to the status quo destroys relationships and ultimately causes the harm we are trying so hard to avoid. Athaliah teaches us that if we are just trying to "survive," we are not trusting God.

Let's start this chapter with a prayer. If you can say this out loud, please do. *"God, please protect my family and me from backlash. Please forgive me for seeking control more than your will. Finally, please heal the damage I have caused in my relationship with you and others. Amen."*

HISTORY AND OVERVIEW

At the beginning of the last chapter on Shuna, we covered over 150 years of history, from Naomi's grandson David becoming King of Israel through the division of Israel into two kingdoms after Solomon's death. Both Shuna's and Athaliah's stories are from the same time in history, about 842 BC. While Shuna taught us how to use our gifts and abilities for God's glory, Athaliah's story is about the danger of seeking significance for ourselves through position, control, and false gods. King Joram, the king who helped Shuna regain her land, and Athaliah were children of the wicked King Ahab and his equally notorious wife, Jezebel. "Jezebel was a pagan priestess who installed Baal worship as Israel's official religion."[108] King Ahab "did more evil in the eyes of the LORD than any of those before him. He not only considered it trivial to commit the sins of Jeroboam, son of Nebat, but he also married Jezebel, daughter of Ethbaal, King of the Sidonians, and began to serve Baal and worship him."[109]

King Ahab was taught the importance of political maneuvering by his father, Omri. Historians view King Omri as a powerful and capable political leader who expanded the Kingdom of Israel and

---

[108] NIV The Student Bible, Zondervan Grand Rapids MI
[109] 1 Kings 16:30-31

created liaisons with other powerful nations such as Assyria. Leaders of surrounding kingdoms referred to Israel as the "Kingdom of Omri" for nearly 150 years after his reign.[110] Kingdom building and expansion of power were family values passed from Omri to his son Ahab. To create a political alliance with the Kingdom of Judah, Ahab contracted for his daughter Athaliah to marry Jehoram, the future King of Judah, while he was still a teenager. The marriage of Athaliah to Jehoram was a political coup for the descendants of Omri. Omri had simply been the commander of Israel's army before a military coup made him King of Israel. He knew how tenuous the position of king was for a usurper, so he trained his son Ahab to watch his back and maintain his power and rule at all costs. Athaliah's marriage to Jehoram was the perfect way to maintain control and ensure their continued reign. It established a treaty between Israel and Judah and ensured that Ahab's descendants would sit on King David's throne and join the lineage of the true King.

Do you think family values of status or a need for power can be communicated from one generation to the next?

As you think about your family – can you think of either good or bad values that were given to you from your parents or grandparents? Please write out your examples.

LIKE MOTHER – LIKE DAUGHTER

Athaliah was raised to value power and position over all other relationships. She had learned from her mother Jezebel's use of power for her own glory and influence.

Please read 1 Kings 21:1-16 to get an idea of what kind of woman Jezebel was. How would you describe her?

A little more background read 1 Kings 18:4 - What did Jezebel do?

What do you think Athaliah learned to value from her mother?

---

[110] http://www.jewishencyclopedia.com/view.jsp?artid=67&letter=O

Athaliah had learned from her mother how to be a "take charge" woman. Jezebel taught Athaliah that manipulation and lying were ways of maintaining power and the throne. She was a woman who did whatever it took to get what she wanted. Her motto was probably, "If it is going to get done, I have to do it myself." Life was about survival; Jezebel used her power and position to ensure her family's needs and wants were met regardless of the consequences for other people.

Do you think that it is okay to make choices based on a need to survive? Why? Why Not?

I have realized that making a choice on the need to survive means I am choosing not to trust God. Here's what I've learned, a "survival mentality" is a matter of the heart rather than actions. For example, Shuna's choice to leave her home was based on faith rather than a need to survive, though it might look like a way to protect herself and her son. Likewise, when Miriam and the Israelites went to their Egyptian neighbors and asked them for money and provisions for their journey, this was an act of faith even though it could be perceived as a means to get what they wanted. Their actions, based on faith and obedience to God's Word, resulted in their survival and blessings; but their motivation was to please God, not just to survive or get a blessing. When we act in faith and obedience to God, He is responsible for our survival. Jesus died that we might have abundant life; He wants us to live abundantly, not just survive.

If you feel the need to tell a lie, check your motives with this question, "Am I acting in fear or in faith?"

A survival mentality that comes from a lack of faith often leads to lying and distortion of God's Word. Remember how Abraham lied to Pharaoh about Sarah being his sister? Rather than having faith in the Lord, his fear of Pharaoh led to Sarah's enslavement in a harem. If you ever feel the need to lie, check your motives with this question, "Am I acting in fear or in faith?"

Athaliah's mom, Jezebel, lied and misused God's Law as a tool that led to Naboth's murder. Lying and distortion of God's Word are always clues that someone isn't depending on God. Rather than submitting to God as the ultimate Ruler, Jezebel used religion as a means of power and control, even though she denied the sovereignty of God and purposefully destroyed the prophets of God. Like many deceptive people, she used God's Law to manipulate others rather than a way to know and love God.

Jezebel wasn't the first person to use religion for her own selfish benefit, and she won't be the last. Jesus warned his followers, "Watch out for false prophets. They come to you in sheep's clothing, but inwardly they are ferocious wolves. By their fruit you will recognize them. Do people pick grapes from thorn bushes, or figs from thistles? Likewise, every good tree bears good fruit, but a bad tree bears bad fruit. A good tree cannot bear bad fruit, and a bad tree cannot bear good fruit."[111] People will

---

[111] Matthew 7:15-18

distort and use the Word of God for their own benefit. Knowing God's Word will help us defend against lies and deception.[112]

As a younger woman, Athaliah watched her mother support the worship of false gods, and she learned she couldn't trust the false gods, Baal and Asherah, because they couldn't even create fire during a drought.[113] She could only rely on herself. Success was about maintaining power and position, regardless of the cost or destroyed relationships.

Though Athaliah saw the brutal consequences of her mother's choices, she chose to continue to live like her parents. Just because our parents have certain values--good or bad--does not mean that we must value the same things. Every day, we have a choice. We can choose who we will serve and what will be our number one priority. Will we choose to serve God as Lord and Master, or will we look for our security in the false gods of control, power, position, and influence? Will we go about our days striving to take care of ourselves and get things done according to "my will and my way," or spend our time trusting God and believing that His will and His way will lead to greater blessing and freedom than we could ever imagine? Giving up our need to control others and get our way is a huge step in trusting God. It means that we are letting go of the controlling and manipulative ways that seem to protect us from hurt and pain. It means letting go of lies and techniques that got us what we wanted when it seemed like no one else cared about us. It means giving up our survival mentality.

Trusting God means that we believe God is in control and that He will take care of us better than we can take care of ourselves. God will protect us from being hurt and heal our pain because He is God, our Healer. God will provide the clothes and food we need because God is our Provider. He will protect our families and us because he is our Shield,[114] our Refuge, and our ever-present help in trouble.[115] God will give us abundant life filled with love, peace, and contentment.

Please take some time to pray and ask God to show you areas you had a survival mentality. Pray and repent for your lack of faith, your dishonesty and manipulation. Ask God to help you trust that He will take care of you and provide for your needs and to open your eyes to His protection and provision. Pray for His will to be done.

---

[112] Matthew 4:1-11
[113] 1 Kings 18:16-46
[114] Genesis 15:1
[115] Psalms 46:1

Week 2

HOW NOT TO INFLUENCE YOUR HUSBAND

Social influence is a popular topic in marketing circles. We can see it on Instagram, Pinterest, and Tik Tok; even LinkedIn.com includes blogs from "Influencers." Marketers are trying to tap into the power of influence because affects the movies we see, the car we buy, and even our laundry detergent.

As women, we have been gifted with the power of influence on our children, husband, and friends. Just as Eve handed Adam the fruit in the Garden of Eden, our approval and encouragement to do good or bad things can significantly impact the people we are close enough to influence. As we will learn, Athaliah was a bad influence on her young husband, Jehoram, and on her son, Ahaziah. We can learn from Athaliah's poor choices as a mom and a wife to use the influence God has given us for good and to guard against unhealthy patterns in our family history.

Athaliah's marriage to Jehoram was a political coup for the House of Omri and was a way to ensure their children were rightful heirs to the throne.

Please read 2 Kings 8:17-18 and answer the following questions-
How old was Jehoram when he became King?

How long did he reign?

Based on this passage, what type of influence did Athaliah have on her husband?

Now, please read 2 Kings 8:25-26.
How old was Jehoram and Athaliah's son Ahaziah when he became King?

Jehoram was 32 years old when he began his reign as King of Judah and he reigned for 8 years and died when he was 40 years old. Ahaziah was 22 when he became king which means Ahaziah was born when Jehoram was 18 years old. According to the passage we read in 2 Kings 8, Jehoram followed the ways of the kings of Israel because he married a daughter of Ahab. Athaliah's family had a significant influence on her young husband.

Please read 2 Chronicles 21:1-6 and summarize what Jehoram did after he became King. Why do you think Jehoram did this to his brothers?

Jehoram's massacre makes no sense based on his family history. The leadership of Judah had transitioned peacefully through four generations for almost 90 years. He was a direct descendant of the throne of David. He was the eldest of his brothers and the rightful heir to the throne. Jehoshaphat even gave each of Jehoram's brothers gold, silver, and cities to keep peace among the brothers.

However, based on Athaliah's family history, this massacre makes total sense. Everyone is a potential threat to the throne for a family of usurpers. Wiping out Jehoram's brothers means more control and power. 2 Chronicles 21:6 says that Jehoram "walked in the ways of the house of Ahab because he married a daughter of Ahab. He did evil in the eyes of the Lord."

Athaliah's influence on Jehoram cannot be understated. Jehoram's father, King Jehoshaphat, was a godly man who did right in the eyes of the Lord. He was a prayer warrior and a military leader; God gave him peace throughout the land. Yet Jehoram chose not to follow in his father's footsteps; instead, he decided to follow his wife's lead.

> **When we are in survival mode and not trusting God, we actually seem to create what we fear and construct a vicious cycle as we fight to survive.**

Jehoshaphat's legacy of peace and success was ravaged by Athaliah and Jehoram's power-hungry lifestyle. Jehoram and Athaliah thought they could prevent conflict over the throne by killing off his brothers, but their desire for control resulted in a loss of control. The countries of Edom and Libnah which had been under control during his father's reign rose up against Jehoram and established their own kings.[116] The Philistines and Arabs attacked Judah and carried off all the goods in the king's palace, as well Jehoram's other wives and all of his sons except for Ahaziah, the youngest.[117] It is striking to me that the thing they feared most seemed to manifest itself in their lives even though they thought their actions would ensure their power and control. When we are in survival mode and not trusting God, I have noticed that we actually seem to create what we fear and construct a vicious cycle as we fight to survive.

Jehoram may have been King, but Athaliah was the boss of the house. She led her husband into the worship of false gods. The strife that afflicted the house of Ahab because of her family's sin and

---

[116] 2 Chronicles 21:8-10
[117] 2 Chronicles 21:16-18

idolatry latched on to Jehoram and his family. Athaliah used her influence on her husband to influence him toward wicked things and away from the worship of God.

We have a great deal of influence on our husbands. Though they may be the head of the house, our priorities and focus can significantly affect their spiritual growth and perspective. King Solomon was tempted to follow other gods by his wives[118] and our behaviors can tempt our husbands toward Christ or away from Him. Herodias convinced her daughter and husband to have John the Baptist's head chopped off and displayed on a platter.[119] In contrast, Queen Esther used her influence with her ungodly husband to save the lives of thousands of people.[120] Our choices and our priorities can sway our husbands whether or not they are believers.

Our choices **and our priorities influence our husband whether or not they are believers.**

Each of us will stand before God and give an account of how we used our God-given position as a wife for His kingdom and His glory. We are challenged by 1 Peter 3:1-6 to "Be good wives to your husbands, responsive to their needs. There are husbands who, indifferent as they are to any words about God, will be captivated by your life of holy beauty. What matters is not your outer appearance—the styling of your hair, the jewelry you wear, the cut of your clothes—but your inner disposition. Cultivate inner beauty, the gentle, gracious kind that God delights in. The holy women of old were beautiful before God that way, and were good, loyal wives to their husbands."[121]

Based on 1 Peter 3:1-6 written above, what are some good ways we can influence our husbands towards the things of God?

How can our actions prevent our husband from seeking after God?

As wives, we have a significant influence on our husbands. There is nothing wrong with beautiful clothes or jewelry, but only "holy beauty" will captivate our husbands and draw them closer to God. In contrast, behaviors such as hypocrisy, not letting God be in control, and selfishness can push someone away from God.

Our choices strongly affect the rest of the family. Ask God to guard the words you speak so that your husband hears encouragement and not judgment. We can create an environment of strife and

---

[118] 1 Kings 11:4-8
[119] Mark 6:18-28
[120] The Book of Esther
[121] 1 Peter 3:1-6

discord or a place of calm and peace. We set the tone of our family by having integrity and being gentle instead of harsh and demanding. To use our godly influence in a non-manipulative way, we need to align our opinions with the Word of God and trust that just as God can change the course of a river, He can change our husband's heart and attitude.[122]

HOW NOT TO ENCOURAGE YOUR CHILDREN

Not all kids of bad parents turn out bad, and not all kids of good parents turn out good. However, parents do significantly influence their children's life choices. Athaliah used her influence on her son Ahaziah.

2 Chronicles 22:3 says, "Ahaziah was twenty-two years old when he became king, and he reigned in Jerusalem one year. His mother's name was Athaliah, a granddaughter of Omri. He too followed the ways of the house of Ahab, for his mother encouraged him to act wickedly."

Please re-read the scripture above and underline the word "encourage." Based on the scripture above, how did Athaliah parent her only son?

I was struck by the word "encourage" in this verse! Here are some other scriptures where the word "encourage" is used.

Please underline the word <u>encourage</u> in each verse and circle what they were encouraged to do like the following example.

Deuteronomy 3:28 But commission Joshua, and <u>encourage</u> and strengthen him, for he will lead this people across and will cause them to inherit the land that you will see."

2 Chronicles 32:6, 7 He appointed military officers over the people and assembled them before him in the square at the city gate and encouraged them with these words:7 "Be strong and courageous. Do not be afraid or discouraged because of the king of Assyria and the vast army with him, for there is a greater power with us than with him.

Acts 22 23 When he arrived and saw what the grace of God had done, he was glad and encouraged them all to remain true to the Lord with all their hearts.

---

[122] Proverbs 21:1

Romans 15:4 For everything that was written in the past was written to teach us, so that through the endurance taught in the Scriptures and the encouragement they provide we might have hope.

Titus 2:6 Similarly, encourage the young men to be self-controlled.

We can encourage people around us. We can inspire each other to have hope and help each other not to be afraid or discouraged. Through encouragement, we can motivate others remain true to the Lord.

We can also encourage others to have self-control in challenging situations. The root meaning of self-control is not about "being the boss of yourself"; instead, it is related to the concept of being potty-trained. Unlike a baby who cannot control himself when he has to go, having self-control means you can "hold it." One definition of self-control is "the virtue of one who masters his desires and passions, especially his sensual appetites." When I think back to those long potty-training days, I was vigilant in encouraging the desired behavior and used many different rewards. Just as we motivate our children when they are potty training, we need to encourage older kids as they learn to flee temptation and master their desires and passions for worldly pleasures.

If we are surrounded by people making foolish choices, we will be harmed even if we are not making the same bad choices.

Godly encouragement builds up. As First Thessalonians 5:11 says, "Therefore encourage one another and build each other up, just as in fact you are doing." Paul writes in 2 Corinthians 13:10-12, "This is why I write these things when I am absent, that when I come I may not have to be harsh in my use of authority—the authority the Lord gave me for building you up, not for tearing you down. Finally, brothers and sisters, rejoice! Strive for full restoration, encourage one another, be of one mind, live in peace. And the God of love and peace will be with you." These scripture passages show that God has given us the authority to build others up, not tear them down.

Just as Athaliah encouraged her son to worship Baal and do wicked things, there are people in this world who encourage us in weakness and selfishness and pull us away from the things of God.

King David writes about such wicked people in Psalm 64:3-5:

"They sharpen their tongues like swords
and aim cruel words like deadly arrows.
They shoot from ambush at the innocent;
they shoot suddenly, without fear.
They encourage each other in evil plans,
they talk about hiding their snares;
they say, "Who will see it?"

We need to be wary and avoid people who encourage us in wickedness and tear us and others down with their words and actions. If we are around people who are constantly making bad choices or people who are destructive and manipulative, we will either become victims or become like them in our behavior because "Bad company corrupts good character." [123]

Proverbs contains godly wisdom that helps us avoid the pitfalls and mistakes people have made throughout history. Please write down the following verses:
Proverbs 12:26

Proverbs 13:20

We need to be careful about who we choose to be our friends. Our relationship with God, our righteousness, is influenced by the friends we keep. When we are friends with evil people and follow their ways, we will be led away from God and forgo some benefits that come from following Him. When we walk with wise people, we become wise, and we will experience wisdom's benefits. If we are surrounded by people making foolish choices, we will be harmed even if we are not making the same bad choices. It is even essential to be careful of what type of shows we watch and beware of the media's influence on how we view ourselves and the world physically, socially, and spiritually. Watching certain movies or TV shows that support ungodly choices can make wrong things seem acceptable.

Can you think of examples from your own life that illustrate the truths of these two Proverbs?

As I read through these two verses, I thought of many situations where I have seen or experienced the truth of these proverbs. I was blessed with wise, godly college friends. Because my friends got up on Sunday morning to go to church, I would get up (usually at the very last minute) and go to church with them. My friends regularly read the Bible, so I started reading the Bible. My friends' actions influenced my righteousness. However, I have also seen the opposite truth. A high school friend went to a different college, and she surrounded herself with friends who didn't seek after God. As she pursued a typical college life, her relationship with God suffered greatly. After college, her heart changed, and she started going to church, and God brought a wonderful man into her life. They are happily married and

---

[123] 1 Corinthians 15:33

now minister to college kids. While her story has a happy ending, much heartbreak during college could have been avoided if she had friends who encouraged her to seek the Lord.

A companion of fools suffers harm is both a statement of fact and a warning. I know a girl whose mom and dad were both crack addicts; though she did not choose her parents, she has suffered much harm because of their foolish choices. She spent Christmas with her grandmother because her mom was in jail. She never knew when her mom would be home, and when she was 15, her mother died of a drug overdose. When the people around us make foolish choices, sometimes we will suffer in small ways, and sometimes we will have to deal with the long-term consequences of their choices.

The benefits from wise choices will trickle down to everyone around us.

Similarly, the benefits from wise choices will trickle down to everyone around us. Children whose parents and grandparents have made wise choices will benefit generations to come.[124] My sister Christy and her husband have made wise financial choices, and as a result, they can give abundantly to those in need. One year, she and her family packed 60 shoeboxes for Operation Christmas Child. www.samaritanspurse.org/occ that went to children in Mali, Benin and Haiti. Her wise financial choices have not just blessed her family but have influenced children from all over the world. For my sister's little girls, abundance and giving generously are a normal part of their lives.

Ask God to show you ways that can be a godly influence on your children and other young people. Please write down what He reveals to you and the first step you need to take to accomplish it.

As I write this, I am struck by the fact that much of what we consider "normal" life is often a consequence of the environment and people we have around us. For example, my sister Joan worked as a bartender, and she would tell me stories of people's foolish choices, broken bones, and blackouts, all normal things in that environment. They are a typical part of that life, just as intrigue and the continual struggle for power were Athaliah's "normal" life.

Our definition of normal should not be determined by our culture or by what the people around us or our family have always done. We need to be wary of anything that depends on human tradition rather than Christ.[125] Instead of trying to be like everyone else, we are called to be like Christ, holy and set apart for His higher purpose.

---

[124] Proverbs 13:22
[125] Colossians 2:8

Have you allowed tradition, and what is "normal" to define how you make choices? Pray and ask God to show you how to be holy in every part of your life.

God has recently shown me patterns in my family that I thought were normal but were actually verbal abuse. Growing up, my mom frequently yelled at us kids, and my dad would discount and trivialize my mom's concerns. Chronic forgetting was also an unhealthy family pattern. Wikipedia contains this list of items that are considered verbal abuse. "Verbal abuse includes the following: countering, withholding, discounting, verbal abuse disguised as a joke, blocking and diverting, accusing and blaming, judging and criticizing, trivializing, undermining, threatening, name-calling, chronic forgetting, ordering, denial of anger or abuse, and abusive anger."[126] Reading through this list was incredibly painful. I realized that much of what I considered normal family conversation instead was hurtful verbal abuse.

When I became a parent, I decided that I would not yell at my kids, but I still continued to trivialize and discount things that upset my husband, and worst of all, I would chronically forget things.

What is normal **should not be determined by our culture nor by what the people around us nor by what our family has always done.**

Realizing that my unhealthy communication patterns were also verbally abusive and on the same list, as yelling, name-calling, and abusive anger was humbling. I wanted to justify my actions and rationalize them as not that bad. I also wanted to point out my husband's faults and make excuses for my behavior. But God has shown me that I am responsible for my actions, and just as He convicted me and is helping me to be more like Him, I have to trust his power and ability to work on the issues in the people around me. My responsibility was to repent and apologize for the hurt that I was causing by forgetting things or by trivializing other people's concerns, not convict or condemn those around me.

MIRROR MIRROR

God has shown me a powerful way to respond when I see unhealthy patterns in other people. The key to helping other people is based on Luke 6:41-42, "Why do you look at the speck of sawdust in your brother's eye and pay no attention to the plank in your own eye? How can you say to your brother, 'Brother, let me take the speck out of your eye,' when you yourself fail to see the plank in your own eye? You hypocrite, first take the plank out of your eye, and then you will see clearly to remove the speck from your brother's eye."

---

[126] http://en.wikipedia.org/wiki/Verbal_abuse

Based on these two verses the first step to helping someone else is to _____.

God calls us first to take the plank out of our eye because if we can see sin or weakness in someone else, we have either been exposed to that sin or are justifying our own sin. People with similar sin patterns tend to stick together because we tolerate each other's weaknesses to a certain point. However, since all sin is destructive, eventually, we will see our husband's or our friend's sin for what it is, and it will bother us.

When we see an unhealthy pattern in another person, our first response must be to repent of what we see in others. We need to pray, "God forgive me for _____." It is essential for *you* to repent of the sin you see in your *spouse's* life because biblically, you are one flesh. If your husband has an anger problem, you have an anger problem. If your husband is impatient, you are impatient. You are one, and God will not be able to work on your husband to get the plank out of his eye until you get out of His way by repenting of the sin you see in your husband's life.

"But Penny, he has the problem, not me." I can hear you say. Not true, you have the problem because you have to live with him! If you truly don't have the problem, repenting should be easy because you are already on the right path. The word "repentance" means to turn from self to God. It reverses our thoughts from an unhealthy sin-filled pattern to God's way. However, for me, often, that feeling of "It's his problem" is actually a sign of pride. So next, I have to repent of pride; I pray, "God, please forgive me for having pride and please help me focus on you and not on myself."

People with similar **sin patterns tend to stick together because we tolerate each other's sin to a certain point.**

As Christians, we are members of a royal priesthood,[127] which means we are responsible for extending God's mercy to the people around us who are cut off from fellowship with God and other people because of their sins. My Old Testament Survey professor, Dr. Laniak, explained, "The role of the priest was to be a bridge between sinful people and a merciful God." Just as the priest on the Day of Atonement[128] first had to confess and repent of both intentional and unintentional sins by making the first sacrifice for himself before he could minister to the people around him, we need to follow the same pattern. First, we need to confess our sins, both intentional and unintentional. Then, we can provide a bridge to the mercy of the Lord to other people.

Identifying and repenting of the sinful patterns that we see in our families and other people will provide healing and blessing for generations to come. Though it was incredibly upsetting when I realized my history of being verbally abusive, I know that God has broken an unhealthy family pattern.

---

[127] 1 Peter 2:9
[128] Leviticus 16:3, 6

He has begun to heal our family and create new communication styles for our two boys, the next generation, and their children so that our home is a place of blessing, where our words will be kind and build one another up and where the truth is spoken in love. I desire that Ephesians 4:15 will be true about our family, "we will speak the truth in love, growing in every way more and more like Christ, who is the head of His body, the church."

Take some time to pray and ask God to reveal unhealthy sinful patterns in your life that need to be healed and ask Him to replace them with healthy and holy attitudes and actions.

Week 3

WHO **NOT** TO ASK FOR ADVICE

My friend Sarah, a Spanish teacher, said something amazingly simple but profound about the inheritance we unintentionally give our children, "Our kids speak English because we speak English." In the same way, the "languages" of life, relationship patterns, and values have been passed down to us just along with our ability to speak English.

One of the hardest things we are called to do on our faith journey is breaking away from unhealthy family traditions and ungodly influences. Even if we realize the choices our parents and grandparents made were based on human tradition and their need for control, it is tough to let go of patterns we have grown up with. But, as we will learn in this chapter, the only way to escape unhealthy traditions and behaviors is to replace them with God-given gifts that can create lasting blessings for generations.

Athaliah's story continued when her son, Ahaziah, became king after his father died "to no one's regret."[129] Though Ahaziah was the youngest of his father's children, he was the only one to survive a massacre by Arab raiders that resulted in the death of all of the older sons of Jehoram.[130] Ahaziah's "normal life" was strongly influenced by his mother Athaliah's family. Ahaziah turned to relatives in his

---

[129] 2 Chronicles 21:20
[130] 2 Chronicles 22:1

mother's family as advisors and "did evil in the eyes of the Lord, as the house of Ahab had done for after his father's death, they became his advisors to his undoing."[131] The end of his brief one-year reign came about because he joined forces with his Uncle Joram, King of Israel, to fight against the King of Aram. After Joram was wounded in the battle, Ahaziah went to see him.

Both 2 Chronicles 22:7-9 and 2 Kings 9:1-10:17 tell the story of the end of the descendants of Ahab and the death of Athaliah's son Ahaziah. Please read one or both of these passages and summarize what happened.

God told Elisha that Jehu, a commander in Israel's Army, was to be the next King of Israel. Elisha sent a prophet to anoint Jehu and give him a message from the Lord God of Israel, "I anoint you King over Israel, you are to destroy the house of Ahab and I will avenge the blood of my servants the prophet and all the Lord's servants shed by Jezebel." Jehu then killed Ahaziah's uncle, King Joram, with a shot from a bow and arrow, and he was left for dead in the field that his mother had connived to get from Naboth. Next, Jehu made sure the 70 descendants of Ahab were killed so that every male relative of Ahab was cut off and the house of Ahab would be no more.

Jehu also killed the officials of Judah and the sons of Ahaziah's relatives who were traveling with Ahaziah while he was visiting Joram. Ahaziah was fatally wounded by Jehu, and his servants brought him back to Jerusalem to be buried. Ahaziah followed the unhealthy patterns of his mother's family. Sadly, after his father died, he turned to his Uncle Joram rather than God.

Continuing in our ancestors' sin and unhealthy choices is the course of least resistance. One of the hardest things we can do is break away from past harmful family traditions and ungodly influences in our families. Just as Ruth made a conscious decision to leave her land, her people, and her gods and chose to follow the God of Naomi, we have to decide to follow Jesus regardless of our family history and tradition. Remember, in the chapter on Naomi, we learned that Jesus is our Redeemer, just as Boaz was Ruth and Naomi's kinsman-redeemer. Our Redeemer paid the price to set us free from the slavery of our sins and our ancestors' sins.

Please look up 1 Peter 1:18 - 19 and answer these questions.
What were we redeemed from?

What is the source of our redemption?

---

[131] 2 Chronicles 22:4

Do you really understand that Jesus redeemed you with His *blood* to save you from the empty way of life handed down to you through your forefathers? Just as you may have inherited good things like brown eyes and curly hair from your ancestors, foolish and worthless patterns of living are also passed down. To experience the complete inheritance God intends for us, we have to let go of the worthless things we have inherited from our ancestors to make room for the good things God has for us.

After Moses and Miriam's death, God used Joshua to bring the Israelites into the land of their inheritance. Just before dying, Joshua called the leaders of Israel together. He reminded them of their deliverance from slavery and idolatry that went all the way back to the time of Abraham. Joshua 24:14-15 says, "Now fear the LORD and serve him with all faithfulness. Throw away the gods your ancestors worshiped beyond the Euphrates River and in Egypt, and serve the LORD. But if serving the LORD seems undesirable to you, then choose for yourselves this day whom you will serve, whether the gods your ancestors served beyond the Euphrates, or the gods of the Amorites, in whose land you are living. But as for me and my household, we will serve the LORD."

> *Let go of worthless* **things inherited from our ancestors to make room for the good things God has for us.**

Joshua presented them with a choice; they could serve the false gods of their ancestors, the false gods of their current generation, or choose to serve the Lord. The leaders of Israel during Joshua's time decided to serve the Lord. We have to make the same choice every day.

As believers in Christ, we have been redeemed and saved from the slavery of foolish traditions of our forefathers, but our salvation is not a guarantee that we are living in freedom. When the chains fell off Peter's wrists, he could have ignored the messenger from God and stayed in prison. Instead, he got up, put on clothes, and followed the angel to freedom. [132]

Living a life of freedom requires action. Jesus has set us free from the slavery of sin, but we will continue destructive and unhealthy behaviors that we have picked up from our culture and remain trapped in our past if we don't take hold of our new legacy of godliness and freedom.

Please read Ephesians 4:20-24. Please answer the following questions.

What are we supposed to do with our former way of life?

What are we supposed to do with our new selves?

---

[132] Acts 12:7

The Message paraphrase of this passage tells us that "everything with the old way of life has to go." We are to "Get rid of it!" The Greek word in this verse that is translated as "cast off" or "put off" means to throw away or cast aside. The idea behind this word is the same as the castoff pile of clothes that no longer fit at the bottom of my closet; they are castoffs. Why would I wear those damaged, ripped, or too tight clothes when I have a valuable new wardrobe filled with righteousness and holiness? We need to throw away the things of the past, throw off anything that hinders us and sin that entangles us[133] from living the life that God has secured for us.

Please read each of these passages and <u>cross out</u> what we are to "throw off, put aside, rid yourselves, strip off, and cast off."

Here is an example:

Romans 13:12 The night is nearly over; the day is almost here. So let us put aside the ~~deeds of darkness~~ and put on the armor of light.

Ephesians 4:25 Therefore each of you must put off falsehood and speak truthfully to your neighbor, for we are all members of one body.

Colossians 3:8 But now you must also rid yourselves of all such things as these: anger, rage, malice, slander, and filthy language from your lips.

Hebrews 12:1 THEREFORE then, since we are surrounded by so great a cloud of witnesses [who have borne testimony to the Truth], let us strip off and throw aside every encumbrance (unnecessary weight) and that sin which so readily (deftly and cleverly) clings to and entangles us, and let us run with patient endurance and steady and active persistence the appointed course of the race that is set before us, (AMP)

James 1:2121 So get rid of all the filth and evil in your lives, and humbly accept the word God has planted in your hearts, for it has the power to save your souls. (NLT)

Is there anything that God has called you to cast off in order to embrace the blessings He has for you?

---

[133] Hebrews 12:1

THE NEXT STEP

I was weeding my yard this morning and pulling out a noxious weed called nuthatch. It has a blade that looks like grass until it grows much taller and takes over the yard. At the surface, the plant looked like a few innocent blades of taller grass but pulling it out revealed a two-inch root ball and created a gaping hole in my yard. I realized that if I didn't re-seed with good seed or cover the hole with mulch, I would have just been "tilling" the soil for any errant seed that blew into that hole.

Making sure nuthatch or another weed didn't grow in that hole meant that I had to intentionally put something in the spot to replace what had been taken out. When we put on the Lord Jesus and clothe ourselves in compassion, kindness, humility, gentleness, and patience, we will prevent weeds from growing in our hearts and damaging our relationships with others.

Casting off the things that hold us back is the first step of an ongoing process toward living in freedom but to complete the process, we need to be intentional about filling the gaps in our life with godly things. This is important because even though we are set free from the bondage of sin and death and are in Christ a new creation, we can still be prone to weakness in certain areas.

We need to be aware that choices made by our parents and grandparents can become places of weakness and areas that are particularly prone to spiritual attack. My friend Laura described these areas of weakness as "landing strips" that give the attackers a place to grab a foothold.[134]

Just a few short generations after Joshua led the Israelites into their inheritance, the people of Israel were seduced by the gods of their ancestors and the false gods of the people around them. The Israelites chose to return to their slavery because they were arrogant and stiff-necked, they refused to listen to God, and they failed to remember His miracles.[135]

Please read the verses below. Circle what we are to put on and ~~cross out what we are to take off.~~

Romans 13:12-14 "The night is nearly over; the day is almost here. So let us put aside the deeds of darkness and put on the armor of light. Let us behave decently, as in the daytime, not in carousing and drunkenness, not in sexual immorality and debauchery, not in dissension and jealousy. Rather, clothe yourselves with the Lord Jesus Christ, and do not think about how to gratify the desires of the flesh."

---

[134] Ephesians 4:27
[135] Nehemiah 9:16-17

Colossians 3:12 -14 "Therefore, as God's chosen people, holy and dearly loved, clothe yourselves with compassion, kindness, humility, gentleness and patience. Bear with each other and forgive one another if any of you has a grievance against someone. Forgive as the Lord forgave you. And over all these virtues put on love, which binds them all together in perfect unity."

Ephesians 6:11-17 "Put on the full armor of God, so that you can take your stand against the devil's schemes. For our struggle is not against flesh and blood, but against the rulers, against the authorities, against the powers of this dark world and against the spiritual forces of evil in the heavenly realms. Therefore put on the full armor of God, so that when the day of evil comes, you may be able to stand your ground, and after you have done everything, to stand. Stand firm then, with the belt of truth buckled around your waist, with the breastplate of righteousness in place, and with your feet fitted with the readiness that comes from the gospel of peace. In addition to all this, take up the shield of faith, with which you can extinguish all the flaming arrows of the evil one. Take the helmet of salvation and the sword of the Spirit, which is the word of God."

My college friend Becky has a creative way of looking at the world. As we discussed this study, she said, "You know many Christians are spiritual streakers. We might have our helmet of salvation on, but we aren't wearing anything else!"

Not only do we have to cast off the past habits and destructive family patterns but to protect against attack and areas of weakness, we are to "put on," get dressed, or clothe ourselves in a new way of life, one of holiness and righteousness. We must let go of the behaviors and attitudes in the past and put on the whole armor of Christ. These verses encourage us to put on characteristics of Christ. He is our Truth, Peace, Salvation, Righteousness, Peace, Righteousness, and the Word.

Pray and ask God to help you put on Jesus Christ so that His character transforms you.

WEEK 4

How **NOT** to Grandparent

Athaliah was an ungodly influence on her husband and an awful mother, but her grand-parenting skills took her to new lows. Let's continue reading about her to discover how she could go to a place I would never imagine.

Please read 2 Chronicles 22:8-10 and summarize what happened.

What was Athaliah's response to her son's death?

Athaliah decided to destroy the whole royal family of the house of Judah. Did she do this out of grief because her son had been killed therefore no one should live? Did she do it in response to Jehu's massacre of her brother and other relatives?

The Contemporary English Version of the Bible provides a little more insight through its translation of this verse, *"As soon as Athaliah heard that her son King Ahaziah was dead, she decided to kill any relative who could possibly become king."* Her objective was to prevent anyone else from becoming king. She wanted the throne, she wasn't of royal blood and "if one of the young princes became king, his mother would supersede Athaliah in the dignity of queen mother."[136]

Athaliah takes resisting change to a whole new level. For Athaliah, this massacre was all about retaining her position and power; these royal heirs were in her way and would usurp her power. With them out of the picture, she would finally be the ultimate ruler. She wouldn't have to take a back seat and rely on her influence with her father, husband, or son to get what she wanted. She would be the boss, the queen, and nothing could stop her. For her, killing was a small thing to gain ultimate control of the throne.

---

[136] Jamieson, Robert; A.R. Fausset; and David Brown. "*Commentary on 2 Chronicles 22.*". Blue Letter Bible. 19 Feb 2000. 2011. 26 Jan 2011.
<http:// www.blueletterbible.org/commentaries/comm_view.cfm? AuthorID=7&contentID=2270&commInfo=6&topic=2%20Chronicles& ar=2Ch_22_1 >

Athaliah is a role model for what not to do. I struggle to understand how anyone could do this. How could she take lives just to maintain her position and power? I hate change and resist it mightily, but I don't think I would physically hurt someone just because I didn't want my life to change.

So, how we can learn to embrace change from a bad example like Athaliah? The first thing we can learn, which may seem kind of obvious, is to not resist change to the point of killing someone. This appears to be a reasonable goal, but it has been a challenging and life-altering struggle for millions of women. In Liz Curtis Higgs' book, *Really Bad Girls of the Bible*, she starts her chapter on Athaliah by telling the story of Regina Banks, a driven, successful businesswoman who finds out that her 15-year-old daughter is pregnant and arranges for her daughter to get an abortion. Regina's concern for her position and reputation ultimately ended her daughter's life and that of her twin grandchildren.

For millions of us, dealing with change, fear of the unknown, shame, or desire to turn back time and keep things the same have resulted in destruction and death, maybe not as apparent as Athaliah but still just as heart-breaking. However, we can take heart that God will be glorified no matter what we have done. God had the victory regardless of Athaliah's actions and our choices.

If the Holy Spirit has brought to mind choices that elevated your plans, your need for control, your reputation, and your desires over God's will, please take a minute to pray and ask for God's forgiveness. Repent of damaging your relationships and ask God to give you grace and give you beauty for ashes and the oil of joy for mourning.

IT ALL BELONGS TO GOD

The next lesson that we can learn from Athaliah is that everything belongs to God. It seems so simple to want to be in control of our lives and our bodies, our money, and our time. Yet God has another answer: our lives, our bodies, our money, and our time are not our own. They are His.

Please read the following verses and <u>underline what belongs to God.</u>
1 Chronicles 29:11 - "Yours, O LORD, is the greatness, the power, the glory, the victory, and the majesty. Everything in the heavens and on earth is yours, O LORD, and this is your kingdom. We adore you as the one who is over all things. (NLT)

Psalm 24:1- The earth is the Lord's, and everything in it, the world, and all who live in it;

1 Corinthians 6:19-20- Do you not know that your bodies are temples of the Holy Spirit, who is in you, whom you have received from God? You are not your own; 20 you were bought at a price. Therefore honor God with your bodies.

Everything in the world and all the people in it are the Lord's. Everything is His. Specifically, you are not your own. Not only did God create you, but He also redeemed you. He paid the price for you with the precious blood of Jesus; therefore, we don't have the sovereignty to say, "This is my body, I'll do what I want; this is my money. I'll spend it as I want; this is my house, my rules my way."

Our desire for control destroys relationships with others because it first destroys our relationship with God. When we put ourselves on the throne, just as when Athaliah established her kingdom in Judah, we are exalting ourselves rather than God. There can only be one Lord in our life. 1 Chronicles 29 continues in verse 12, "Riches and honor come from you alone, for you rule over everything. Power and might are in your hand, and it is at your discretion that people are made great and given strength. (NLT)

God is sovereign. If we are trying to control/ rule over things and people, we are getting in the way of God's rule. Satan took this to the extreme. Satan tried to ascend to a throne above God and make himself like the Most High[137] but instead, he was thrown down and fell like lightning from heaven.[138] Satan's desire for control led to an uprising in heaven but ended in his ultimate destruction. When we try to ascend to the throne of God (el) and make ourselves like Most High (Elyon) and LORD Master (Jehovah), we are putting ourselves above God.

> *Our desire for control* **destroys relationships with others because it first destroys our relationship with God.**

Pause for a moment and pay attention to this: your need for control over your body, money, spouse, children, grandchildren, and home has the same root as Athaliah's need for power and Satan's desire to be Ruler of all. If someone would describe you as a controlling person, that means you are exalting yourself over God in those situations. God is Ruler over EVERYTHING.

Are there areas of your life where you need to be in control? Why is this so important to you?

When I answered this question, I realized that much of my need for control came out of fear. I was afraid that something terrible would happen if I didn't have control in a particular area. I was worried that I or someone I loved would get hurt. I was afraid that I wouldn't get what I wanted and wouldn't achieve my dreams. I was scared that if I trusted God with all areas of my life, He would take something away that I loved or make me do something I didn't want.

---

[137] Isaiah 14:12-15
[138] Luke 10:18

One area I really struggled with was the area of birth control. I was paranoid of becoming pregnant. As a teenager, I saw the heartbreak caused by rebellious children, and as the oldest of five, I saw the sheer amount of work that went into raising kids. I was convinced that there were enough children in this world, and I didn't want any of my own. I made sure my husband knew this when we got married, so I religiously took my pill every day.

I was in control and was convinced of my beliefs. Yet, I felt God saying, "Penny, do you trust me?" I knew God loved me and wanted the best for me. I knew His Word said, "Children are a gift from the Lord,"[139] though my experience growing up had proven otherwise. I even knew my desire for control in this area was in direct conflict to His command to multiply.[140] I knew He desired to give me good gifts,[141] but I was so scared. "Do you trust me?" It was a gentle question, a reminder of my place and His sovereignty and His love. After much prayer, I answered, "Yes, I trust you. I trust you with my body which will forever be changed; I trust you with my heart which could be desperately broken by a child, I trust you with my career, and I trust you know the best for me. I trust you even if I don't understand."

All of us must ask, "Do I trust God in EVERYTHING?"

Do I trust God to take care of my loved ones?

Do I trust God to provide for financial and physical needs?

Do I trust God to change the heart of my children, boss, or husband?

Do I trust God to give me the desires of your heart?

Do I trust God to elevate me to positions of influence in my work and community?

Do I trust God to heal me?

Do I trust God to love me and take care of me?

Do I trust God to_____?

Do you trust God in everything? Why not? Pray and ask God to help you trust Him in everything.

To truly embrace change is to trust God. As Jesus prayed, "not my will but your will be done."[142] To trust God, whatever happens, even if it is not what we want, is to know that He is sovereign, just, kind, loving, and patient. He is Our Creator, Our Healer, Provider, Our Master, Our Savior, and Redeemer.

---

[139] Psalm 127:3
[140] Genesis 9:7
[141] Luke 11:13
[142] Luke 22:42

If you have made past choices that were based on fear rather than faith, pray and ask God to forgive you and bless you with his best. He has already taken the punishment for your sins and has His amazing grace waiting for you. There is nothing that you have done that can separate you from the love of God. He knows our weakness and our sins. Yet, he has forgiven us and set us free from guilt and shame.

God has a fairy tale ending planned for each one of us. Our past choices do not limit God's grace. Even in the most impossible situations, God has a plan to bless us and give us hope and a future.

The end of Athaliah's story shows God's ultimate control and sovereignty. Imagine living in Jerusalem during Athaliah's rule, King Ahaziah had died, and the wicked Queen Athaliah was on the throne after massacring the rightful heirs to the throne. It seemed as if there was no hope. Yet God had a plan.

Please read all of 2 Kings 11 to learn the rest of the story and write down who was saved.

Athaliah thought she had destroyed anyone that could take her place on the throne. But God used Ahaziah's sister Jehosheba to preserve Joash, the future King of Judah. Jehosheba stood in the gap for the baby Joash. She and her husband knew that even during the terrible, wicked rule of Athaliah, God was still in control. His will is sovereign.

God's plan and purpose will not be thwarted; God will bring good out of a bad situation. I know people who feel like their mother, sister, or boss should be named Athaliah. Pray for God's justice to be done. Be patient. Do not lose hope. He is just, and he will prevail no matter how powerful any evil force appears. At times, it seems wickedness will win, but its reign of terror is just for a moment while the Lord reigns on high forever and ever. Just as God used Jehosheba and her husband, Jehoiada, God will use us to do great and mighty things for His Kingdom and His Glory. We just have to take courage[143] and say, "Yes, God, I trust you."

LEARNING TO EMBRACE CHANGE FROM ATHALIAH

Athaliah's resistance to change didn't alter God's plan or alter God's promise to King David that his ancestor would be on the throne. God is Sovereign; and even in the most hopeless circumstances, God will provide a way. Athaliah's resistance to change and need for control destroyed relationships with her husband, children, and grandchildren. She tried to control people and circumstances. Because she did

---

[143] 2 Chronicles 23:1

not trust God as her ruler, she used her influence on her husband to accomplish her will rather than God's will. She encouraged her son to trust her family connections and false gods rather than the True God. She did not want to give up her power and position and tried to kill everyone who could take it from her.

To embrace change starting with trusting God, no matter how hopeless or difficult the situation. When we trust God rather than ourselves, our money, our influence, and our resources, He will show His power in mighty and miraculous ways. The times that I have stepped out in faith and trusted God, He has directed me on a path that was so different than anything I would have chosen, yet it was better and more wonderful than anything I could have ever imagined.

HOW HAVE YOU LEARNED TO TRUST GOD THROUGH STUDYING ATHALIAH?

CHAPTER VII

ENCOURAGING FRIEND

HOLY AND UNASHAMED

Lived about 50 BC to AD

But you are a chosen people, a royal priesthood, a holy nation, God's special possession, that you may declare the praises of him who called you out of darkness into His wonderful light. 1 Peter 2:9

Week 1

Elizabeth

Let's pretend that we have stepped into a time machine and traveled over 800 years from the reign of Athaliah to just before Jesus was born. Over a millennium has passed from the reign of King David to the births of John the Baptist and Jesus. In the following three paragraphs, we'll cover the highlights of the millennia. After many warnings from various prophets for idolatry and unfaithfulness to the Lord and occasional times of repentance, Jerusalem fell to the kingdom of Babylon in 586 BC, during the reign of King Zedekiah, Athaliah's great, great, great, great, great, great, great, great, great, great-grandson.

However, the conquest of Jerusalem continued, and in 539 B.C., Jerusalem became a part of the Persian Empire when Babylon fell to Persia. After 70 years of Jewish exile, the Persians allowed the people of Judah to return to Jerusalem and rebuild their city and Temple. Priests once again offered sacrifices in the rebuilt Temple. The people of Judah were allowed to live in their homeland and worship God even though they were still officially under Persian rule. During this time, about 430 B.C, the final book of the Old Testament, Malachi, was written. It exhorts God's people to leave their complacency in worship and offerings. It prophesies that God would send a messenger "who will prepare the way before me. Then suddenly the Lord you are seeking will come to His Temple, the messenger of the covenant whom you desire will come."[144]

The Bible is silent during the next 400 years. From historical documents, we know that during this time, the land of Judah was ruled by Alexander the Great, the Ptolemies of Egypt, and the Seleucids of Syria. In 166 BC, the Jews led by Judas Maccabees revolted against the Seleucids because "Jewish sacrifice was forbidden, sabbaths and feasts were banned, and circumcision was outlawed. Altars to Greek gods were set up, and animals prohibited to Jews were sacrificed on them. The Olympian Zeus was placed on the altar of the Temple."[145] Within three years of this revolt (now celebrated in the feast of Hanukkah), the Maccabees gained control of Jerusalem and the Temple.

Descendants of Judas Maccabees' father Matthias led Judah until 63 B.C., when Pompey, a Roman general, captured Jerusalem and the provinces of Palestine. The Romans appointed Herod as

---

[144] Malachi 3:1
[145] http://en.wikipedia.org/wiki/Maccabees

king over Judea in 40 B.C. During this time of Roman rule, the Jews were required to pay taxes to Rome but could worship the Lord in the Temple. Herod renovated and expanded the Temple in 19 B.C. During Herod's reign, the role of the High Priest was a political appointment given by Herod to bolster his rule and authority. The duties of serving in the Temple fell to the priests, descendants of Miriam's brother, Aaron.

Elizabeth lived during the time of Roman rule. She was married to a priest. Elizabeth is "old" because, as the King James Version tactfully puts it, she is "well stricken in years."[146] Her husband even calls her "old," and as we will see, this is never a wise thing to say about one's wife.

During this chapter, I hope you will grow to love and appreciate Elizabeth's role as a friend and a mentor to Mary, the mother of Jesus. Elizabeth's dedication of her life to be holy and set apart for God gave her a unique ability to rejoice with and encourage Mary as she was coming to terms with God's call on her life as the mother of the long-awaited Savior.

Elizabeth's story begins in Luke 1:5-7. Please read the following verses and fill in the blanks of the questions.

"In the time of Herod king of Judea there was a priest named Zechariah, who belonged to the priestly division of Abijah; his wife Elizabeth was also a descendant of Aaron. Both of them were righteous in the sight of God, observing all the Lord's commands and decrees blamelessly. But they were childless because Elizabeth was not able to conceive, and they were both very old. Once when Zechariah's division was on duty and he was serving as priest before God, he was chosen by lot, according to the custom of the priesthood, to go into the Temple of the Lord and burn incense. And when the time for the burning of incense came, all the assembled worshipers were praying outside."

Who was Elizabeth's husband?

Who was Elizabeth a descendant of?

Elizabeth and her husband are described as "righteous," what do you think that means?

Did they have any children?

What was Zechariah chosen by lot to do?

---

[146] Luke 1:7 (KJV)

Elizabeth was married to a priest named Zechariah. He belonged to the priestly division of Abijah, who was a descendant of Aaron, Moses, and Miriam's brother. Elizabeth was also a descendant of Aaron. As the daughter and wife of a priest, she understood the privileges and responsibilities of being of the priestly tribe, the Kohanim.

> "The status of Kohen was conferred on Aaron, the brother of Moses, and his sons as an everlasting covenant. During the 40 years of wandering in the wilderness and until the Holy Temple was built in Jerusalem, Kohanim performed their priestly service in the portable Tabernacle. Their duties involved offering the daily and Jewish holiday sacrifices, collectively known as the Korbanot in Hebrew, and blessing the people in a ceremony known as Nesiat Kapayim ("Raising of the hands"), the ceremony of the Priestly Blessing.
>
> A Kohen may become disqualified from performing his service for a host of reasons, including -but not limited to Tumah, Marital defilements, and Physical blemishes… Torah verses and Rabbinical commentary to the Tanach imply that the Kohen has a unique leadership role amongst the nation of Israel -in addition to the common knowledge that the Kohen is to officiate the sacrificial activity in the Temple (the Korbanot), the Kohen is assumed responsibility of being knowledgeable in the laws and nuances of the Torah and accurately instructing those laws to the Jewish people."[147]

When King David was about to transfer the leadership of the nation of Israel to his son Solomon and the opportunity to build the Temple, he organized the priests into 24 Temple service rotations by family. Each family of priests was required to serve in the Temple for one week in the order that was determined by lots during King David's rule.

Zechariah was chosen by lot among all the priests serving that week to offer incense to the Lord in the Temple. This was a significant honor. Incense was the symbol of the prayers of the people. Revelation 5:8 describes heaven, "the twenty-four elders fell down before the Lamb. Each one had a harp and they were holding golden bowls full of incense, which are the prayers of God's people. Psalm 141:2 states, "May my prayer be set before you like incense; may the lifting up of my hands be like the evening sacrifice." Offering incense was a once-in-a-lifetime opportunity. It was as close to the presence of God that any priest, other than the High Priest, would ever go because the table of incense was just outside the door of the Most Holy Place in the Temple, the Holy of Holies.

For Elizabeth and Zechariah, righteousness meant following all of the laws and commands given to Moses for the people of Israel and the additional rules and regulations for priests.

---

[147] https://en.wikipedia.org/wiki/Kohen

When I read the word "righteousness," I think of the phrase "right relationship with God." Through Christ, we have righteousness, a right relationship with God. For Elizabeth and Zechariah, the only way they could have a right relationship with God was through the law. By following the law with all of their heart, they showed their desire to have a relationship with God.

Elizabeth and Zechariah lived a holy life. They were faithful in following all of the laws and commands that God had established for His people. And they also had to live to a higher standard because they were Kohanim. As descendants of Aaron, priests were given the privilege of offering sacrifices to the Lord on the altar. Just as Temple sacrifices had to be pure and without blemish, so the members of the Kohanim had to be pure and holy.

Through Christ we have righteousness- a right relationship with God through Christ.

Reading about the rules and regulations that Elizabeth and Zechariah lived with as Kohanim was a little hard for me to connect with until I read the following paragraph from Lauren Winner's memoir, *Girl Meets God*. I loved what she wrote about her crush on a boy named Aaron Farmer, who, like Elizabeth and Zechariah, was also a descendent of the high priest. It helped me understand the idea of being set apart and the unattainability of holiness.

"I was half-smitten with Aaron Farmer all through college. I have never known if he was half-smitten with me. If circumstances were different, we might have been married years ago with a baby already and living here in New York and visiting his parents all the time. It was never possible, though, because the Farmers are Cohanim. They are descended from the line of the high priests of Israel, those men who when the Temple still stood, performed all the most important sacrifices, and on the most holiest days soaked in a mikvah and removed their shoes, and entered the kadosh kadoshim, the Holy of Holies, what Latinist call the sanctum sanctorum. They entered into that spot, and the uttered God's ineffable name. There is no Temple anymore, but Jews know that one day there will be a Temple again, so the cohanim, the priestly class must be kept distinct, and pure, and separate. Priests must be found and called on when the time comes.

Cohanim are subject to all sorts of special rules that don't apply to other Jews, they cannot enter cemeteries, lest they become contaminated by the impurities of corpses, and they cannot marry converts. That I had grown up thinking I was Jewish did not matter; I was a convert, and Aaron Farmer was off-limits. We bantered and conversed endlessly but we rarely talked about what I took to be our kindredness. We never kissed. I never told him I sometimes looked at him across his mother's table and just wanted to touch his face. Joan and I discussed it once, discussed how it could not be and I wished— because I wanted to be her daughter as much as because I fancied being his wife—that it could be."

Lauren Winner knew her crush Aaron was set apart and different than other boys. He had a calling on his life and was lived by a higher standard of behavior.

Though we are not descendants of Miriam's brother Aaron like Aaron Farmer and Elizabeth's husband Zechariah, we are still called to be holy because we are members of a royal priesthood. Please look up 1 Peter 2:9. How does this verse apply to your life?

God has chosen us and made us a royal priesthood, a holy nation; we are God's special possession to declare His praises. We are made holy through Christ[148] because He fulfilled the law once and for all. Therefore, just as Elizabeth and Zechariah were set apart for God's service, you and I are also called to be holy and set apart.

The word "holy" means "set apart." It means that we need to separate ourselves from the patterns and evil desires of the past. It also means that we are to be used for God's purposes and plans, not our own. The priests were "holy" because they were set apart from the other Israelites; only priests could offer sacrifices to the Lord. Living a holy life meant that they had to give up certain things, such as going to a cemetery to visit their parent's graves, and it meant that they would receive unique tangible and spiritual blessings during the week of their service in the Temple.

Elizabeth and Zechariah obtained holiness by following the law; however, we are given holiness through Christ, which comes from a right relationship with him. Philippians 3:9 tells us that we do not have a righteousness that comes from the law, "but that which is through faith in Christ—the righteousness that comes from God on the basis of faith." Our right relationship (righteousness) with God is an unearned gift through Christ that should result in holiness in our lives.

Please look up 1 Peter 1:14-16 answer these questions. What does God call us to be?

What should we do with our desires?

*What do you think keeps people from being holy?

---

[148] Hebrews 10:10

We are called to be holy because God is holy. Living a holy life means that we no longer conform to the evil desires we had when we lived in ignorance. The Message paraphrase puts these verses this way, "Don't lazily slip back into those old grooves of evil, doing just what you feel like doing. You didn't know any better then; you do now." It is easy to slip into old comfortable patterns of living and make self-centered choices rather than God-centered choices. We lean on our own understanding rather than asking God what He wants us to do.

> **Satan uses fear to keep us from God's best. Without trust in who God is, His character and His love for us it is nearly impossible. .to obey him.**

Though I know God has called me to be holy, I am scared of such a life. I would love to be "good" or even "great," but "holy" is scary and alienating. I am afraid of being set apart and different from everyone else. I am worried that people will think I am weird if I live my life wholly for the Lord and if I am set apart from the culture or other people. I have realized that my fear of rejection and being judged by people is a form of idolatry because I am valuing other people's opinions above God. However, I still struggle to desire God's high opinion over people.

I am also terrified of the accountability of being "holy." If I am "set apart" and do unholy things, what will people say; will they see my hypocrisy and weakness and doubt God? I am also afraid of being set apart for God's purposes. Being holy means that God will use me for His purposes and plans, not my own. Just as the priests, bowls, and knives in the Temple were holy and only used for according to God's commands, so my life would be solely for God's purposes and plans. Zechariah gave up two weeks a year in service in the Temple and every day gave up rights to big and small things- what he ate, how he styled his hair, even who he could marry, to name a few. This challenges me to ask, "Am I willing to give up whatever God calls me to give up for His plans and purposes because He has called me to be holy?"

Like Elizabeth and Zechariah, are you willing to do whatever God calls you to do to be holy? If not, what are you afraid of? What is holding you back?

For me, this boils down to a question of trust. Do I trust that He has called me to be holy because He loves me and wants to bless me? An old hymn contains the line, "Trust and obey for there's no other way to be happy in Jesus but to trust and obey." Satan uses fear to keep us from God's best. Without trust in who He is, His character, and His love for us, it is nearly impossible to obey him.

We have to know that He is our Creator, He is our Lord, He is our Provider, and He is our Master in order to trust that He loves us. When He calls us to obey him, it is out of His desire for us to experience his magnificent plans, to prosper us, give us hope, and bless our future. The truth is that

God's desire for obedience is not to punish us and keep us from "fun, cool things" but instead to protect us and give us better things than we could ask or imagine. Obedience equals blessings.

Deuteronomy 28:1-14 contains a list of the blessings we will receive for obedience. Please write out these blessings in the space below.

The blessings that God has stored up for you are incredible. He wants to give you financial resources, bless your work, protect your resources and belongings, and secure victory over enemies. He will bless your children and your descendants and even bless the people who live around you in the city and the country. Wherever you go, you will be blessed. Verse 11 sums the blessings up "The Lord will grant you abundant prosperity—in the fruit of your womb, the young of your livestock and the crops of your ground—in the land he swore to your ancestors to give you." God's plan starts with abundantly blessing us, but experiencing His blessings requires our obedience. Our desire for Him must be greater than our desire for anything else.

God requires holiness because He wants to have a connection with us that is deep and intimate. Matthew 5:8 says, "Blessed are the pure in heart, for they will see God." The word "pure" relates in a Levitical sense to items that are "clean, the use of which is not forbidden, imparts no uncleanness."[149]

Our purity ensures that God can use us for His purposes and plans, just as the priest used only utensils in the Temple for God's purposes. Our purity and holiness will allow us to see and experience God in new and surprising ways. On the other hand, impurity keeps us from fully being used by God. Holiness is for our blessing so that we can know God more because He is holy and be used by God for even greater things.

Wrap up this week by praying and meditating on God's call for you to be holy. Then, ask God to show you the blessings He has for you and the places of unholiness keeping you from those blessings.

---

[149] http://www.blueletterbible.org/lang/lexicon/lexicon.cfm?Strongs=G2513&t=KJV katharos

Week 2

SHAME ON ME

A friend recommended watching Brene' Brown's TED Talks on shame and vulnerability. TED talks are brief lectures from innovative thinkers. I must admit I didn't think I would get much out of her speech until she described "the warm wash of shame."[150] In an instant, I remembered the feeling of shame washing over me. As a kid, I felt it when I was called "Skinny Pinny" on the playground and when I realized that I wasn't asked to a birthday party my classmates had attended. As an adult, I felt it after realizing that I had just met 25 new people with spinach stuck on my teeth. It stalks me when I can't remember someone's name who obviously remembers me. I still cringe remembering how I went to a friend's house for Bible Study two *days* late! As a mom, I felt it when I realized at lunchtime that it was St. Patrick's Day, and my kids weren't wearing anything green. Recently, I was embarrassed to tell my son's soccer coach that we would be 40 minutes late for a match because I put North Albemarle Middle School in the GPS instead of North Asheboro Middle School. Ugh! These are the times I can share; other times of embarrassment I can't even bring myself to put on paper.

I realize I am not alone in feeling this way. Over six million people have watched Dr. Brown's 20-minute TED talk on Listening to Shame, and 24 million have listened to her talk on vulnerability. Before her talk, I didn't understand the differences between shame and guilt and the impact shame can have on our lives. Shame is a feeling that tells us, "Something is intrinsically wrong with me either because of who I am, choices I have made, or because of things that have been done to me." My mother-in-law, a wise older woman, simply defines shame as "some people don't think they are worthy."

As I did more research, I found an article in *Psychology Today* that pointed out that shame can take many forms. It can be shyness, discouragement, embarrassment, self-consciousness, or inferiority.[151] A common trigger for shame is comparison. As we will soon read, shame is an underlying theme in Elizabeth and Zachariah's story. Though they both lived holy and righteous lives, they were not blessed with children. Even in modern times, couples who struggle with infertility ask, "What is wrong with me that I can't have kids." Testing hormone levels, sperm counts, and ovulation cycles helps answer this question from a physiological perspective but doesn't get to the heart of shame surrounding infertility.

---

[150] https://www.ted.com/talks/brene_brown_listening_to_shame?language=en
[151] https://www.psychologytoday.com/blog/your-zesty-self/200905/what-we-get-wrong-about-shame

Zachariah's and Elizabeth's public shame of infertility was amplified by God's call to be holy. A holy life was supposed to result in God's blessings like fruitfulness and many children, but Elizabeth and Zachariah had no children. In his priestly work, Zachariah also had the shame of being an older man who hadn't been chosen to offer incense in the Temple. Since his early 20s, he served in the Temple twice a year and two times a day during his week of service, lots were drawn to see who would offer the incense. It was a once-in-a-lifetime opportunity.[152] Over 700 times, he faced disappointment and questions about his worthiness as he saw younger and younger men get chosen to offer incense. The clock was ticking; at age 50, he would no longer be able to serve in the Temple.[153] Time was running out.

The amazing thing to me is that Zachariah didn't lose heart, and he continued to hope that this time he would be chosen. Just like a single woman who risks heartbreak and shame as she continues to try to catch a bride's bouquet long after her friends have gotten married, Zechariah kept himself holy and ready to serve in case his lot was drawn. The book of Leviticus outlines all the rules and requirements for a priest to serve; if he had "forgotten" to do even one thing, he could have avoided the potential disappointment of not being chosen. Yet, he didn't lose hope and continued to seek after God.

How do you handle being ashamed, discouraged, or disappointed? Do you withdraw, escape, get angry, or put-up walls?

My natural response to disappointment and shame starts with pulling away but goes through all these stages. When I have done something embarrassing, I want to avoid the people who saw me in an awkward moment. When people have disappointed me and let me down, I withdraw; I don't want to ask them for help or depend on them. My walls come up, and I decide I am better off without them. I feel vulnerable and hurt when God doesn't answer my prayers, and He seems to let tragedies occur. It hurts to think about when He didn't heal a friend's daughter, and when growing up, we struggled financially though my parents did all they could. So, I create my version of the Job and friends pity party. I ask, "If God is all-knowing, all-powerful, and has unlimited resources, why hasn't he answered my prayers?" Then I start to blame. I wonder if it is something that I did, or a family member failed to do. Once I rule out those possibilities, I get mad because life is not fair.

Elizabeth and Zachariah may have wondered if some sin in their spouse's life kept them from God's blessing. I am sure they examined their own hearts to see if there was any impurity in them. At times, they must have gotten mad at God, angry when they saw irresponsible people become parents, when fools were blessed in their careers, and when others who had no desire for righteousness seemed

---

[152] ttp://www.sefaria.org/Mishnah_Tamid.5.1
[153] Numbers 8:24-26

to have the life they wanted. It is hard to keep going, keep putting yourself out there, and keep trusting God after 25 years of disappointment. But they did, and God was faithful, answered their prayer, though not in their timing or even the way they expected. His plan for their blessing was more remarkable than they could have imagined.

Zachariah didn't allow his shame, disappointment, and discouragement to harden his heart. He didn't give up hope that God could use him and answer his prayers. As a result, he was ready and able to serve in the Temple when "he was chosen by lot, according to the custom of the priesthood, to go into the temple of the Lord and burn incense."[154]

His willingness to be vulnerable and put himself out there instead of checking out or calling in sick enabled him to experience God's presence in a way that few people in the nation of Israel could comprehend. Elizabeth and Zachariah were able to expand their view of God and His involvement in their lives in a miraculous way just because he was willing to be disappointed, willing to keep trying, and willing to follow what God had called him to do. Even after 25 years of waiting, he made himself vulnerable and didn't lose hope that God could use him.

Romans 5:3-5 shows the importance of hope. You may have read this passage before; this time underline how these two different translations use "shame" and "disappointment."

"Not only so, but we also glory in our sufferings, because we know that suffering produces perseverance; perseverance, character; and character, hope. And hope does not put us to shame, because God's love has been poured out into our hearts through the Holy Spirit, who has been given to us." (NIV)

"We can rejoice, too, when we run into problems and trials, for we know that they help us develop endurance. And endurance develops strength of character, and character strengthens our confident hope of salvation. And this hope will not lead to disappointment. For we know how dearly God loves us, because he has given us the Holy Spirit to fill our hearts with his love." (NLT)

Our hope has to be built on God's love for us even during great suffering, after deep disappointment, when promises were not fulfilled, children aren't healed, and dreams don't come true. This is hard. It means we have to be vulnerable, get ready and keep going even if it means disappointment and embarrassment.

Brene` Brown points out that the antidote to shame and disappointment is vulnerability. Rather than pulling away from God, we must draw closer. We need to depend on Him more; we need to trust

---

[154] Luke 1:8-9

him more, and we need to love him more. Only if we draw closer to God will we experience the promise found at the end of Roman's 5, that "we know how dearly God loves us." When we place our hope on God's love, sovereignty, and perfect understanding, we will have abundant life regardless of our circumstances.

Is there a place where you have been disappointed, ashamed, or discouraged, so you have pulled back and stopped trying, stopped hoping and stopped believing? Don't lose heart. Be brave and vulnerable. Put your hope in God – this hope does not disappoint or put us to shame.

Zachariah was ready to be used by God when the time came. He was about to have an experience with God that would leave him speechless. Please read Luke 1:9-22 and answer the following questions.
What was Zechariah doing when the angel appeared to him?

What did the angel say to Zechariah about his prayer?

What was Zechariah's response?

What happened to Zechariah?

Why do you think this happened to Zechariah?

*If you were Elizabeth, what would you think?

Zechariah was offering incense and prayers to the Lord. The angel said God had heard his prayer and that his wife Elizabeth would have a child. As I thought about this passage, I wondered if Zechariah's prayer was for his wife even more than for a child. Zechariah had finally been given this once-in-a-lifetime opportunity. He used it to pray for his wife, who may have given up hope over the years of shame and disappointment. She may have questioned why God had not blessed them with a child—asked why God had not allowed Zachariah to offer incense and wondered if something was wrong with them.

Even though Zechariah was a priest who had just experienced a face-to-face conversation with an angel, he still had some doubt that God would answer his prayer, which is why his voice was taken from him, but God still answered his prayer. Prayer opens our eyes to see God's hand at work. Zechariah's prayer opened his eyes to see two seemingly unrelated events, losing his voice and Elizabeth's pregnancy, were God's work.

Zechariah's doubt didn't change the fact that all things are possible with God. Doubt doesn't stop God from working. There isn't one right way to pray. One of my favorite prayers is, "I believe. Help my unbelief."[155] Your husband may not pray exactly the way you want, but when you ask him to pray for you and the things that are important to you, you are being vulnerable and humbling yourself to his leadership in this area and trusting God to work in and through your husband's life. God has given our husbands a special honor and responsibility of interceding for their wives and children. When our husbands pray for us, they are acknowledging God's lordship over their lives. God is the ultimate authority and is in control. Don't let your standards of how someone should pray, keep you from reaping the blessings of having your husband pray for you. Even if it is not always comfortable, ask your husband to pray for you for both big things and little things. Just as God did amazing things in Zechariah's and Elizabeth's lives, He will do amazing things in you and your husband's life.

ELIZABETH'S VIEW OF THE LORD

Let's read what happened next in Luke 1:23-25. "When his time of service was completed, he returned home. After this his wife Elizabeth became pregnant and for five months remained in seclusion. "The Lord has done this for me," she said. "In these days he has shown his favor and taken away my disgrace among the people."

Elizabeth uses the word "Lord" to acknowledge her disgrace being taken away Elizabeth uses the word "Lord" to acknowledge her disgrace being taken away. "Lord" in Greek is *kyrios* which is the equivalent of Jehovah – κύριος. [156] This means having power or authority. The one to whom a person or thing belongs, about which he has power of deciding; master, lord

    a) the possessor and disposer of a thing

    1) the owner; one who has control of the person, the master

    2) in the state: the sovereign, prince, chief, the Roman emperor

    b) is a title of honor expressive of respect and reverence, with which servants greet their master

    c) this title is given to: God, the Messiah

---

[155] Mark 9:24
[156] http://www.blueletterbible.org/lang/lexicon/lexicon.cfm?Strongs=G2962&t=KJV

Elizabeth's understanding of the Lord went beyond Master and Sovereign to become personal. Foundational in understanding the word "Lord" is the idea of a relationship. Just as a servant had a relationship with their master or an employee had a relationship with their boss, Elizabeth knew that the Lord had miraculously intervened in her life. The Lord had power and control over every part of her life.

Her miracle pregnancy was more than an unexpected blessing. It redefined her life and changed her identity. When Elizabeth exclaimed, "He has taken away my disgrace," she was referring not just to her situation but who she was. The idea behind "*Oneidos*" which means shame or disgrace includes both the disgraceful thing/action and one's identity, status, and reputation. Disgrace was a horrible thing. This is an incredibly painful experience that goes beyond just feeling bad about a situation and is comparable to the mourning and devastation caused by rape.

Please read the following verses to gain some additional understanding of Elizabeth's pain. Write out what disgrace meant in each of these passages.
Genesis 30:22-23

Isaiah 54:1,4

The two previous verses give insight into the concept of disgrace, but Tamar's heartbreaking betrayal by her brother in 2 Samuel 13:10-14 expanded my view of disgrace. Read this passage, and then write out your thoughts on the impact of disgrace on a woman's heart.

The disgrace of infertility was compared to the disgrace and shame of rape. It was humiliating and incredibly painful. Just as Tamar's innocence and identity was changed through her brother's violent act, Elizabeth's life was clothed in pain and shame. Elizabeth and Tamar's situations were not their fault, but they bore the stigma and shame of disgrace.

Just as the Lord took away Elizabeth's disgrace and shame, Jesus died on the cross to take away our disgrace and shame. Psalm 69:9 is quoted in Romans 15:3, "For even Christ did not please himself but, as it is written: 'The insults of those who insult you have fallen on me.'" This means the insults, abuse, shame, and disgrace from those who hurt you were carried by Christ to the cross. Jesus is our hope and identity even in the most painful situations.

There is no shame or disgrace that Christ did not remove when he died on the cross for our sins. The verbal and physical abuse Christ endured during and before his crucifixion means that he has taken the pain and suffering on himself. His crucifixion and resurrection fulfilled the prophecy in Isaiah 25:8, "He will swallow up death forever. The Sovereign LORD will wipe away the tears from all faces; he will remove His people's disgrace from all the earth. The LORD has spoken."

If you struggle with disgrace and shame, please memorize these verses to refute Satan's attacks that say, "Who do you think you are?" or "You are unworthy" with the sword of God's Word. Jesus has removed His people's disgrace – just as Zachariah's and Elizabeth's disgrace was taken away—so your disgrace, shame, and pain from abuse have been removed by Christ's death and resurrection. You are holy. In Christ, you have a new identity.

The insults, abuse, shame, and disgrace **from those who hurt you were carried by Christ to the cross. There is no shame or disgrace that Christ did not remove when he died on the cross for our sins.**

Please write out 2 Corinthians 5:17.

In Christ, you are a new creation. The old you is gone. Your holiness and righteousness are based on what Christ has done for you, not because of anything you have or haven't done. Just as Elizabeth did not do anything to have her disgrace miraculously removed from her life, you don't have to do anything either. He has done it all.

Pause for a moment to think of the most disgraceful or shameful thing you have done or that has been done to you. You are forgiven, made clean, and without shame. Jesus died on the cross to take away your shame and disgrace. Completely. All of it. Through His sacrifice, you are holy, clean, and forgiven. Please take a minute to read Psalm 69 and write out a prayer of thankfulness to God for setting you free from shame and disgrace, healing you, redeeming you, and giving you His name and blessing.

Week 3

NOTHING IS IMPOSSIBLE WITH GOD

Some of my greatest joys have come from seeing my friends being blessed. I was filled with joy as I watched my friend Chris fulfill her dream of being a bride in a beautiful wedding ceremony under a live oak tree on her 40th birthday. I was amazed at God's provision when we realized that my friend's adoptive son was conceived the exact month her husband and she signed up with an adoption agency. After years of hard work, I was excited for my friend Dawn to get a fantastic promotion. I celebrated my oldest son making the 8th-grade soccer team after getting cut in 7th grade.

Just thinking about the times that God miraculously provided for my friends' finances, how He has healed them, and the small miracles they share every day fills me with joy. This week's Bible Study will show us the amazing grace of God and the joy that we receive when we reach out to encourage others, just as Elizabeth reached out to Mary, the mother of Jesus.

Let's read Luke 1:26-40 to find out what happens next.
When the angel appeared to Mary, how far along in her pregnancy was Elizabeth?

How did Mary respond to the news that she was to be pregnant?

Elizabeth's pregnancy was a touchstone in Mary's life. When Mary found out she was chosen to be pregnant with Jesus, she asked, "How is this to be?" The angel told her two things would prove that the baby was the Son of the Most High. First, the Holy Spirit would come on her, and the power of the Most High would overshadow her. Second, her relative Elizabeth would have a child in her old age. Elizabeth had spent the first five months of her pregnancy in isolation, and in her sixth month, Mary hurried to see her. Elizabeth's pregnancy confirmed the word of the Angel Gabriel to Mary. It also confirmed that God could do anything- including a virgin becoming pregnant.

Luke 1:37 contains a remarkable promise. Please write out Luke 1:37 in the margin.

This is an amazing verse. Here's what it says in multiple translations of the Bible.

For nothing is impossible with God.(NIV)

For with God nothing will be impossible.(NKJ)

For no word from God shall be void of power.(ASV)

For everything spoken by God is possible. (HNV)

For no word from God will ever fail.(NIV 2011)

For with God nothing is ever impossible and no word from God shall be without power or impossible of fulfillment.(AMP)

Elizabeth's pregnancy was proof that nothing was impossible with God and that no word from God shall be without power. Elizabeth's pregnancy confirmed that the angel was not a figment of Mary's imagination; it confirmed that the angel was telling the truth and that the baby she was carrying was the Son of the Most High God. Elizabeth's pregnancy was a miracle that blessed and took away her disgrace, but God intended it for the more significant benefit of encouraging Mary so that she would believe and would be able to face the hardships and struggles to come.

God works in multiple **places, people, and times to empower multiple blessings according to His will.**

Six months before the angel appeared to Mary to tell her that she would have a son named Jesus, God sent the angel to Zechariah so that Mary would have the proof she needed. This reminded me of a principle that I learned about how God works: God works in multiple places, people, and times to empower multiple blessings according to His will.

MIRACLE BIRTHS

Here's a story from my life that reminds me of this principle. Every year 8-10 of my friends from college have our annual "Girls' Weekend." It is 24 hours of food, fun, and encouragement in life and the Lord. We laugh and talk about the stuff of motherhood and marriage; but there is always an undercurrent of Christ throughout our discussions.

Several years ago, we were together for a time of great joy. My friend Laura brought her tiny two-month-old son, David, to our get-together, and two other friends were pregnant. The rest of us were glad to be done with our child-bearing years, except for our friend Karena.

Karena had struggled with infertility for several long and heartbreaking years. Long before she ever married, she dreamed of being a mom. She held baby David on her chest throughout the weekend, dreaming of holding her own baby boy one day. As I went to sleep Saturday night, I couldn't get the picture of Karena holding this tiny baby on her chest out of my mind. I cried out to the Lord, "Lord, why isn't she a mom? She desperately wants a baby; please help her." Gently, I heard the Lord answer,

"It is her time." I went to sleep wondering what that meant; was it her time to have a baby, or was it time to let it go? I didn't know.

On Sunday morning, as our weekend was wrapping up, all the girls except Amee laid hands on and prayed for Karena. Amee stood on the side of the room and just observed us. It was Amee's first visit to Girl's Weekend. Amee had joined us that year because as I was planning our get-together I felt like we should open our group to guests, so I sent an e-mail to the regulars and asked them to pray about inviting a friend to our group. Loren felt called to invite her neighbor Amee who had lived on the hall with us our freshman year. While many of us grew closer to Christ during college, Amee chose a more typical college path that didn't involve God. So, this praying and laying on of hands was completely outside of her comfort zone.

The rest of us circled Karena and prayed for her. We prayed for God's will, whether it meant pregnancy or not, and we prayed that God would take away this desire if it were not God's will for her to have a baby. We prayed for God's blessing and encouragement and rejoiced in God's love for our friend. Soon after the prayer was over, everyone headed home.

A little more than a month later, Karena sent an e-mail to the group, "Hello everyone. I want to start by saying how encouraged I was after the last girl's weekend. Thank you all for praying for me. I left feeling such peace! I did not think I would be writing this e-mail so soon...but...I am pregnant! The doctors are doing the standard hormone test thing every 3rd day because of my early miscarriages, but everything looks really good so far. I am 5 weeks so I would be due the first week of February. ...Anyway, I do not have a lot of time, but I wanted to give everyone an update and say THANK YOU and please keep praying for me. I am really nervous but at peace at the same time...it is weird. Love, Karena

Six months passed. Karena kept us updated with prayer requests, ultrasounds, and the joyful news that she was expecting a boy. Just before Christmas, we received an e-mail from Amee with the news that she had lost her job, and she was writing to ask us to pray for her and her family. She wrote, "I'm not sure how we are going to get by. That's why I am turning to you. I have seen firsthand how your power as women of faith has helped each other through tough times. So, I am asking for you to pray for us. That we may find a solution for all of the problems are facing." Karena's healthy baby boy was born in January, and Amee's tentative request for prayer led to her discovering Jesus. At our most recent Girls' Weekend, she joined us in the middle of the circle as we prayed, rather than on the outside looking in.

I shared this story with you to talk about the two miracles that began that spring morning. The first miracle was the miraculous birth of Karena's baby boy, but the bigger miracle was the new birth of our friend Amee. Karena could have become pregnant at any time without us ever praying for her because nothing is impossible with God. But instead, He waited so that we would all experience the miracle of two births. He knew that when hard times come and doubts rise, Amee and the rest of us would need a touchstone; a time that we can look back on that helps us to trust and to believe that everything God says is true, that God is real and not a figment of our imagination, a time we are certain that God answered prayers and performed a miracle, and that nothing is impossible for our Lord.

CONFIRMATION AND ENCOURAGEMENT

God used Elizabeth's pregnancy to encourage and confirm God's Word to Mary. When we have asked others to pray with us and to pray for us, and then share what God is doing in our lives, the miracle of God's blessings are multiplied, our faith is strengthened, and our ability to trust God grows.

Please read Luke 1:41-45 and answer the following questions.
What happened to Elizabeth when she heard Mary's greeting?

What did she say to Mary to encourage her?

Elizabeth felt her baby leap in her womb when Mary called out her greeting, and Elizabeth was filled with the Holy Spirit. God then gave her unique insight into Mary's situation. She realized that Mary was pregnant and the mother of her Lord. She commended Mary because she believed that the Lord would fulfill His promises to her. In contrast, the angel prophesized that Zechariah would lose his ability to speak because He did not believe what the Lord told him.[157]

What was Mary's response in verses 46-55?

Mary responded to Elizabeth with praise to God. She glorified God and praised him for all that He was doing for her and His people. Finally, she had someone to rejoice with to celebrate the marvelous thing that God was doing in her life. Elizabeth provided a haven and a place of encouragement that allowed Mary the freedom to rejoice in the miracle inside her.

Can you think of times when God has brought a woman into your life with whom you could share good news, who rejoiced with you, and encouraged your faith in God? Take a minute to let her know how she blessed you. If you can't contact her, say a quick prayer of thanks for her.

---

[157] Luke 1:20

Please write out Romans 12:15

As we encourage each other in our faith, we need to rejoice in the goodness of the Lord in our friends' lives. Sharing our joy with others is so important that the word "Rejoice" appears over 100 times in both the NIV and King James Versions of the Bible. It is a command and a response. When we share what God has done for us with others, we can encourage them to trust that God can do exceedingly and abundantly even greater things for them.

Elizabeth's joy-filled response helped Mary trust God. When we share the good things that God has done for us with other people, we can "re-enjoy" the blessing and the people we share our joy with are blessed to learn more about God's goodness. For example, Jesus told the parable of a woman who loses a very valuable coin; he ended the story with the woman calling her friends and neighbors together to say, "Rejoice with me; I have found my lost coin."[158] The idea behind the prefix "re" is to do something again- i.e., redo, return. So, "to rejoice" means to feel the joy again. The woman had the initial joy of finding the coin; then, her happiness was multiplied because she could rejoice with her friends.

> *When we are authentic* with others, they will be able to mourn with us in the hard times and rejoice with us in the times of blessing.

I am hesitant to share my blessings at times because I don't want people to think I am bragging. The proper heart in sharing blessings requires us to not seek glory for ourselves but instead to give glory for what God has done. God calls us to rejoice with those who rejoice and mourn with those who mourn.[159] It is much easier to rejoice with someone who has shared her hard times and good times. When we are authentic with others, they will be able to mourn with us in the hard times and rejoice with us in the times of blessing. By remembering past struggles, we are better able to appreciate the current blessings in our friends' lives and our own life.

"Rejoice with those who are rejoicing" is a command because our natural self is more likely to be envious or jealous of someone else's blessings than to celebrate them. Our natural selves are not the best guides; my boys don't naturally want to do laundry and I want to eat dessert every meal. Though it may go against our natural inclination to rejoice with certain people, the Holy Spirit can empower us with joy (a fruit of the Spirit) to be obedient and rejoice with those who are rejoicing.

The antidote to envy is giving glory to God. His resources aren't limited. Celebrating that God has blessed someone else, should remind us of how He has blessed us and will continue to bless us in the future. We have much to thank God and praise him God for. We can rejoice because of the great things God has done. Rejoice for the wondrous things he has made. Rejoice because of His love.

---

[158] Luke 15:9
[159] Romans 12:15

Rejoice because of His provision and protection. God calls us to rejoice with others because when we rejoice with our friends, we get to enjoy and celebrate the blessing again and again.

This week look for opportunities to rejoice with the people God has put in your life. Share a blessing you have received and ask them to tell you about a blessing they have recently experienced. Your request will allow them to re-joice and will allow you to join in their joy! Write down a summary of a blessing you or a friend experienced so you can read it and rejoice again.

Week 4

Is there a story behind your name? When I was pregnant with my youngest son, my husband and I looked through our family records for names that had a historical connection and weren't too off the wall like Washburn or Holloway. I also looked up the meaning of each name because I hoped it would communicate our heart for our baby's character.

We settled on John William because both names had historical significance in our families and honored our fathers and grandfathers. Plus, both had great meanings. John means the "LORD is gracious," and William means "Determined Protector." Because his Grandpa was also named John, we planned to call our new baby, "Jack." This plan worked for five years, but the day before kindergarten started, Jack decided he wanted to be called by his real name. So, from that point on, "Jack, Jack" as his older brother called him, became John.

Finding the perfect name consumes the attention of expectant parents everywhere. I am sure that Mary and Elizabeth talked about family names and the meaning of the names for the babies in their wombs. These moms were in an unusual situation because an angel had told them what to name their boys. I am sure they wondered how Elizabeth's baby John would live up to his name "Yaweh is gracious," and Jesus would fulfill the meaning of his name "Yaweh saves."

Luke sums up Mary's encouraging visit to Elizabeth with this simple sentence, "Mary stayed with Elizabeth for about three months and then returned home."[160] However, when Mary left Elizabeth's home, she went back to a very different environment.

Please read Matthew 1:18-19. What was waiting for Mary when she returned home?

If this was Joseph's initial response to her pregnancy, how do you think the rest of the town treated her?

Mary's time with Elizabeth provided a blessed respite from the shame of divorce and the stigma of an illegitimate child. People would question Mary and Joseph's purity and faithfulness to God. Rather than shaming and disgracing Mary, Elizabeth rejoiced in the Lord's goodness and celebrated the blessing of the coming Messiah.

Share your thoughts on Elizabeth's role in providing a place without shame and encouraging Mary.

One of the greatest gifts we can give the people in our lives is to love them as Christ loves them. Elizabeth was able to see and celebrate the work of God in Mary's life, and she was able to confirm God's Word to Mary. She encouraged Mary and rejoiced with her. As an older woman, she had lived years in shame and disgrace because of her infertility. Her painful past allowed her to provide a safe, grace-filled place for Mary, unlike society that would hide her pregnancy or stone her for assumed infidelity. As we learn to embrace change, we need to remember Elizabeth's example of love for Mary.

> **One of the greatest gifts we can give the people in our lives is to love them as Christ loves them.**

One of the ways that God will redeem our lives is to use our healed places of shame and disgrace to bless and encourage others. After the Lord gave Elizabeth a new identity without shame, she could minister to Mary in her place of need. Both Mary and Elizabeth's lives illustrate how God can take our shame-filled identities and past and transform them into a place of blessing for us, our families, our friends, and the world. If you ask God to be glorified in places of shame and disgrace in your past, He will use them to bless and lead others to a new identity in Christ.

---

[160] Luke 1:56

THE MIRACLE BABY IS BORN

Elizabeth's story continues with the birth of her son John. Please read Luke 1:57-66 and summarize what happened.

What did everyone assume the baby's name would be?

What did Elizabeth say the baby's name was?

What happened after Zechariah wrote out the baby's name?

Everyone assumed this miracle baby would be named after his father, Zechariah, but Elizabeth told everyone the baby's name would be John. Though Zechariah could not talk, he could write, so he wrote out the baby's name, John. Immediately, his mouth was opened, and he began praising God.

Elizabeth and Zechariah's neighbors and all the people who lived in the surrounding area were amazed and filled with awe regarding the birth of the baby John. Everyone wondered about John's destiny because they knew that the "Lord's hand was with him." The idea of the Lord's hand being on John is an interesting concept. The Greek word for hand in this passage is *cheir*. This word literally means "hand as the part of the body; it also contains the idea of the Lord's involvement in our lives and His power." In the Bible, *cheir* is used to connote several things-

    1) by the help or agency of any one, by means of any one

    2) fig. applied to God symbolizing His might, activity, power

    a) in creating the universe

    b) in upholding and preserving (God is present protecting and aiding one)

    c) in punishing

    d) in determining and controlling the destinies of men[161]

The people in the community realized that God was actively involved in John's life. God, the Creator, had miraculously created this baby; God, in His might and power, would protect and help this child; and God had a special plan and destiny for him.

Just as the Lord's hand was on John, filling him with power, protecting him, guiding, and directing him, in the same way, God's hand is on your life. A song I learned as a child proclaims, "He's got the whole world in His hands." This simple lyric contains an important truth. God has got it all

---

[161] http://www.blueletterbible.org/lang/lexicon/lexicon.cfm?Strongs=G5495&t=KJV

under control; He doesn't grow tired; His arm is not too short; He can do anything; and He is all-powerful. When life is difficult and hard, when you feel weak and out of control, remember; "He's got you and me sister in His hands, He's got the little, bitty baby in His hands, He's got the whole world in His hands."[162]

After nearly 300 days of silence, Zechariah regained the ability to speak. Luke 1:67-69 contains a beautiful passage of praise to our Lord. Everyone who has been redeemed from shame and made holy by the blood of Jesus has much to praise God about. Please read what he said, and then take a minute to personalize this passage by filling the blanks with your name.

68Blessed (praised and extolled and thanked) be the Lord, the God of Israel, because He has come and brought deliverance and redemption to _____!

69And He has raised up a Horn of salvation [a mighty and valiant Helper, the Author of salvation] for _____in the house of David His servant--

70This is as He promised by the mouth of His holy prophets from the most ancient times [in the memory of man]--

71That _____ should have deliverance and be saved from our enemies and from the hand of all who detest and pursue us with hatred;

72To make true and show the mercy and compassion and kindness [promised] to our forefathers and to remember and carry out His holy covenant [to bless, which is [ad]all the more sacred because it is made by God Himself],

73That covenant He sealed by oath to our forefather Abraham:

74To grant us that _____, being delivered from the hand of our foes, might serve Him fearlessly

75In holiness (divine consecration) and righteousness [in accordance with the everlasting principles of right] within His presence all the days of our lives.

76And you, _____ little one, shall be called a prophet of the Most High; for you shall go on before the face of the Lord to make ready His ways,

77To bring and give the knowledge of salvation to His people in the forgiveness and remission of their sins.

78Because of and through the heart of tender mercy and loving-kindness of our God, a Light from on high will dawn upon us and visit

79To shine upon and give light to those who sit in darkness and in the shadow of death, to direct and guide our feet in a straight line into the way of peace. (AMP)

---

[162] Boatner, Edward "He's Got The Whole World in His Hands*" Spirituals Triumphant Old and New* Sunday School Publishing Board. 1927

Here's what this passage says to me: The Lord has delivered you, redeemed you, saved you, rescued you from the hand of your enemies, shown you mercy, compassion, and kindness so that you can serve him fearlessly, in holiness, righteousness all the days of your life by sharing the knowledge of salvation through the forgiveness and remission of sins so that those who sit in darkness and the shadow of death will instead find peace! Praise the Lord!

As we read in the introduction to this chapter, 400 years before John was born, Malachi prophesied that a messenger would come to prepare the way for the Savior. Just as God had a plan and a purpose for the baby John long before he was in Elizabeth's womb, God has a plan for your life. Elizabeth's story is a reminder that following God's plan may not always be easy, but it is always the best. Elizabeth and Zechariah lived with the disgrace of infertility for decades. The Bible says John the Baptist grew up in the wilderness until he appeared publicly in Israel.[163] Some Bible scholars believe that Elizabeth's husband, Zechariah, was killed by Herod. Elizabeth raised John in the wilderness to avoid the infanticide ordered by King Herod after the visit by the wise men who told of the birth of the Messiah.[164]

> *God has a plan* for your life. Elizabeth's story is a reminder that following God's plan may not always be easy, but it is always the best.

God gave this family a significant role in the story of Christ's birth. Elizabeth, Zechariah, and John all suffered greatly. Still, the years of discomfort and pain were insignificant to the eternal blessing that God poured out on all humanity because of their faithfulness. Elizabeth was blessed to provide a place of encouragement for Mary and know that the arrival of the Messiah was imminent.

John the Baptist had the unique privilege of baptizing the Son of God, seeing the Holy Spirit descend on him, and hearing God's voice audibly proclaim, "This is my son, whom I love, with him I am well pleased."[165] Though John the Baptist was martyred for speaking the truth, he was privileged to proclaim the life–changing message, "Behold the Lamb of God who takes away the sins of the world."[166]

God has set each of us apart for specific blessings and a mission. Our age or life expectancy does not limit the impact we can have on the Kingdom of God. Whether we are old like Elizabeth or young like Mary, every minute of our lives can be lived for His glory and bless others. Each of us has a particular purpose – God will use your places of disgrace and deformity to point others to Christ, just as the Lord used Zechariah's loss of a voice to highlight the Lord's message and allowed Elizabeth to encourage Mary.

---

[163] Luke 1:80
[164] Matthew 2:16-18
[165] Matthew 3:16-17
[166] John 1:29

We are called to be holy because God is holy. He has called you to holiness so that you can be used to bless other just as God used Elizabeth to carry baby John and to rejoice with Mary.

You are a member of a royal priesthood like Zechariah, and your offering of praise and prayer is like incense to our Lord. Wherever you live and whatever you do, God can use you to bless others if you are willing to be used by Him for the purpose that He has planned for you. you.

HOW HAVE YOU LEARNED TO TRUST GOD THROUGH STUDYING ELIZABETH?

CHAPTER VIII

PRAYER WARRIOR

PROPHETESS OF HOPE

Born about 100 BC

Do not conform any longer to the pattern of this world, but be transformed by the renewing of your mind. Then you will be able to test and approve what God's will is—his good, pleasing and perfect will.
Romans 12:2

Week 1

Anna

Churches in our area host Salvation Army overflow shelters for homeless women during the winter. For a week, nine women spend the night in our church. Teams of volunteers prepare dinners, stay at the church with the women, and drive them to and from our building to the Salvation Army Center every morning and evening.

For a couple of years, I was one of the drivers; I enjoyed getting to know the ladies during the 20-minute trip to our church. One week, all the official volunteer spots were filled up, so I just went to the church to hang out with the ladies. The nine ladies were a mix of ages and races. I didn't ask the ladies why they were homeless or how they ended up in a shelter; I figured that was none of my business.

But several women shared how they had grown up in Charlotte, and we talked about high schools and popular radio stations. A mother and her 18-year-old daughter explained that they had moved to North Carolina from Detroit with the hope that the 18-year-old would be able to attend college here. One of the ladies talked about moving between Belgium, South Carolina, and Tennessee during her high school years because her Dad was a mechanical engineer who worked in tire manufacturing. Another woman talked about how she had owned a house in Columbia, SC for 13 years but "things happen," so now much of her stuff was in storage and with friends.

I particularly enjoyed getting to know an older woman named Annie. She had lived for a while in Brooklyn, New York. However, she had grown up in Charlotte and attended Second Ward high school. I thought I knew all the Charlotte-area high schools, but I had never heard of her school. So that night, I went online to read about her school, which was established in 1923 as a high school for black children in Charlotte. It was closed in 1969 when Charlotte desegregated its school system.

After our service on Sunday, I saw Annie. I told her that I hoped she would come to visit our church again.

With a little embarrassed shrug of her shoulders, she said, "Hopefully not like this."

"I agree," I said, "but it would be wonderful to see you again." Then I brought up the story of Anna.

"Annie," I asked. "Do you know the story of Anna in the Bible? There were two remarkable people in the Temple when Mary and Joseph took Jesus to be dedicated. Simeon, a prophet, had been told by God that he would not die until he saw the Messiah. The other person was…,"

"Anna, the prayer warrior," Annie quickly finished my sentence.

"That's right, but did you realize that just like you, she was living in the Temple. She was 86, and for most of her life, she did not have a home, yet God allowed her to be the only woman other than Mary to see the baby Jesus and know that He was the Messiah! Just as God blessed Anna though she was living in the Temple, He will bless you."

Annie looked at me with understanding. Amid her personal pain and a lifetime of suffering that had led to the embarrassment of living in a church, she understood the blessing of seeing and knowing Christ.

UNDERSTANDING ANNA

By studying the prayer warrior, Anna, we will learn about the importance of trusting God to take care of us, seeing God, and encouraging others. We will also discover background information about Anna's home in the Temple and the reason for the two sacrifices required after giving birth: the sin offering and the burnt offering. We'll learn about why Joseph and Mary took Baby Jesus to the Temple. Finally, Anna will help us discover the two powerful keys to embracing change: prayer and fasting.

Anna was a woman of deep faith even though she had experienced tough times that would cause most people to doubt God. She was born sixty years after the Maccabean revolution, and the miracle in the Temple that is now commemorated during the Jewish celebration of Hanukkah.

Political and personal tragedy highlighted her life. When Anna was in her early 20s, a struggle for the leadership of Jerusalem resulted in the Romans taking control of her homeland. Anna's husband may have died during the civil war and attack by Rome. She was left homeless without a husband or family; she had no one to take care of her.

Anna lived in the Temple and had suffered great heartbreak, but she never lost hope. Four hundred years had passed since the final book of the Old Testament, Malachi, had been written, yet Anna trusted that God would carry out his plan to save His people even though her circumstances proclaimed a hopeless situation. It is remarkable that she continued to believe God's Word and promises even after seeing her country's political and spiritual leaders become pawns of the Roman authorities. She was confident that the Messiah would come to set His people free from the bondage of sin and death.

THE TEMPLE

Let's start with some background information on Anna's home, the Temple. Naomi's great, great, ... grandson King Solomon built the First Temple nearly a thousand years before the birth of Jesus. When Jerusalem fell in 586 BC, Solomon's Temple was ransacked, and many of the gold and precious items in it were taken by King Nebuchadnezzar and his armies to Babylon. About 70 years later, during the time of Ezra and Nehemiah, the exiles in Babylon were returned home to rebuild the Temple. Unfortunately, this Second Temple was less magnificent than the one Solomon built.

Five hundred years passed between the return of the exiles from Babylon and the birth of Jesus. During that time, the Second Temple fell into disrepair. To curry favor with the Jews and the Romans, King Herod began an expansion of the Second Temple in 20 BC. It was an elaborate undertaking intended to build his prestige and win favor with the Romans because the Romans valued architecture. It took Herod 40 years to rebuild the Temple, which means at Jesus' dedication, the Temple was nearly 50% completed. During the rebuilding, Herod expanded the outer courts and added the Royal Stoa, an ancient type of covered market.

N

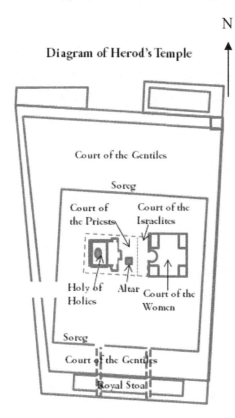

Diagram of Herod's Temple

Various courts in the Temple were reserved for certain groups of people. Anyone who was ceremonially clean could be in the "Court of the Gentiles." It was the most public part of the Temple. The next court was the "Court of the Women"; only Jewish women and men were allowed in this area. The "Court of the Women" had a balcony that allowed women to observe the sacrifices and the "Court of the Israelites." Only ritually clean Jewish men were allowed in the "Court of the Israelites." The "Court of the Priests" contained the Holy Place where Zechariah offered incense and the Holy of Holies. The High Priest was allowed to go into the Holy of Holies once a year. The entire Temple was a holy place dedicated to the worship of God.

Based on paragraph above, please highlight the places on the diagram to the left that Anna could go in the Temple.

On the drawing of the Temple, you should have highlighted the Court of the Gentiles and the Court of the Women. Anna was not allowed in the Court of the Israelites, the Court of the Priests, or the Holy of Holies.

The Temple was a segregated place, and if you were Jew, Gentile, male, or female determined how close you could get to the presence of God. A thick curtain separated the presence of God in the Holy of Holies from the daily offerings of the priests.

Please read Mark 15:37-38 and record what happened in this passage.

The thick curtain, called the "Veil" in some translations, was supernaturally split-in-half at the moment Christ breathed his last breath on the cross. This verse records a significant moment of transformation in our relationship with God. The Book of Hebrews further explains that Christ became our High Priest and entered the Holy of Holies behind the curtain on our behalf.[167]

> *In Christ,* there was no segregation or limits based on race or gender on who could be in the presence of God.

Paul explains the transformation that occurred in our relationship with God and others in Galatians, a letter to new believers who were Greek gentiles by birth. He wrote, "So in Christ Jesus you are all children of God through faith, for all of you who were baptized into Christ have clothed yourselves with Christ. There is neither Jew nor Gentile, neither slave nor free, nor is there male and female, for you are all one in Christ Jesus."[168]

Take a minute and underline this sentence above, "There is neither Jew nor Gentile, neither slave nor free, nor is there male and female, for you are all one in Christ Jesus."

This is a revolutionary statement. Paul, who had grown up under the Law was writing to uncircumcised, unholy people in Galatia to make sure they knew that everyone was the same in God's eyes. In Christ, there was no segregation or limits based on race or gender on who could be in the presence of God. Anna's access to God in the Temple was limited to the Court of Women, but Christ's birth would change her and every other person's ability to experience the presence of God in their daily lives.

1 Corinthians 6:19-20 says, "Don't you realize that your body is the Temple of the Holy Spirit, who lives in you and was given to you by God? You do not belong to yourself, for God bought you with a high price. So you must honor God with your body."

How does knowing Anna's story, change your view of the Temple?

---

[167] Hebrews 6:19-20
[168] Galatians 3:26-27

Week 2

OFFERING SACRIFICES

I am a wimp. For instance, my brief collegiate soccer career ended before our first match because I ran into our goalkeeper at practice; she was fine, and I became the team manager. Stubbing my toe brings extreme agony, angry squawks, and a desire for vengeance. When it was time to give birth to my oldest son, I demanded an epidural as soon as I set foot in the hospital. I am not a hero. I had nothing to prove. I didn't care if it made the process longer. The pain of stubbing my toe makes me furious at myself, I couldn't imagine giving birth without pain medicine! All you ladies who have are super heroes.

I praise God that I am alive during a time when pain medicine is readily available. I love taking a hot shower and my comfortable bed. As you read this chapter, think about what life would have been like over 2000 years ago as a woman—no doctors, pain medicine, sanitary items, or even running water.

In last week's chapter, we looked at the physical layout of the Temple and the separation that people had from God. We learned that because of Jesus, everyone has access to the Holiest Place and that in Christ, there is neither male nor female, Jew or Gentile, slave, or free. In Christ, we are righteous and holy.

Anna's story intersects with new mom Mary's dedication of her baby Jesus at the Temple. Please read Luke 2:21 and summarize what happened in this verse below.

Like his cousin John, Elizabeth, and Zechariah's son, Jesus was named and circumcised on the 8th day after his birth. This was according to the Law given to the people of Israel. "The LORD said to Moses, "Say to the Israelites: 'A woman who becomes pregnant and gives birth to a son will be ceremonially unclean for seven days, just as she is unclean during her monthly period. On the eighth day, the boy is to be circumcised. Then the woman must wait thirty-three days to be purified from her bleeding. She must not touch anything sacred or go to the sanctuary until the days of her purification are over."[169]

Please read Luke 2:22-24. When did Joseph and Mary take Jesus to the Temple?

---

[169] Leviticus 12:1-4

What were the two reasons they took Jesus to the Temple?

Joseph and Mary took Jesus to the Temple to be dedicated to God after "the time of their purification" had been completed, 33 days after Jesus was circumcised. They offered two sacrifices and dedicated Jesus to God. God required[170] the firstborn to be dedicated to the Lord to acknowledge God's sovereignty and to commemorate God's protection for the Hebrews' firstborn during the first Passover when Moses and Miriam and the rest of the Israelites were preparing to leave Egypt.

Jesus was about six weeks old when he was brought into the Temple to be dedicated because Joseph and Mary waited until after their 'Time of Purification." This time of purification gave mothers a chance to recuperate from the child's birth. Though Leviticus was written over 3,000 years ago, even now, when a mom gives birth, she is typically allowed to stay out from work by her doctor for about six weeks.

Though we are no longer under the Law since Jesus is the fulfillment of the Law, when I read the Bible, I try to understand God's heart when He established the Law for His people. It says in Deuteronomy that the Law was meant to bless us. The Law often established protections for women during a time when brute force was typically how men protected and established their rights.

So how could this time of purification be a blessing? Imagine living in a rural society with no stores, hospitals, or restaurants. Life would be very hard. Having a break for nearly six weeks after giving birth would be a blessing, especially when some parents had to travel long distances by donkey or camel to Jerusalem to dedicate their baby. Six weeks would be a blessing before such a bumpy ride!

When Mary and Joseph arrived at the Temple, they were required to offer two sacrifices- the burnt offering and the sin offering. These offerings were based on Leviticus 12, "These are the regulations for the woman who gives birth to a boy or a girl. But if she cannot afford a lamb, she is to bring two doves or two young pigeons, one for a burnt offering and the other for a sin offering. In this way, the priest will make atonement for her, and she will be clean." I found a good explanation of these two types of offerings from the website *Judaism 101*.[171] As you read the descriptions of these sacrifices, remember that a Jewish person wrote this explanation, so he did not spell the complete word "God" out of respect.

Olah: The Burnt Offering

"An olah is completely burnt on the outer altar; no part of it is eaten by anyone. Because the offering represents complete submission to G-d's will, the entire offering is given to G-d (i.e., it cannot be used after it is burnt). It expresses a desire to commune with G-d, and expiates

[170] Exodus 13:1, 11-15
[171] http://www.jewfaq.org

sins incidentally in the process (because how can you commune with G-d if you are tainted with sins?)."[172]

Based on this definition, what did the Burnt Offering symbolize?

Chatat: Sin Offering

"A sin offering is an offering to atone for and purge a sin. It is an expression of sorrow for the error and a desire to be reconciled with G-d. The Hebrew term for this type of offering is chatat, from the word chayt, meaning "missing the mark." A chatat could only be offered for unintentional sins committed through carelessness, not for intentional, malicious sins."[173]

Did you pick up the idea from the definition of the Chatat that sin involves the unintentional mistakes that everyone makes? Sin is a part of our life, not because we intend to fail or to do harm but because we are not perfect. Sin is a part of our lives because no matter how hard we try, there are times when we will "miss the mark" and unintentionally make mistakes. I used to think sins were the big bad things like lying and stealing. In fact, God established another sacrifice, the Guilt Offering, and the process of restitution for the "big bad things" like stealing or intentionally hurting someone. Sin is the little stuff; the result of being human, of not being perfect, and not knowing everything.

Why would someone offer a Sin Offering?

*Why do you think God had women make these two offerings after giving birth?

These offerings symbolized submitting to God's will and acknowledging how we unintentionally miss the mark. Mary had to make a sin offering and a burnt offering to be reconciled with God. The Burnt Offering symbolized Mary's desire to have a right relationship with God. It was also an acknowledgment that she wanted God's ways and God's will in her life. Just as the lamb or dove was fully given over to God, the sacrifice symbolized Mary's willingness to be fully dedicated to the work that God had for her.

Mary was human just like each of us, and so she had to make a sin offering, not because giving birth is a sin but because the process can bring out almost any woman's sinful natures. If most of us were

---

[172] http://www.jewfaq.org/qorbanot.htm
[173] ibid

honest, we would say in the same situation, far from home in a stable, we would have certainly thought and maybe even said many impure things. I certainly would have. Though Mary rejoiced at being the mother of Jesus during the actual labor and delivery in a stable surrounded by animals and far from home, she may not have been perfect in word, thought, or deed. Even with our hearts fully committed to the Lord and His work, we still make mistakes. Some people would argue that Mary may not have sinned while giving birth, but we need to remember God established the Sin Offering after giving birth so that every woman could be made right with God after such a trying time. Not everyone was as righteous as Mary. Making these offerings a requirement for every woman meant that no one was singled out for something that was a completely normal response to pain and giving birth.

WHAT IS SIN?

When I was a freshman in college, a friend asked me, "What is sin?" Answering this simple question was much more difficult than I imagined. My friend brought up the idea that much of what we consider "bad" is just cultural. Whether we are sticking a particular finger in the air, showing the soles of our feet, or even saying certain words, "Ever been to Phuket?", those things may be wrong in one culture but fine in another. Even the big bad ones like killing, lying, and stealing are debatable in times of war and capital punishment.

How would you answer the question, "What is sin?"

"What is sin?" has been rumbling through my mind for 20 years. For a while, I defined sin as selfishness. This made sense to me. We've all made selfish decisions at one time or another in our life. As toddlers and teenagers, our selfish desires are most evident. So, without a doubt, selfishness is a component of sin. But I've now realized since doing this study that sin is even more fundamental than selfishness.

Even with our **hearts fully committed to the Lord and His work, we still make mistakes.**

Sin carries the idea that no matter how hard we try, we unintentionally make mistakes; we can never be perfect all the time, in every part of our life. We are not perfect, whether we are giving birth, raising children, going to school, working in our jobs, spelling, singing, eating, sleeping, talking, praying, giving, driving, exercising, or fighting. We may be very, very, very, very good, smart, strong, giving, and loving. But we have made a mistake at least once, gotten less than 100% on a test, forgotten something, done a less than perfect job on a project, said something we shouldn't have, or sung off-tune just one note. That is being human and being human means that we are not perfect.

Please read Romans 3:22-24 and write out verse 23.

Please read my paraphrased version of Romans 3:23 below and circle the words that describe any time when you have been less than perfect.

"for all have sinned (been impatient, forgetful, selfish, absent-minded, careless, imperfect, unforgiving, lethargic, undisciplined, regimented, controlling, independent, gossipy, judgmental, permissive, resentful, weak, flippant, unintentional, slow, flawed, hasty, lazy, harsh, unloving, unknowing, bitter, foolish, insensitive, obtuse, unfeeling, thoughtless, inconsiderate, uncaring, thick-skinned, offensive, inattentive, rude, arrogant, clumsy, uncaring, passive, reckless, tactless, proud, indelicate, impulsive, _____) and fall short of the glory of God,

The Message put these verses this way, "Since we've compiled this long and sorry record as sinners (both us and them) and proved that we are utterly incapable of living the glorious lives God wills for us, God did it for us. Out of sheer generosity, he put us in right standing with himself. A pure gift. He got us out of the mess we're in and restored us to where he always wanted us to be. And he did it by means of Jesus Christ."[174]

God provided the sin offering and the burnt offering as a means for His people to be reconciled with Him and other people. Sacrifices were necessary because everyone makes mistakes. When we make mistakes and cause hurt or pain, something inside us knows we need to make restitution to be reconciled with God and with the people we have hurt or offended.

Jesus has revolutionized the sacrificial system. Just as Jesus as our High Priest provided the way for everyone (male, female, enslaved person, freeman, Jew, and Gentile) to come into the presence of God by dividing the curtain outside the Holy of Holies, His blood and death on the cross have provided an eternal sacrifice for our sins. We no longer have to make animal sacrifices. His sacrifice once and for all took away our guilt and sin and made us right with God (righteous.) Romans 3:22 says, "This righteousness is given through faith in Jesus Christ to all who believe." Our right relationship with God is not obtained through our ongoing sacrifices but through belief in Jesus Christ, who made himself to be our sacrifice.

Romans 5:8 says, "But God demonstrates His own love for us in this: While we were still sinners, Christ died for us." It is a pure gift. Not because we are close to perfect but because he is perfect, and he loved us in spite of our sin of _____ (fill in the blank with any sin.)

---

[174] Romans 3:23-24 MSG

LIFE WITHOUT SIN- DESIRING PERFECTION

Have you ever wanted to be perfect, even if only for a moment?

Maybe not altogether perfect in every way; but wished just for a moment to have perfect hair, a perfect body, a perfect family, a perfect house, perfect clothes, perfect health, perfect happiness, perfect love, or perfect teeth. So, you bought the clothes, wore the make-up, read the books, cleaned the toilets, ate your vegetables, wore braces, straightened or permed your hair, exercised, and/or dieted—all that for the hope of a moment of perfection.

We can trace how these deep longings for moments of perfection started in childhood, stretched through our teens, and follow us today. They develop at such a young age, long before we realize it. Here's an example of how it begins. One spring day, I took my three-year-old son John to a park with a giant sandbox. It is a fun beach-like escape since we live many hours from the ocean. He started making a castle fortress in one part of the sandbox, and three little girls were building a castle together in another corner. The girls were working toward their grand design when one little girl said in amazement, "Look, everyone, this one is perfect. The sides are so smooth. Look." I glanced at her creation. The tower's sandy sides were smooth, and the imprint of bricks and windows from the bucket was perfectly embossed. She had a momentary taste of perfection in the tumultuous work of sandcastle construction.

Perfection isn't **about how things look or function but about becoming all that God created us to be in Him.**

Whether we are little girls or older women, we still seek perfection because God made us for perfection. Our desire for perfect clothes, hair, relationships, etc., is a desire that goes back to the Garden of Eden to the time before sin entered the world. Our desire for perfection is a longing to be free from sin, death, decay, and sickness because we were created to be perfect.

Please look up and write out Hebrews 10:14

Just so this sinks in, let's personalize this verse. Please put your name in the blank-
Hebrews 10:14 for by one sacrifice JESUS has made Perfect forever _____ who is being made holy.

One day in eternity, we will live in a perfect house with perfect bodies. But, in the meantime, let's reframe those moments when you wish for more in relationships, clothes, and hair as a heartfelt wish for more of Jesus, the Perfecter of our faith.[175]

By seeking after Jesus, our perfectionist desires that get stuck on food, clothes, kids, houses, and zits will be transformed into a desire to know Him more and be more like the one who is utterly perfect. In the process, we will learn that perfection isn't about how things look or function but about becoming all that God created us to be in Him.

Deuteronomy 32:3-4 captures this idea perfectly. Please write it out and meditate on it.

Our God is so great. He is steadfast, and His works are perfect. Including you and me, He is just, faithful, and does no wrong. "No wrong" means *nothing wrong*. Perfect. Always faithful. Oh, praise the greatness of our God *Our desire for perfection is truly a desire for God who is perfect.* As we grow closer to God, our perception of true perfection will be transformed, and we will become more like Him.

Spend some time praising God because he is perfect and holy. Give Him your desire for perfection and control. Thank Him because He sacrificed Himself for our sins and made us perfect, holy, and righteous.

Week 3

AN AMAZING PROPHECY

Have you ever had the feeling you need to stop what you are doing and pray for someone? Not too long ago, I felt called to pray that my friend Emily would have enough Vitamin C. It was a silly prayer, and I wondered if I was projecting my need for Vitamin C into my prayers for her. But I would pray for her to find good sources of Vitamin C every time I ate some. God had used it to help me regulate my cortisol levels and sleep, but I had no idea why I was praying for her.

---

[175] Hebrews 12:2

About a month after my Vitamin C prayer compulsion began, I had a chance to catch up with her. She told me that she had gone to the doctor's office, and the day after her appointment, the doctor contacted her with an urgent request to come back in. Her blood work had revealed a severe iron deficiency. Then she looked at me and said, "Guess what my doctor told me I needed to absorb the iron?" I had no clue. "Vitamin C!" she exclaimed. I was overwhelmed. God knew what she needed and brought it to my mind to pray for her. When we act in obedience to the prompting of the Holy Spirit, we can fully experience God's blessings.

In the past couple of weeks, we've learned about Anna's home in the Temple and why Mary and Joseph took Jesus into the Court of Women to be consecrated and make the sin offering and burnt offering. In the process, we've learned that Jesus, as our High Priest, has broken down the barriers between people and God. Last week, we also learned that Jesus became our sin offering and removed our sins and guilt for eternity. Though we will never be perfect, Christ in us is perfect, and we can rest secure in that marvelous fact.

In this chapter, we will learn more about Anna and her encounter with Jesus. Just before Mary and Joseph met Anna in the Court of Women with baby Jesus, something remarkable happened.

Please read Luke 2:25-35 and answer the following questions.

Why did the Spirit move Simeon to praise God?

What did he prophesy about Jesus?

How does this relate to your life?

Imagine being told by God that you would not die until you saw the Messiah, the consolation of Israel. Then, finally, when you are old, the Holy Spirit says to go to the Temple to see the baby. Simeon believed God's promise that he would see the Messiah and acted on God's Word by being obedient in going to the Temple. He didn't question that a poor carpenter and young girl could be the parents of the Messiah. He simply believed and rejoiced. He knew that he had seen the salvation for the people of Israel and all nations, a light for all the people in the world, including you and me.

Are you willing to act on what God has revealed to you?

God has rewarded me when I believed Him and acted in faith according to His will. He opened doors for my first book proposal to be read by a well-known Bible study author's editor by showing the editor's face on the Jumbotron in a 10,000-seat auditorium.[176]

Another time, God told me to pray for a near-stranger who was getting a divorce and to ask a mutual acquaintance I barely knew to pray with me for the couple. It seemed to be an impossible situation. I didn't even know if the woman I asked to pray with me was a believer or if she would think I was crazy. She said, "Yes," and over the next year, we met and prayed. God did a miraculous work, and the family we prayed for is now back together. Who knows what miracles God has for you to experience and the blessings He has in store for other people if you are willing to act on what God has revealed to you?

Anna was another remarkable person in the Court of the Women along with baby Jesus, Mary, Joseph, and Simeon. To learn more about Anna, please read Luke 2:36-38 and answer the following questions.

Who was Anna? How old was she? Did she have a husband or children?

Where did she live?

What did she say about the redemption of Jesus?

How was her relationship with God changed that day?

Why do you think Anna lived in the Temple?

*Why do you think she fasted?

Annie, the woman I wrote about at the beginning of this chapter, called Anna a prayer warrior." Why do you think she said this?

Luke used the word "prophetess" to describe her. What do you think it means to be a prophetess?

---

[176] http://pennynoyes.blogspot.com/2009_08_01_archive.html

Anna's life situation was challenging. She was an 84-year-old widow, and either her husband had left her without any resources, or her home had passed to her husband's family, and she couldn't live with his relatives. Since she lived in the Temple, Anna spent her days fasting and praying. It is likely that she fasted because she had no food except that which was given to her by the people worshiping at the Temple who shared their sacrifice with her. Every bite she took was solely dependent on God's provision through the people around her.

She was basically a homeless woman living in her church. She was completely alone. She probably didn't have any children, or they had predeceased her. If a woman didn't have a child after being married for seven years, she would have been branded as infertile and unmarriageable.

"Widows and orphans lacked the economic, legal and physical protection a man provided in that society. To be both a widow and childless is a double hardship. Such a woman had no husband to be provider and protector and also has no son or even prospects of a son to carry on the family name and to support her in old age... In societies where the basic social unit was headed by the father... those without a father or husband were social misfits."[177] By her society's standards, she was worthless; She was homeless and had the double shame of being a widow and childless.

Every bite she took **was solely dependent on God's provision through the people around her.**

I struggled with the sentence above about Anna being worthless because she wasn't worthless, she was precious to God. Her relative age, wealth, health, success, and contribution to society were inconsequential compared to the magnificence of God. Her value came from being made in the image of God.

God has created all of us with intrinsic value, though many of us struggle with our sense of worth. Anna's grief and the loss that she experienced during her 86 years reminded me of friends who lost homes to bankruptcy, were laid off and felt abandoned by employers, became widows because of their husband's sickness or suicide, and have felt like failures in the face of childlessness. Amid their pain and grief, they felt like misfits, isolated by their hardships and situation.

Who are you without your house, career, husband, or child? Who are you after your dreams of marriage and family are shattered, and you become a widow after only seven years? Who are you when your home is no longer yours? If the only safe place you can live is the Temple? What comforts you when the only food you eat is given to you by kind people who invite you to share in their fellowship offerings? How do you rejoice when they are celebrating the good things the Lord has given to them while you have nothing?

---

[177] Brand, Draper, England, *Holman Illustrated Bible Dictionary*, Holman Bible Publishers Nashville, TN 2003, pg. 1671

As women, we often find our identity in our dreams of a home, marriage, and children. Who are you when everything is stripped away?

Have you or a friend experience such a situation?

How did their self-image change?

Did their dreams change?

What was the biggest adjustment?

I realized that during mourning, my friends often pulled away. Their identity had changed so dramatically they didn't believe that anyone could really accept them anymore.

*What are some practical ways you can help someone who has lost their sense of self and their worth see their intrinsic value to God?

God values and loves each of us so much. Not because of what we have, what we can do, or where we live. He loves us because He created us in his image. Every person represents a unique facet of God's majesty and beauty. He passionately values us; He sent His son for us so that He can have a relationship with us and bless us. Even during earth-shattering loss and incredible hardship, His love never fails.

Anna was the least of the least, yet God loved and valued her so much. Although she was a woman who had nothing, she received an incredible gift from God, the opportunity to see and recognize the Messiah. Though many other people had prayed to see the Savior, God chose to bless this woman with the life-changing privilege of holding the Messiah even though she was a poor, homeless woman living in the Temple.

Anna's story causes me to wonder, "Why does God seem to bless people in such different ways?" The quick answer is that God is Sovereign. God blesses whom He blesses, and God has specific blessings for each of us. But the way God provides is not always the way we expect or think we deserve.

A broader perspective helps us understand that one person might perceive something as a blessing, and another person would see the same thing as a burden. As a result, life often doesn't seem fair. Why did I have kids when so many friends have struggled with infertility? Why are some kids born to loving, healthy parents and other children grow up as AIDS orphans in sub-Saharan Africa? When we struggle with tough questions about Anna's life and the unknowns in each of our lives, we must hold onto the promise that God has not forgotten us, we are not worthless, and He is working all things together for the good of those who love Him and are called according to His purpose.[178]

Trusting God with the tough questions and the unfairness of life is a way to find peace and live a joy-filled life regardless of our circumstances. As we seek first the kingdom of God and His righteousness, all the other things we stress about will be given to us. Just like Anna, God has a plan and unique purpose for each of us—no matter our life situation—whether we are married, widowed, or single; living in a home or a church; with or without children; rich or poor; succeeding or struggling. He will take care of us and fulfill our heart's desires because He loves us.

> *God has a special plan* and purpose for each of us- no matter what our life situation is—He will take care of us and fulfill our heart's desires because He loves us.

Anna didn't have abundant resources to give generously; she didn't have a house like the Shunammite woman to offer hospitality, and she probably wasn't a dancer or singer like Miriam. Though she lacked material resources, Anna did have a valuable gift. She was a prophetess; this means she was a female prophet. Biblical prophets were often given the ability to see the current situation of God's people. For instance, prophets could see the consequences of sin and idolatry before it happened. Most Biblical prophecies dealt with the condition of God's people and the consequences that would happen if they continued on a path away from God. This prophetic gift is similar to my husband's ability to anticipate danger when my little boys climbed in precarious places. He was able to see the imminent danger if they continued on their current risky path. It often seems like common sense, if we don't realize that it is God who has given us this intuition. If God has given you this gift, use it and give him the glory or pride will lead to greater problems. If you don't use it, you will lose it like the man who buried his talent.

Anna's relationship with God changed that day in the Temple. God gave Anna and Simeon the ability to see that an average daily occurrence at the Temple, a baby being dedicated in the Temple, was the answer to their prayers for the Messiah. Their God-given perspective transformed a normal situation into a vision that included the entire world's salvation through this tiny baby, Jesus. Though Anna was not even allowed in the Court of the Israelites, she could stand face to face in the presence of the Most High. She was able to have Jesus' tiny hand wrap around one of her gnarled fingers and feel the hands

---

[178] Romans 8:28

that one day would be pierced for all of our sins and mistakes. At age 84, God used her to carry out His mission and proclaim His message to the women and men who came into the Temple. Even though she did not have a home, husband, or children, God had given her a purpose. She was a prophetess and a prayer warrior. She spent her days praying and fasting for the redemption of Israel. Just imagine the impact that she had after coming face to face with the Messiah. Hope had come.

Regardless of your age, God has a mission for you to bless others and use the gifts that He has given you for His glory. Don't underestimate God's ability to use you, whatever your life situation. Take a minute to think about and write down ways that you can bless others with the resources and gifts that God has given you.

Week 4

TWO KEYS TO EMBRACING CHANGE

Despite her challenging situation, Anna's continued hope and ability to embrace change came from two significant spiritual practices in her life: Prayer and Fasting. The first time I remember fasting was when I "did Lent," in college. I didn't know much about it but my friends were all doing it, so I decided to join in. Loren decided to give up chocolate, but I knew that would be too hard for me. I gave up drinking soda because I didn't really like it that much. Or so I thought. Over the course of the next forty days, I realized I did like soda with pizza and burgers. Giving up anything was a lot harder than I realized and it gave me a tiny taste of the glory that Jesus had given up before coming to earth as a baby. In the years since college, I have learned a lot more about the power and privilege of fasting.

How do you think praying and fasting helped Anna during her years in the Temple?

*Have you practiced praying and fasting? What are some of the benefits that you have experienced in your life?

Prayer and fasting allowed Anna to trust that God would take care of her. It redirected her attention from the poverty and desolate situation that she was in and allowed her to see and hear God more clearly. It opened her eyes to the revelation that the baby Jesus was the Messiah, the Redeemer of Israel, a privilege given only to one other woman, Mary. Despite her physical poverty, she had spiritual riches that she could use to bless others. Prayer and fasting opened Anna's eyes, ears, and heart to see God's work in hopeless circumstances.

TRUE FASTING

When we read about Mary making her sacrifices at the Temple, it is easy to imagine that Anna's temporary home was like a modern-day church, a building that people visited weekly to worship God through songs, giving offerings, and listening to a 25-minute sermon. It's time to erase that image from your mind when you think about the Temple. Instead, you need to imagine something closer to an all-you-can-eat steak buffet or the smells and excitement of a Texan's annual whole steer BBQ. Imagine the smell of steaks grilling, spices sizzling in the heat, and the excitement of a meal with friends and family. Since the Temple was the place where sin offerings, guilt offerings, and fellowship offerings were offered to God, the scent of well-done beef, lamb, and dove continually filled the air.

Faithful worshipers of God would bring their sacrifices to the Temple and give a portion of it to the priest, and then depending on the type of sacrifice, they would have a cookout with their friends and family. After making the sacrifices, it was a time of celebration. Sins were forgiven, and hearts were restored by a right relationship with God. It was time to kick back and enjoy some grilled meat.

Fasting is a spiritual practice that involves refraining from food. I can hardly imagine how hard it was for Anna in this environment. She was too poor to buy food. She depended on the generosity of strangers who came to the Temple to share their sacrifices with her. On days that no one shared their offering with her, she responded with prayer and fasting.

Though Anna was called to a lifetime of intermittent fasting, for most of us, a spiritual fast typically lasts for a certain amount of time. Fasting was done in various ways throughout the Bible. When Jesus fasted, he ate nothing.[179] for forty days. Paul, Esther, and Ezra fasted for three days and did not eat or drink.[180] Daniel participated in a partial fast when he abstained from the meats and items from the royal table. One of my friends goes to a church that has a "Daniel fast," which gives up meat

---

[179] Luke 4:2
[180] Acts 9:9, Ezra 10:6, Esther 4:16

and sweets, every January to refocus the leadership and members of the church. I have several friends who participate in Lent- which is a partial fast for forty days before Easter. I believe that fasting has immense physical and spiritual benefits, but please talk with your doctor before beginning any fast if you have health problems.

Please look up the following verses and summarize why they fasted.
Luke 4:1-2, Matthew 4:1-2

2 Chronicles 20:3

1 Samuel 7:3-6

Esther 4:16

Jesus fasted for 40 days to prepare for being tempted in the wilderness before beginning his public ministry. The Israelites fasted in the face of a battle. As a sign of repentance, the Israelites turned back to the Lord, fasted, confessed their sins, and put away false gods. Esther fasted and had all the Jews fast before she approached the King to seek deliverance for her people from Haman's decree.

Fasting helps us experience God more fully. Fasting provides an avenue for seeking God's will in a specific matter. Fasting combined with repentance draws us closer to God. Fasting takes our focus off physical things like food and our body and helps us refocus our energy and mind on the things of God.

I have seen some of the most powerful benefits of fasting in healing broken marriages. For example, friends, whose husbands told them that their marriages were over and stopped being intimate, applied the wisdom of 1 Corinthians 7:5, which I paraphrase, "The only reason for depriving your spouse of sex is prayer and fasting." Since their husbands didn't want to fulfill the physical side of the marriage, my friends got serious with God and fasted for months. God was faithful to restore their marriages. A Bible study note, looking at the Greek lexicon for this verse, not all include νηστεία which means fasting,.[181] But, I can confidently tell you that if you are seek after God through both fasting and prayer, a transformation will occur in your marriage.

---

[181] https://www.blueletterbible.org/kjv/1co/7/1/t_conc_1069005

Why would we sit around feeling hopeless and sorry for ourselves when we have the God of Hope on our side? Don't trade the comfort of food for the presence of the Comforter. Prayer is powerful but combining it with fasting adds another level of depth and focus. In my experience, a fast isn't so much about food or drink but instead about changing my heart and focusing on God. Filling ourselves with God's Word is an essential part of fasting.

When Jesus was fasting in the wilderness and tempted with food, he quoted a verse from Deuteronomy 8:3. Please write out what Jesus said in Matthew 4:4.

For a spiritual fast to be effective, you need to refrain from food and fill yourself with the Word of God—the Bread of Life.

Please read John 6:35 and write it below.

Jesus is the Bread of Life. We need to fill ourselves with His Word and His presence when fasting. When doing an all-day fast, I have found that I am able to focus on Jesus and not focus on food when I read the Bible during mealtime. It truly becomes my daily bread. I supplement my "meals" with praise music and prayer times. Prayer, praise, and reading the Bible help me focus on God.

For partial fasts, like Lent, I use those tugs of attraction towards the things I have given up to draw me to Jesus and help me focus on His sacrifice. It is valuable to replace what I have given up with something God tells me to do. Usually, I add something that the Holy Spirit has already been prompting me to do; one year, it was reading the Bible daily, and another year, it was writing every day.

Is there something you feel the Holy Spirit prompting you to do or to give up?

In the chapter on Athaliah, we looked at scriptures that encourage us to put off the things of this world and to put on spiritual gifts like love, peace, and patience.[182] I believe that letting go of things and putting on new behaviors amplifies the benefits of the fast. Fasting for Lent provides the structure I need to do what God had already told me to do. When I fast for Lent, I am not perfect. I have slipped. I have accidentally eaten chocolate though I gave it up. Other times, I have forgotten to do my daily Bible reading. When I realized my mistake, I was remorseful and humbled by my imperfections, but

---

[182] Colossians 3:8-14

immediately, grace flooded my heart. I realized that Christ has forgiven all my sins (unintentional mistakes) and that His sacrifice on the cross means that my actions aren't the source of my salvation. Jesus has done it all and paid the ultimate price.

When doing a spiritual fast, what we give up, how much, and how long we fast are secondary to having a heart that is seeking to know God, experience His presence and feel his power in our lives in a real and tangible way. As we pray and fast, God will even tell us what we should abstain from.

> *We often seek our own will* and just go through the motions of seeking God when we are praying and fasting.

One year for Lent, I decided to fast one day a week. After my first day of fasting, I completely binged; to sink to such depths after such a spiritual high was heart-breaking. I was filled with remorse at my depravity. As I was praying and repenting, I heard God say, "Are you serious?" When I said "Yes," He said, "Give up sugar." This one act of obedience changed my life for many years to come. As I fasted, I learned that He cares about the food we eat and the clothes we wear, and that just as He established the sacrifices for Israelites, He will let us know how we should fast. Now, whenever I feel called to begin a fast, I stop to pray and ask Him what I need to put off and what I need to put on.

One important note- Spiritual fasting is not a quick fix. Several of my friends look at fasting as a diet or a "cleanse." While eliminating things from your diet may have some physical value- spiritually, it is a bad practice. In fact, thinking that you could lose weight on a fast is only going to send you down a slippery slope of focusing on yourself rather than on God.

Another potential motivation for fasting is using it as a way to control God. Seeing fasting as a strategy to get what we want rather than focusing on God is not a new problem.

Please read Isaiah 58 and write down your thoughts on fasting for our benefit versus doing what God has called us to do.

Isaiah 58 records some of the dangers of going through the motions of fasting and praying but missing the heart of seeking to know God and do His will. However, we often seek our own will and just go through the motions of seeking God when we are praying and fasting. God told His people in Isaiah 58 that they were fasting and dressing in sackcloth and ashes as an outward sign of repentance, but they weren't doing what He wanted. "This is the kind of fast day I'm after: to break the chains of injustice, get rid of exploitation in the workplace, free the oppressed, cancel debts. What I'm interested in seeing you do is: sharing your food with the hungry, inviting the homeless poor into your homes, putting clothes on the shivering ill-clad, being available to your own family.[183] This chapter in Isaiah highlights the problem of fasting and praying to avoid doing God's will after He has already told it to us.

THE IMPORTANCE OF PRAYER

Fasting without prayer is just a diet. Prayer is intrinsic to the Christian life, but people often wonder if there is a right way to pray. Some churches recommend reading prayers written by priests or experts and others value popcorn prayers and extemporaneous thoughts.

 Please write out what you think it means "to pray."

 Following are three verses that talk about praying. I removed the word "pray" from each of them so that you could put your definition of "to pray" written above in these verses. Does it make sense?

"So do not _____ for this people nor offer any plea or petition for them; do not plead with me, for I will not listen to you. Jeremiah 7:16

But when you _____, go into your room, close the door and _____ your Father, who is unseen. Then your Father, who sees what is done in secret, will reward you. (Matt 6:6)
As for other matters, brothers and sisters, _____ for us that the message of the Lord may spread rapidly and be honored, just as it was with you. (2 Thes 3:1)

Therefore confess your sins to each other and _____for each other so that you may be healed. The prayer of a righteous person is powerful and effective. (James 5:16)

To me, the phrase "ask God" substitutes well in each of these verses. The Jeremiah verse gives us a clue to the meaning of prayer by using synonyms like "petition" or "offer a plea." Prayer is simply asking God to intervene in a situation. He can heal us, save us, bless us, prosper us and expand his kingdom. Prayer has immense power because God has unlimited resources. Nothing is impossible with God.

However, sometimes asking God to intervene is a waste of breath. For example, in the first verse from Jeremiah, the people of Judah were reaping the consequences of years of idolatry. Therefore, whenever you pray, it is important to ask for God's will to be done in the situation. God knows the

---

[183] Isaiah 58:6-9 MSG

beginning and the end. A prayer warrior knows the power of prayer comes from God's resurrection ability. The good news is that even in hard situations like the one in Jeremiah, God ultimately was going to bless his people. As Jeremiah 29:11 says, "For I know the plans I have for you," declares the Lord, "plans to prosper you and not to harm you, plans to give you a hope and a future." Asking for God's will rather than your own provides immense peace and freedom when things don't go the way you want.

To pray means to ask God for his will in your life and other people's lives. It acknowledges that you need God's help; you can't change the situation, and He can. Here's a way to decide what to pray for "Is there anything you can do better without God's help?" For me, the answer is no, so I pray about everything. We pray and ask God to answer our prayers because He can.

Anna was a prayer warrior because she knew the power of prayer came from God's resources and abilities. God knows the future, He knows other people's hearts and intentions, He has unlimited resources, and nothing is too hard for Him.

Over the course of this study, we have touched on just a few of the numerous names and character traits of God.

We learned from Eve- He is our Creator, He is our Lord, He is our Helper

From Sarah- He is Faithful, He is God Most High, God Almight

From Miriam- I Am- LORD, He is our Healer, He is our Provide

From Naomi-He is Kind, He is our Redeemer

From the Shunammite Woman- He is a Giver, He Lives

From Athaliah-He is our Protector and Shield, He is Sovereign

From Elizabeth- He is Holy, He is our Righteousness, He is our Hope.

From Anna- He is our Messiah and Savior, He is our High Priest, He is our Sacrificial Offering.

From Lois we will learn- He is the Word, He is Good, He is Jesus.

From _____ what have you learned about God.

(Your Name)

POWERFUL PRAYERS

To pray means to ask God for something. That seems pretty straightforward, but I have found I can quickly fall into a "gimme, gimme" trap where my prayers are just a list of wants and needs. When my prayers are focused on my desires, they feel pretty shallow and petty. Many years ago, I learned an acronym to help ensure my prayers have a proper balance. The word "Pray" forms the outline.

P is for Praise- Praise and exalt God for His character, His resources, His miracles, His power, His majesty, His holiness, His love. Praising God gets your focus off your limitations and the situation. Jesus did this when he prayed – Our Father in heaven, hallowed is your name.[184]

R is for Repent- We have to repent of our sins, imperfections, unforgiveness, and unrighteousness, just as the priest had to make an offering for his sins before interceding for the people. We need to ask God to forgive our sins and trespasses as we forgive others.[185]

A is for Ask- This is really the heart of praying. Asking means that we need God to intervene in a situation. We need his help. It requires humbling ourselves to His power and sovereignty. Jesus modeled the need for daily asking for God's help when he prayed, "Give us this day our daily bread" and "Lead us not into temptation but deliver us from the evil one."[186]

Y is for Yield- Yielding your request to God puts the responsibility for that situation where it belongs – on God. You can pray as Jesus prayed, "Not my will but your will be done on earth as it is in heaven." Prayer has immense power, but with power comes responsibility. Prayer is a weapon. By asking for God's will to be done in the situation, we can see the direction that God wants it to go.

Take a minute right now to stop and pray through this outline for yourself and for a loved one.

Prayer provides a supernatural connection and the power for spiritual breakthroughs. "Prayer is our way of communicating with God. God deeply wants to have a relationship with each of us. Prayer builds our relationship and is a means of directly contacting God, our Creator, Healer, True Love, and Best Friend- any time we want. Communication is the lifeblood of any relationship. Through prayer, we can share our heart's desires, concerns, and interests to our Heavenly Father, God."[187]

Psalm 139 captures how intimately God knows us. Please read this psalm and jot down all the ways that God knows you.

God knows everything about you, when you sit down and when you get up in the morning. He has known you since you were created in your mother's womb. Even in the darkest places, you cannot hide from Him. His love is always with you, reaching up to the highest heavens and down into the depths of the sea. Oh, how He loves you and has forever loved you.

---

[184] Matthew 6:9
[185] Matthew 6:12
[186] Matthew 6:11,13
[187] Noyes, Penny, *Responding to God*. Open Door Publishing Hendersonville, NC 2009 pg. 95

Prayer is a conversation. Just as you can talk with a friend, you can talk with God. The best thing about talking with God is that He knows you intimately and loves you passionately. He completely understands you. He knows your heart, dreams, hurts, and fears because He made you. So, as you read God's Word and seek to know God, praying will become easier because you understand His heart and His great love for you.

EMBRACING CHANGE THROUGH PRAYER AND FASTING IN AN ORDINARY LIFE

Anna was widowed after seven years of marriage; she was homeless. She was worthless in the eyes of society, yet in God's eyes she was a precious messenger of His love to the people who came into the Temple. Her focus on God through prayer and fasting allowed her to see Jesus and to know that he was the Messiah. Jesus, our ultimate sacrifice, paid the price for all of our sins and imperfections; he provided the connection to God through His righteousness.

Anna was a woman who regularly prayed and fasted. Her heart to know God was rewarded with the opportunity to see Jesus face to face, know that He was her Redeemer, and hold the hand of the answer to her prayers for the Salvation of Israel. When we pray and fast, God will reveal himself to us in new and amazing ways. God has used prayer and fasting to deliver His people, guide them, show His love, and strengthen them. As you seek to know God and trust Him, prayer and fasting are valuable and powerful ways to grow closer to God during change.

HOW HAVE YOU LEARNED TO TRUST GOD THROUGH STUDYING ANNA?

CHAPTER IX

GRANDMOTHER OF GENUINE FAITH

TEACHER AND LOVER OF THE SCRIPTURES

Lived about 10-50 AD

That precious memory triggers another: your honest faith—and what a rich faith it is, handed do wn from your grandmother Lois to your mother Eunice, and now to you! And the special gift of ministry you received when I laid hands on you and prayed—keep that ablaze! God doesn't want us to be shy with His gifts, but bold and loving and sensible.
2 Timothy 1:5-7 MSG

Week 1

Lois

Before taking my two boys to meet my friend at a nice restaurant, I discussed proper table manners with them, including my rule, "No technology at the table while eating." I explained that being on their devices was rude and disrespectful to the people at the table. Then my youngest, John, said, "But mom, you do it." Ugh! I had been caught red-handed. He's right. I'll sit at the table and check the weather, or if my husband and I are having a discussion and need to look up a fact, one of us will pull out a phone to look things up. When I am out to lunch with a friend, I'll happily pull out my phone to show them a cute picture. I'll even keep my phone on the dinner table if I am expecting a call. My son called me out on my double standard because he intuitively knew that there was something wrong with my hypocrisy.

My eight-year-old pointed out one of the great inconsistencies of life; we will often tell someone the right thing to do and don't do it ourselves. Even as Christians, we don't practice what we preach. Instead, we excuse our hypocrisy with a mental explanation that somehow our situation is different. Therefore, it is okay to use our cell phones at the table, not wash our hands or talk behind someone's back. We make excuses for our compromises but are upset by doctors who smoke, police who break the law, and ministers of the Gospel who act in ungodly ways. Hypocrisy at any level is offensive unless we are the ones being hypocritical.

This chapter will study Lois, a remarkable grandmother who stood out in her community as a woman of sincere faith. Surrounded by hypocrisy, Lois was a woman of integrity who lived out her faith in such a genuine way those around her, including her daughter and her grandson, chose to follow Jesus. Lois left a godly legacy by passing on her love and knowledge of the scripture to multiple generations.

Lois is a great role model. Studying Lois will help us answer tough questions such as, "Why does God allow bad things?" and "How can we trust God in suffering?" Lois will also teach us about the importance of not being hypocritical. We will also learn about faith, the foundation for trusting God during difficult circumstances and all of life's unknowns. Finally, we will discover Lois's secret that allowed her to pass down her faith to her family in a genuine way that transformed the world.

A WOMAN OF SINCERE FAITH

Our key scripture passage for Lois comes from 2 Timothy 1:5-7. Please read these verses and write down any facts you can ascertain about Lois.

Let's find out a little more information about this family in Acts 16:1. Please look up this verse and fill in the blanks.

Paul came to Derbe and then to _____, where a disciple named _____ lived, whose mother was _____ and a _____ but whose father was a _____.

One more verse to provide insight into this family.

2 Timothy 3:15 "How from _____ you have known the Holy Scriptures…"

I chose to include Lois in this study because she was Timothy's grandmother. She provides an admirable role model for us as we get older because she was able to pass down a godly legacy to her daughter and her grandson. In 2 Timothy, the Apostle Paul wrote to encourage the young pastor Timothy and specifically mentioned Timothy's sincere and honest faith, which had been handed down from his grandmother, Lois, to his mother, Eunice, and finally, to him. Lois was a woman of sincere faith who shared her faith with her daughter and grandson, Timothy. Even though Eunice's husband was Greek and not a believer, and they lived in Lystra, which was far from Jerusalem, Timothy had studied the scriptures since he was very young. Timothy must have been taught the scriptures by his mother and grandmother since he learned them from infancy. Three generations of blessing! What an amazing legacy!

KNOWING GOD'S WORD

Lois and her grandson Timothy embraced Paul's message of Good News that Jesus Christ was their long-awaited Messiah because they knew the Holy Scriptures. In 2 Timothy 3:15, Paul wrote to Lois' grandson, Timothy, "How from infancy you have known the Holy Scriptures…." This is a remarkable statement to make about a half-Jewish and half-Greek boy raised in a city hundreds of miles away from Jerusalem.

As I thought about this, I realized what a truly remarkable statement this was. Lois was a Jewish foreigner in a small Roman outpost that didn't even have a synagogue. Timothy's father was Greek, and Lois' husband was likely Greek or Roman since her daughter Eunice was named after the Roman Goddess of Victory, Nike. With little help from her husband, Lois raised her daughter and helped raise her grandson to know the scriptures from infancy.

How do you think Lois taught Eunice and Timothy the scriptures?

This may seem like an easy question to answer; She knew the scriptures, so she taught them to her daughter and grandson. But dig a little deeper, and it gets a bit more complicated. How did she know the Scriptures? Could she read? Did she have a copy of the Holy Scriptures (the Old Testament) in her house?

These are interesting questions that can only be answered by supposition. The Jewish diaspora used a Greek translation of the scriptures called the Septuagint (LXX) during Lois's life. The Septuagint is widely quoted by Jesus and the writers of the books of the New Testament. "By the 3rd century BC, the Jewish people were widely dispersed and primarily within the Hellenistic world. Outside of Judea, many Jews may have needed synagogue readings or texts for religious study to be interpreted into Greek, producing a need for the LXX...The Septuagint enjoyed widespread use in the Hellenistic Jewish diaspora and even in Jerusalem, which had become a rather cosmopolitan (and therefore Greek-speaking) town."[188] A quick summary of this paragraph: Jews throughout the Greek-controlled regions did have some access to the scriptures.

However, it is doubtful that Lois, as a woman, would have had the ability to read in Greek or Hebrew. The most probable answer to how she learned the scriptures was by memorization. She would have memorized large amounts of scripture through both recitation and singing as a young girl. The scriptures were a part of her daily and weekly life. For example, she would have memorized Psalm 126 because it was recited as a blessing before meals as part of the *birkat hamazon*. Every New Year (Rosh Hashanah), the community would read the story of beginnings in Genesis, so as a young girl, she learned the stories of Adam and Eve and Abraham and Sarah. On special celebrations and holidays, Lois and the whole Jewish community would recite Psalm 113-118 (called Hallel).

As a very young girl, Lois learned Deuteronomy 6:4-9, the words found on a scroll in a *mezuzah* attached to the doorposts of her house. Please read Deuteronomy 6:1-9 and write verses 4-7 in the margin.

This passage of scripture was memorized by everyone in the community who physically could because it simply stated the most important tenants of their faith. Young and old would recite this passage as part of the Shema both in the morning and at night. "The Lord is one" was a critical concept when Moses taught it to the Israelites after leaving Egypt. It was important to Lois because she was surrounded by

---

[188] http://www.orthodox-christianity.com/2010/12/on-the-septuagint/

worshipers of Zeus, Hermes, and Nike. It is a critical concept for each of us to impress on our hearts since we live in a society that wants us to "coexist" and asserts that all religions are equal.

As Lois memorized this passage of scripture and inscribed it on her heart, she put the words "Love the LORD your God with all your heart and with all your soul and with all your strength" into action. As we learned from Paul's endorsement, she also made sure to teach them to her daughter and her grandson. As she went about her daily work, when she walked to get water from the town well and sat by the fire in the evenings, she shared her love of God and told her children and grandchild about the one true God. Lois' life modeled the scriptures lived out for her family and all the people in the town.

*What has helped you to learn the Scriptures?

*What are some ways that parents and grandparents can teach the Scriptures to their kids and grandkids?

For all of us, memorizing scripture has an immense value that goes beyond a mental exercise. When we allow God's Word to enter our hearts and minds, we are connecting with Christ, The Word who became flesh. On his blog, Mike Glenn of Brentwood Baptist Church put it this way: "We memorize scripture because they are the most important words ever written. And something happens to you – in you – when you hold the words of God in your mind. The words seep from your mind into your heart and when they seep down into your heart, God's Word begins to shape and reshape, that is TRANSFORM you as a person. They literally become the words that you think, the words that you say and the lens through which you view life."

If you want to embrace change, you have to trust God;

If you want to trust God, you have to know God;

If you want to know God, you have to know His Word.

When my friend Emily, who is more of an expert on rhetorical logic than I am, read my quote above, she explained that the following statement logically should be, "If you want to know His word, you have to embrace change. We can best live out our faith and come to know Christ, the Word, more intimately by embracing change. It is only through life's changes that we get to see and understand the fullness of Christ.

REAL LIFE STORIES

Lois was able to pass on her faith and belief in God to her daughter and grandson because it was an authentic faith. When Lois memorized the Shema, she learned that she was to share God's Word with her children, and she was to "Talk about them when you sit at home and when you walk along the road, when you lie down and when you get up."[189] As a young girl, her parents taught her how God had delivered their ancestors from Pharaoh and provided manna in the wilderness; these "stories" trained her to recognize God's presence and provision in Lystra. When we understand how God works and who He is-kind, loving, merciful, and good-by studying the Bible, we can recognize His provision, protection, healing, and blessing in our everyday life. Then we can share with our family and friends about how God has personally provided for us, how he has healed us, delivered us, blessed us, and made us holy. This not only encourages our faith and glorifies God, but it also helps others learn how to live out their faith.

My friend Joyce is in the process of downsizing and finding new homes for many of her precious belongings. Each item in her house has a story about a dear friend, a wonderful trip taken, or a gift from a loved one. As she shares the stories, these items that were beautiful in their own right take on a special value that goes beyond the actual value of the item. I cherish the stories about the things in her house because I cherish her. In the same way, we must be diligent in cherishing what God has done for us and teach our children and others to value what God has done for us by sharing the stories of our personal deliverance. Deuteronomy 4:9 says, "You must be very careful not to forget the things you have seen God do for you. Keep reminding yourselves, and tell your children and grandchildren as well." (CEV) We should tell stories of the good things God has done for us, just the way we tell stories of our childhood homes or favorite teenage hangouts.

Many years ago, I read God Moments by Alan D. Wright. This book highlighted the ways that God wanted his people to remember His deeds through the seven Jewish festivals: Feast of Unleavened Bread, Passover, First Fruits, Feast of Weeks, Feast of Trumpets, Day of Atonement, and Feast of Tabernacles.[190]

These annual feasts reminded them of God's provision when they lived in tents, God's protection at the Passover, God's removal of sin just as they removed yeast from their homes, and God's blessing at the beginning and end of the harvest. So, I decided to see if our family could do a better job of remembering these God Moments in our life so, on Sunday nights, we would share the times that God had provided for us, when he protected us, and when we had a desire to seek Him.

---

[189] Deuteronomy 6:7
[190] Leviticus 23

I want to challenge you to see if you can remember times when you were able to experience God's hand at work in your life or your family. Take a minute to fill out this chart with examples from your life.

God Moments	My Examples	Your Examples
Amazing Rescue- You were guarded and set free (Passover)	Protected from accident No injury in soccer game Saved from a bad choice	
Holy Attraction –You were cleansed or drawn to something noble. (Unleavened Bread and Yom Kippur)	Chose to study the Bible Turned off the TV Teenage son wanted to go to church Didn't gossip	
Unearned Blessing- You were given a blessing you couldn't attained for yourself. (First Fruits)	Given a wonderful husband and kids Job promotion God provided customers	
Revealed Truth- God spoke to you or led you (Feast of Trumpets and Weeks—Pentecost)	Understood a Bible passage Great sermon at church Christian song ministered to my heart	
Valuable Adversity – God sustained you during a difficult time (Tabernacles)[191]	God carried us through grief God gave peace in trials God gave strength in sickness	

Lois' life has helped me realize that I spend a lot of time giving my children things that don't last. She has challenged me to ask myself, "How can I align my mental, financial, and physical priorities to focus on eternal value?"

Ask God to help you make his Word and his Presence your priority. Spend time remembering the blessings He has given you. Ask Him to bring to mind areas you have resisted Him by resisting change. Repent and ask forgiveness. Hold fast to His Word. Be strong and courageous.

---

[191] Chart modified from *God Moments*, Alan D. Wright Multnomah Publishers Sisters OR 1999 p.54

Week 1

LOIS' BACKGROUND AND HISTORY

Let's learn a little more about Lois, Timothy, and the Apostle Paul, who was named Saul, on our journey to discover the secrets of being women of sincere and honest faith. To start, let's go back in time to fill in the gaps since Jesus' dedication at the Temple with Mary and Anna. After the dedication, Mary and Joseph fled to Egypt for the first two years of Jesus' life. They returned to their homeland and settled in Galilee. Like any young Jewish boy, he went to the Temple with his family on holy days and helped his parents around the home.

While Jesus was growing up in Galilee, another boy was born about 300 miles away in Tarsus of Cilia, now in modern Turkey. This little boy named Saul grew up to be the Apostle Paul. Saul was circumcised on the eight-day as any other Jewish baby boy. Though he grew up in a foreign country that was a long way from Jerusalem, Saul was a devout Jew who studied the Bible at a very young age. As a teenager, he moved to Jerusalem to study under a wise rabbi named Gamaliel and later became a Pharisee, an influential group of religious leaders. Pharisees studied the Law and believed that the way to have a right relationship with God was through obedience to the Law.

While Saul was studying the Scripture in Jerusalem, Jesus was working as a young carpenter. When Jesus was about 30 years old, he was baptized by Elizabeth's son, John the Baptist. At that time, Jesus began his public ministry, which is chronicled in the Gospels of Matthew, Mark, Luke, and John. Jesus' public ministry lasted for about three years until his death by crucifixion and miraculous resurrection to life on Easter Morning in 30 AD.

After the resurrection, Jesus met with his disciples and other followers for forty days before ascending into heaven. While he was still with them, he told them, "Do not leave Jerusalem, but wait for the gift my Father promised, which you have heard me speak about. For John baptized with water, but in a few days you will be baptized with the Holy Spirit."[192] During Pentecost (The Feast of Weeks and revealed truth on the chart last week), the believers were transformed and empowered by the Holy Spirit. This led to a time a great rejoicing and miracles. Jesus healed many people, and their lives were forever changed by believing in Jesus. However, the mass conversions of so many people led to jealousy from established Jewish leaders and the persecution of the believers.

---

[192] Luke 1:4-5

Saul became one of the most fervent Jewish leaders persecuting Christians. He even obtained a permit from the High Priest to capture followers of Christ in Damascus and imprison them. However, on the road to Damascus, Saul had a life-changing encounter with Jesus.[193] In the blink of an eye, God changed Saul from an adversary of Christians into Paul, a follower of Jesus. Like Sarah and Abraham, God changed Saul's name to indicate a change in their relationship. After his transformation, he traveled throughout the Mediterranean region to share the good news of Jesus Christ. Several of his journeys took him across what is now the Turkish peninsula through the ancient crossroads city of Lystra.

As we learned in Week One, Lystra was the town where Timothy, Lois, and Eunice lived. Lystra was a stopping point on the Persian Royal Road; a road used 500 years before Christ to connect cities in modern-day Iraq, Iran, and the coast of Turkey. During Lois's time, the Romans controlled this area and used the road as a post road between the far reaches of their Empire.

> *In the blink of an eye,* God changed Saul from an adversary of Christians into Paul, a follower of Jesus.

Lystra was a small market town and Roman military outpost. Historians believe that most of the people in the town other than Roman soldiers were uneducated Lycaonians who came from a small Anatolian tribe and spoke their own language. Most Bible scholars believe that Lystra did not have a synagogue since Paul first preached outside rather than in a synagogue. This is a significant detail because having a synagogue required a quorum of ten Jewish men. Lois, Eunice, and Timothy were minorities surrounded by Greeks, Romans, and Lycaonians.

Though Lystra was in the Roman Empire, life in Lystra was influenced by mythology and the worship of Greek and Roman gods. Lois is a Greek name that means "more desirable" and "better." Her daughter, Eunice's name, is a derivative of the name Nike, the Roman Goddess of Victory. There was a temple to Zeus in Lystra. People worshiped and feared the pantheon of gods found in Greek mythology. Zeus was the leader of the gods, Hermes was the messenger of the gods, Poseidon was the god of the sea, and Hades was the god of the underworld. They believed these gods could take human form, bring victory in battle, determine success in farming, and facilitate the birth of many children. Though they were gods, they weren't perfect. They had flaws and weaknesses and were selfish and capricious. As a result, the people sought to appease the gods and earn their favor through worship and sacrifice at their temples.

When I was a kid, I enjoyed Greek mythology stories, but I never once believed they were real. Greek myths were no different from Grimm's fairy tales or a Nancy Drew mystery. Movies like The *Little Mermaid, Hercules*, and *Percy Jackson and the Lightning Thief* contain elements of Greek myths and are entertaining but certainly aren't true. However, for Timothy and Lois, Greek myths influenced their city and many aspects of their neighbors' lives.

---

[193] Act 13:9, Acts 9

To get a picture of what life was like for Lois in Lystra, please read Acts 14:8-18. What did Paul do when he arrived in Lystra that amazed the people? Vs. 8-10

Who did they think Paul and Barnabas were? Vs. 12

What did Paul say to the people about himself in vs. 15?

What did Paul say about God in vs. 15-17?

Why do you think knowing this about God was important to the people of Lystra, like Lois, and to people today?

Though Lystra was a part of the Roman Empire, Greek influence on the culture and religious beliefs were pervasive. The people's hopes and dreams of having a relationship with their gods had finally been fulfilled. Zeus had come to their town! They were so amazed by God's miraculous healing of the man through Paul that they decided to worship Paul and Barnabas as the Greek gods, Zeus and Hermes. Even the priest of Zeus tried to worship them and give sacrifices to them!

Paul crushed their false hopes in verse 15 by saying that he and Barnabas were only human but gave them a new hope with good news about the living God. As we learned in our study of Eve, in Genesis 1, "Elohim" is God our Creator. He made everything in the heavens and earth. All creation testifies to His rule and provision. The "good news" that Paul shared with the people of Lystra was life-changing for those who worshipped Greek gods and also for Jewish believers who prayed for the Messiah. Paul had proclaimed that the God who created the heavens and the sea was living. He was alive! This sentence creates a link between "Elohim," the name of God used in Genesis 1 when He created the heavens and the earth to Jesus, who had died and was now living and reigning in heaven.

Imagine how revolutionary this "good news" was for a Jewish woman like Lois, living in a foreign land and dreaming of the Messiah. How did this message change her view of God?

For Lois, living in a foreign land far away from the Temple in Jerusalem, the knowledge that the Messiah had come was life changing. In this passage, Paul makes the connection for all of us between God, who we studied in Genesis and Exodus, our Creator, Provider, and Lord, and the "good news" of Jesus. Jesus, God in the flesh, was the ultimate sacrifice and source of righteousness for all who believed.

Paul's message was equally life-changing for the Greeks and Lyconians living in Lystra: God was good! The Greek word for God is Theos (θεός.) Paul tells the people that God made the heavens, the earth, the sea, and everything in them. Zeus and Poseidon weren't in control of the heavens and the sea- God was. He made it, and he was the Master of it all.

God has shown kindness by giving rain from heaven and crops in their seasons. Acts 14:17 contains the phrase "he has shown kindness" in the NIV; other versions of the Bible, such as the NLT, translate it as "evidence of himself and His goodness." Imagine how amazing this news was to Lois and the other people in Lystra—God is good! They could see evidence of His goodness in His concern for His creation. He was not fickle, selfish, or capricious. He is good, and he does good things for His people. He is the provider by giving plenty of food and filling hearts with joy.

Please look up the following verses and write them out; this may seem redundant, but I want to make sure this concept gets into your heart.
Psalm 25:8

Psalm 86:5

Psalm 100:5

Psalm 106:1

Sometimes it is hard to trust God, so how could knowing about the kindness and goodness of God, help you trust him?

Knowing that God is good, loving, and kind helps me trust Him even in the worst situations. He is sovereign and Lord of all. When things aren't good, I know that they are either the consequences of sin and that God in His goodness will bring justice to the situation or that God will use the hard times for the good in the lives of those who love Him and are called according to His purpose.[194]

---

[194] Romans 8:28

God's goodness helps me trust Him regardless of my immediate circumstances. Today, most people don't believe that Zeus is real or that Poseidon is in the ocean, but many of us don't trust God because, deep down we really don't think that God is good. Deeply hurt people will ask, "If God is good, then why did such a horrible tragedy happen to me or my loved one?" Skeptics will look at the world and say, "If a good God exists, why doesn't He do something about all the wickedness in the world?" I even have friends who believe in God but at the same time feel that God might just have something bad up His sleeve that He will use to get them.

Questions posed by my friends, skeptics, and hurt people shift the focus from God to a focus on sin, evil, and our fallen world. As we learned in Chapter 1, because of Adam and Eve's sin, evil was unleashed in this world. Sin has led to many consequences, including physical suffering, damage to our relationship with God and others, and even changed humankind's relationship with the Earth. Though sin and wickedness have transformed our world and our relationship with God from one that was very good to one tainted by sin, God has not changed. He is good. Rather than focusing on sin, wickedness, and our fallen world, to truly trust God, we have to focus on Him and His unchanging character.

Many of us **don't trust God because deep down we really do not think that God is good.**

Throughout the Bible, God is described as good and what He does is good. The word "good" has multiple meanings; it can mean good as in material items like good food or good land, it also means good as in ethical, the opposite of bad, and it means kind and agreeable. Here is the list I copied from www.BlueLetterBible.com on the meanings of good.

a) pleasant, agreeable (to the senses)

b) pleasant (to the higher nature)

c) good, excellent (of its kind)

d) good, rich, valuable in estimation

e) good, appropriate, becoming

f) better (comparative)

g) glad, happy, prosperous (of man's sensuous nature)

h) good understanding (of man's intellectual nature)

i) good, kind, benign

j) good, right (ethical)

Some churches greet their congregations with the statement, "God is good," and the congregation replies, "All the time. Then the leader responds, "All the time," and the congregation replies, "God is good." As you look through the meanings of "good" above, let the goodness of our God sink into your heart.

For Lois and the other people of Lystra, the knowledge that God is good was life changing. Since God is the same yesterday, today, and forever, He is good. If we allow this truth about God to transform our hearts, it will revolutionize our lives.

God is good. He is all of this and more. To apply this knowledge to your life, write a prayer acknowledging God is good and thanking God for His abundant goodness.

Week 3

GOD IS GOOD EVEN IN HARD TIMES

Soon after preaching about the kindness and goodness of God, Paul's visit to Lystra got really uncomfortable. Paul had an awful experience that seemed to contradict the facts that God is good and kind.

Review Acts 14:8-21 to find out what happened next and fill in the blanks from verse 19 "... They _____ Paul and _____ him outside the city, thinking he was _____.

I would call this a very bad day- worse than any day I have ever experienced – people threw stones at him, then dragged him out of the city and left him to die. Yet Paul got up and went back Lystra and challenged these new believers to remain true to the faith with this statement, "We must go through many hardships to enter the kingdom of God." [195]

---

[195] Acts 14:22

*How would you explain to a friend that God is good even though Paul warned believers in Christ that "We must go through many hardships to enter the kingdom of God?" Please write out your thoughts below.

Being able to answer this question for yourself and your friends is a foundational concept for growing your faith. Here's how Paul explained this idea in a letter to Timothy, Lois' grandson, while looking back on this difficult time in Lystra. He said, "You, however, know all about my teaching, my way of life, my purpose, faith, patience, love, endurance, persecutions, sufferings—what kinds of things happened to me in Antioch, Iconium and Lystra, the persecutions I endured. Yet the Lord rescued me from all of them. *In fact, everyone who wants to live a godly life in Christ Jesus will be persecuted, while evildoers and impostors will go from bad to worse, deceiving and being deceived.*"[196] (Italics mine)

Paul gives the big picture to Timothy. We don't go through hardships and suffering to earn our salvation- Christ did that once and for all on the cross. Hardship and suffering came to Paul because of the Gospel of Jesus Christ. Jewish leaders and unbelievers felt threatened by the message of God's grace and goodness through Jesus Christ, and they violently reacted to this message and nearly killed Paul.

The Lord saved him from all of them, but while he was being dragged out of the city and left for dead, I am sure he wondered why God hadn't intervened before he was attacked. Going through times of suffering for our faith does not mean that we are sinning or out of God's will. The selfish, sinful hearts of the people in Lystra led them to assault Paul. Like Paul, we will suffer through no fault of our own because the people close to us sinned.

Our actions, other people's sins, and unforeseen circumstances do not change God's character. He is good all the time. Hard times and suffering are not proof that God is not good; We can be confident that in the end, just as God rescued Paul, He will rescue us.

*Have you or someone you know experienced times of suffering because of following Jesus and His will?

There have been times that I have lost friends, broken up with boyfriends, and have been left out of social activities because I have stood up for what is right. I faced opposition from people who just didn't understand why I wouldn't go along with the crowd. My friends have also suffered for standing up for

---

[196] 2 Timothy 3:10-13

the Gospel. One public school teacher was threatened because of her faith in Christ. My family and I support missionaries who live in dangerous and hostile environments.

Suffering for the Gospel is one consequence of following Jesus Christ. However, we can be confident because God is good, loving, and kind; the suffering will last only for a short time. Like Paul we can trust that God will rescue us, if not here than in eternity.

As a teenager, I was deeply afraid that if I whole-heartedly sought the kingdom of God, I would be worse off than if I didn't follow Jesus. I now know that not following Jesus leads to much greater pain and the loss of God's blessings for me. Whatever loss I face, it is nothing compared to the surpassing worth of knowing Christ Jesus my Lord.[197]

ETERNAL VALUE

I recently read a true story of the little boy who lived about 30 miles from my home. One Sunday in 1799, he found a pretty rock in a stream. His family used this 17-pound rock as a doorstop until a man from Fayetteville offered to buy the stone, and the boy's father, John Reed, asked for the "big price" of $3.50 (about $65 in current dollars.) The man gladly paid it because he knew the rock was gold worth $3,600 (in 1799). Today, that 17-pound rock of gold would be worth about $490,000!

Jesus pointed out the value of the Kingdom of Heaven in a couple of stories in Matthew 13:44-46. Jesus said, "The kingdom of heaven is like treasure hidden in a field. When a man found it, he hid it again, and then in his joy went and sold all he had and bought that field. Again, the kingdom of heaven is like a merchant looking for fine pearls. When he found one of great value, he went away and sold everything he had and bought it."

In these two parables, Jesus is pointing out the immense value of the Kingdom of God compared to the small cost of the field or the pearl. The man and the merchant were both knowledgeable investors. They understood the immense value of the treasure and the great pearl—having it was worth more than everything else they owned, and the price they would pay was insignificant to the asset's underlying value.

These two parables emphasize the immense worth of the Kingdom of God. What Jesus is saying in these parables is that even if you have to sell your $300,000 house, it is worth it to buy the field with the 17lb lump of gold, worth almost half a million dollars. You have to give up something to pay for the land, but the value of the gold in the field dwarfs the cost of selling your house. In the same way, suffering for the Gospel is worth the eternal glory of the Kingdom of God.

---

[197] Philippians 3:8

In both of these parables, Jesus taught about the immense value and eternal worth of the Kingdom of God. How can you live your life focusing on the eternal rather than the temporary?

I constantly struggle to rightly value the things of God compared to the stuff of life that I can touch and feel. Everything like sports, leisure activities, Facebook, friends, working, cooking, cleaning, and shopping captures my attention. All the things pull me with their immediate benefits and instant gratification. In contrast, focusing on the eternal has cost my time and money. My house might not be as clean, I spend less time on social media, I am invited to fewer parties, and I have less money for myself, but my investment in seeking the kingdom of God and His righteousness will reap eternal rewards.

Though I have experienced moments when standing up for what I believe has been difficult, I can see that my suffering was relatively short-lived compared to eternity. God has faithfully rescued me from difficult and sad times. He has given me so many incredible blessings; a wonderful group of godly friends, a great husband, and the knowledge that I will be a part of the best party ever in heaven one day.

Paul went to Lystra to share the good news of the living God who was kind, good, and so unlike the fickle, capricious, false Greek gods, they worshiped. This Gospel was worth any suffering because it was so immensely valuable. Though Paul faced hardship and persecution, he knew that the sufferings of this life were temporary compared to the eternal glory of the Kingdom of God. He wrote, "For our light and momentary troubles are achieving for us an eternal glory that far outweighs them all. So we fix our eyes not on what is seen, but on what is unseen, since what is seen is temporary, but what is unseen is eternal."[198] The tradeoff between earthly suffering and heavenly glory in the Kingdom of God is of no consequence. An eternity of glory compared to temporary suffering.

Jesus came that we might have abundant life, yet He also said suffering is a part of following him. Take a moment to repent for focusing on the temporal rather than the eternal. Pray and ask God to show you how to embrace an abundant life even while living in a world of heartbreak, loss, and change.

---

[198] 2 Corinthians 4:17-18

Week 4

OPPOSITE OF SINCERE=HYPOCRISY

Lois was a woman of integrity whose actions matched her faith. Paul commended Lois because she had a sincere faith. I looked up the Greek word translated "sincere;" it means "anti-hypocritical." The opposite of sincerity is hypocrisy. Being hypocritical was the default state for most people in the Greco-Roman world, making Timothy's and Lois's genuine faith stand out like sunflowers in a clover field. Hypocrisy means that we aren't being true in our hearts or actions to God. A sincere faith is real and genuine.

I believe that much of the world's frustration with people who call themselves Christians comes from Christians who aren't living out their faith. Our faith in God should affect every part of our lives, how we spend our money, who we hang out with, how we do our jobs, and how we raise our kids.

We can be hypocritical when we have the right external actions and "look the part," but our faith is not sincere in our hearts. In Matthew 23, Jesus attacked religious hypocrisy. He pointed out the hypocrisy of people who would make sure they gave just the right amount of cumin or dill in their offering but didn't practice the more essential parts of the Law like justice, mercy, and faithfulness. These same people would make sure that everything looked good on the outside, but they were full of greed and self-indulgence on the inside.

Have you known people that looked the part, they went to church and said all the right things but on the inside were rotten? How did that make you feel?

James, the brother of Jesus, points out the hypocrisy in people who know the Bible but don't act on their faith. James 2:17 calls this faith "dead." The Message paraphrase puts James 2:14-17 this way,

"Dear friends, do you think you'll get anywhere in this if you learn all the right words but never do anything? Does merely talking about faith indicate that a person really has it? For instance, you come upon an old friend dressed in rags and half-starved and say, "Good morning, friend! Be clothed in Christ! Be filled with the Holy Spirit!" and walk off without providing so much as a coat or a cup of soup—where does that get you? Isn't it obvious that God-talk without God-acts is outrageous nonsense?"

James also warns readers not to settle for a faith that only acknowledges God because even demons do that. When our pastor preached on this passage, he pointed out that demons have a type of faith; they believe in God, they acknowledge that Jesus is the Son of God, and they even know their destiny is Hell.[199] Demons may tremble in fear, but they do not let their faith in God transform their lives through obedience and worship.[200]

In contrast, Abraham and Rahab are commended by Jesus's brother James for demonstrating their faith through their actions.[201] Rahab's story in Joshua 2 is an amazing reminder that no matter what we have done, God can transform our lives through faith. Even though Rahab was a Canaanite and a prostitute, she believed in God and boldly proclaimed that the Lord had given the Israelites the land and that the "Lord your God is God in heaven above and on the earth below."[202] Not only did Rahab believe in God, but she acted on her faith; she hid the spies and then later shared her faith with her family by inviting them to stay in her house when the Israelites attacked her town.

A sincere faith results in a love for God and love for others. When Paul wrote to Timothy as a young pastor, he encouraged him to focus on God's work which is by faith. Please read 1 Timothy 1:5 and fill in the blanks. The goal of this command is _____, which comes from a _____ and a _____ and a _____.

Filling in the blanks (in order) with love, a pure heart, a good conscience, and sincere faith highlights the connection between our love for God and others. A pure heart represents our internal thoughts; a good conscience is related to our outward actions, and a sincere faith is not hypocritical.

Romans 12:9-10 expands on the idea of living in a non-hypocritical way that is based on love with this admonition, "Love must be sincere. Hate what is evil; cling to what is good. Be devoted to one another in love. Honor one another above yourselves."

In the box on the next page is The Message version of this verse. I love it. It makes me think of those signs at *Homegoods* or *Hobby Lobby* that have positive thoughts. It is so much more than a cute saying because it is the living Word of God. Living this way will change your life and the lives of the people around you, just as Lois's family was transformed because of her faith.

Our faith must include a belief in God and Jesus Christ as His Son as the only means to salvation and trust in God that leads to obedience and following God's will. Though our actions don't save us, our salvation should change how we live every moment of our lives. Working out our faith is a process that means we won't always be perfect, but we are becoming more like Christ every day.

---

[199] http://www.foresthill.org/watch-and-listen/weekend-message/faithworks/faith-without-works-is-dead.html
[200] James 2:19
[201] James 2:20-25
[202] Joshua 2:11

I have a friend who recently became a Christian after many years of pursuing what she wanted rather than God. It has been exciting to hear about her enthusiasm and desire to know God more and trust Him more. Her heart has been dramatically changed, yet there are still patterns in her life that some people would say are ungodly.

While my friend's process of becoming holier in her behavior is more obvious than some people's, no matter how long we have been walking with God, we are all still in the process of becoming more like Christ. Unfortunately, at times, we are less than holy; we are not loving; we don't have a pure heart, and we don't choose actions that lead to a good conscience. As a result, we are all potentially vulnerable for a judgmental person saying about us, "How dare she do such and such and call herself a Christian?" Comments like this can be discouraging and can even lead us to embrace a form of hypocrisy that thinks, "I am not going to put myself out in public as a Christian, so people won't judge me." This is the type of hypocrisy I am most prone to do. One example of this in my own life is that I won't put a Christian sticker on my car because I don't want people to judge my driving skills or parking ability, which I must admit aren't all that great. Lines are a suggestion, right?

> *LOVE* FROM THE CENTER OF WHO YOU ARE; DON'T FAKE IT. RUN FOR DEAR LIFE FROM EVIL; HOLD ON FOR DEAR LIFE TO GOOD. BE GOOD FRIENDS WHO LOVE DEEPLY; PRACTICE PLAYING SECOND FIDDLE
> RM 12:9-10 (MSG)

FOLLOW ME AS I FOLLOW CHRIST

The Apostle Paul wasn't perfect, but rather than hiding his faith and avoiding accountability, he let himself be judged by believers and his enemies. He even challenged new Christians to use him as a role model when he said, "Imitate me, as I imitate Christ."[203] People are wired to learn by watching each other, Paul wanted to give us a good example to follow. If we aren't intentional to seek out good examples, we will be enticed by evil.

Paul warned in Philippians 3:17-19, "Brothers, join in imitating me, and keep your eyes on those who walk according to the example you have in us. For many, of whom I have often told you and now tell you even with tears, walk as enemies of the cross of Christ. Their end is destruction, their god is their belly, and they glory in their shame, with minds set on earthly things.

What are the four characteristics of poor role models who are enemies of Christ in Philippians 3:17-19?

---

[203] 1 Corinthians 11:1

1. *Their end is destruction.* They intentionally destroy relationships, create chaos and ruin lives. Much of their life is wasted in pursuit of short-term thrills and material success.

2. *Their God is their belly.* They are motivated and driven by what makes them feel good. They have elevated their feelings over God's Word. Their desires and cravings control how they spend their time, money, and attention.

3. *They glory in their shame.* Enemies of the cross of Christ delight in a distorted sense of right and wrong. They celebrate ungodly behaviors and immoral life choices that they should be ashamed of and shame others for being narrow-minded. They actively recruit others to join them in hedonistic, self-seeking, indulgent, and destructive behavior.

4. *Their minds are set on earthly things.* They are focused on temporal, worldly things rather than the eternal things of God. They have a materialistic focus.

Have you known or read about people who are like this?

It is vital to be careful around such people. Following them will lead you us away from Christ and limit the blessings God has for you.

We all learn by watching. I've learned tennis from watching Pros, other players, and my husband. Kids learn dances from Tik Tok, and my son built a computer after watching YouTube videos. We need to seek out role models, friends, and mentors who will point us to Jesus. And we need to be willing to be a role model, mentor, and friend to others on their faith journey. The people around us are watching and learning from us; so, let's make sure we share the most important thing, Jesus Christ.

If we aren't willing to step up and be held accountable for our behavior, evil people will entice our loved ones and friends down a path to destruction. We don't have to be perfect, but we should be ready to share what we have learned about Christ with others, just like teenagers help their friends learn dance moves and bakers share cooking tips.

As a friend and mentor, being sincere and authentic is more important than being perfect. We can inspire others to learn from our relationship with Christ and invite them to, "Follow me as I follow Christ." Every believer is a living testimony of God's grace and role model for the people around them. Let's start acting like one!

Choosing to follow good role models and being wary of bad influences will lead to blessings in our lives and bless the people around us who are learning from us and imitating our words and actions. Who are some people that may be watching and learning from your faith journey?

How can you intentionally encourage them to follow you as you follow Christ?

JUDGE NOT, LEAST YOU BE JUDGED

I've realized that some of fear of being a spiritual role model comes from living in a culture that constantly judges me for what I eat, wear, or do. As a kid, I felt judged for the clothes I wore, the style of my hair, and what brand of jeans I was wearing. Television shows like "What Not to Wear" and magazine articles on "fashion don'ts" compound that feeling of being constantly judged. Many people in our society have responded to this by saying, "Don't judge me, and I won't judge you." While this defensive response seems to make sense when you feel attacked on all sides, it is unfortunately in conflict with the Bible, which tells us that believers will, in fact judge the world.[204]

"But Penny," I can hear you saying, "What about that passage that says, 'Judge not least you be judged?'" Good question- let's look at it right now.

Please read Luke 6:36-42 and fill in the blanks-

36 _____, just as your Father is merciful.

37_____ and you will not be judged.

_____, and you will not be condemned.

_____ and you will be forgiven.

38_____, and it will be given to you. …

_____ it will be measured to you…….

42 first, _____ and then you will see clearly to remove the speck from your brother's eye.

"Judge not, "Judge not, and you will not be judged" is quoted by many people and perceived to mean the same thing as "Don't judge me and I won't judge you"; however, in context, it is a holy standard issued by Jesus to believers so that we live lives of mercy and integrity even as we hold other believers accountable.

This passage starts with: "Be merciful, just as your Father is merciful." Here's an important concept to add to your understanding of God's character: just as God is good, God is merciful. God's

_____

[204] 1 Corinthians 6:1-3

mercy towards us requires us to be merciful to others. If we fully understand God's mercy to us, we will show mercy in our relationships with others by changing how we judge, condemn, forgive, and give to others.

Two thousand years ago, Jesus was appalled by the hypocritical behavior of the religious elite. Unfortunately, society hasn't changed much. As humans, we easily fall into the trap of judging people by their actions, looks, style of hair, and clothes. Jesus is clearly telling us, "Do not judge." To apply this command, we need to ensure that we are not judging and slandering other believers based on outward appearance because only God knows their hearts. One of my friends realized she would judge someone's church attendance as a measure of their spirituality until she was too sick to go to church then, she realized that even church attendance wasn't a measure of one's heart for God.

As believers, we have been freed from condemnation through Christ's sacrifice.[205] If Jesus does not condemn them, neither should we. We also need to forgive. Living as brothers and sisters in Christ means that we will find ourselves in situations where we get offended and hurt by other believers. Forgiving others starts with being mindful of the great forgiveness that Christ has given us. When we truly grasp His love and forgiveness, it is much easier to forgive others. Finally, we should give generously. "What goes around comes around" is a popular saying that sums up the blessings of giving. Christ generously has given us grace, forgiveness, and everything we need, and we will receive a significant blessing if we follow His example and give generously to others.

My hypocrisy predisposes me to see it in other people, the same way that I am more likely to notice other people who drive the same type of car.

Jesus' command to get the plank out of our eye challenges all of us to not be hypocritical. To do this, we must appreciate the mercy that God has shown to us so that we can show His mercy to others. Finally, we need to understand that we are not to be judgmental even as we are supposed to judge other believers. The only way that we can do this is to follow Christ's command and make sure we judge ourselves. Are we living lives of integrity? Though we are saved by grace, are we holding ourselves to the standard of behavior that non-Christians expect from Christ-followers? Are we excusing mean, selfish, ungodly behavior because we're "not perfect, just forgiven?" If someone identifies a speck in our eye, are we humbly asking Christ to remove it and not justifying our unrighteous behavior? Vigilance in actively seeking and destroying the planks in our lives will allow us to fully experience the gift of seeing clearly and give us the proper perspective and humility to help others experience God's blessings. A humble heart and a focus on God's holiness and amazing sacrifice will allow us to receive assistance when another believer identifies a speck in our eye.

---

[205] Romans 8:1-2

"Judge and you will be judged" in Luke 6:34 is a warning. When we point out the speck in someone else's eye, people around us will feel justified in judging us. Similarly, if we don't have a humble heart when someone points out our sins, our natural response will be to justify our behavior and attack the accuser's credibility. This can create a damaging cycle of antagonism or avoidance. Fear of attack can keep us from fulfilling our responsibility as brothers and sisters in Christ to hold each other accountable to a holy standard.

The key to understanding Luke 6:36-42 is that Jesus is telling us first to judge ourselves before judging others. I have learned through the years that when I see any hypocrisy in another person's life, it is a red flag warning that indicates I need to examine my own life and repent of my sin. My hypocrisy predisposes me to see my sins in other people, the same way that I am more likely to notice other people who drive the same type of car as I do. After God has revealed a place of hypocrisy, I need to repent of my sin, and often, I have had to apologize to the people around me. The wonderful thing is that when I repent, God allows me to experience His grace and, in turn, have mercy towards others in their weakness. We will appreciate God's amazing mercy, grace, and forgiveness only by coming to terms with our sin. Next, by following the model of our Heavenly Teacher, we will be able to extend grace to other believers, our "brothers and sisters" in Christ, even when we encourage them to take the speck out of their eye. Our words and actions will be filled with love, grace, and humility based on the magnitude of Christ's forgiveness to us.

Please take a minute to pray and ask God to reveal any places of hypocrisy in your life. Our amazing God forgives all of our sins. He is so good. After you repent, take some time to embrace God's amazing grace and mercy. He loves you so much- His love never changes, and His mercies never come to an end.

A LASTING LEGACY

I would like to leave behind an enormous inheritance to the people I love and to a bunch of other random people just for fun. Proverbs 13:22 puts it this way, "A good person leaves an inheritance for their children's children, but a sinner's wealth is stored up for the righteous." Not many of us will be able to leave an inheritance to people we don't know, but all of us can leave a legacy that will last for eternity. The Message paraphrase of 2 Timothy 2:1 describes Lois' faith as a rich faith! While there is nothing wrong with leaving an inheritance for our children, grandchildren, and strangers, our goal should be to pass on the most important legacy, a rich faith; but like any other inheritance, we have to have it to give it.

True, genuine, sincere faith draws people to Christ, but hypocritical religion repulses people. Too often, kids are turned off by the hypocrisy they see in their parents' lives. Our minister says that "faith is caught, not taught." If we want to leave a lasting inheritance that stands the test of time, we have to live out our faith—in a real and genuine way—and in the process, we will create a legacy of real and genuine faith for our family, friends, and the other people that God brings into our lives.

As we live out our faith, not just in words but in actions, we must begin by practicing our faith with our families and blessing the people around us. Please read how author Eugene Peterson paraphrases James 3:17-18 in The Message and makes this point about how we should live and love, "Real wisdom, God's wisdom, begins with a holy life and is characterized by getting along with others. It is gentle and reasonable, overflowing with mercy and blessings, not hot one day and cold the next, not two-faced. You can develop a healthy, robust community that lives right with God and enjoy its results only if you do the hard work of getting along with each other, treating each other with dignity and honor."

*Can you think of a person who has this "real wisdom" of a holy life and gets along with others like the person James 3:17-18 describes? Share what you admire about them.

This book started many pages ago with the verse from Titus 2:3-5 "Likewise, teach the older women to be reverent in the way they live, not to be slanderers or addicted to much wine, but to teach what is good. Then they can train the younger women to love their husbands and children, to be self-controlled and pure, to be busy at home, to be kind, and to be subject to their husbands, so that no one will malign the word of God."

Throughout the past chapters, we looked at nine women's lives who have become a model of how to live out our faith. Lois seems to be a woman who lived out this verse in Titus 2. Lois was reverent and received the good news that Paul and Barnabas taught about Jesus and allowed it to transform her life and her relationships with others.

In a hostile environment with a husband who may not have been a believer, she taught her daughter and grandson the Holy Scriptures and was a woman of sincere (non-hypocritical faith) based in love. She modeled how to be self-controlled and pure by not gossiping or being judgmental. Through studying Lois, we learned that we should judge ourselves, repent, and receive God's forgiveness so that even as we hold others accountable, we can show them God's mercy, and no one will malign the Word of God because of our lack of faith or hypocrisy.

HOW HAVE YOU LEARNED TO TRUST GOD THROUGH STUDYING LOIS?

Wrap Up

WE'VE COVERED THOUSANDS OF YEARS OF HISTORY, STUDYING THE LIVES OF NINE WOMEN ON OUR JOURNEY TO LEARN HOW WE CAN EMBRACE CHANGE BY TRUSTING GOD. WHAT IS ONE THING YOU LEARNED FROM EACH OF THESE WOMEN?

EVE

SARAH

MIRIAM

NAOMI

SHUNAMMITE WOMAN

ATHALIAH

ELIZABETH

ANNA

LOIS

PLEASE TAKE A MINUTE TO FLIP BACK THROUGH THE STUDY TO REVIEW WHAT YOU HAVE LEARNED AND TO ANSWER THE FOLLOWING TWO QUESTIONS.

WHAT HAVE YOU LEARNED ABOUT GOD DURING THIS STUDY?

HOW DOES THAT HELP YOU TRUST HIM?

Now to Him who is able to keep you from stumbling and to make you stand in the presence of His glory blameless with great joy, to the only God our Savior, through Jesus Christ our Lord, be glory, majesty, dominion and authority, for all time and now and forever.
Amen. Jude 24-25

Appendix

Sandy Brown's Time Line Tool is a process that involves one asking Jesus' into their life, acknowledging the work of the Holy Spirit, visualizing gathering painful feelings and giving them to Jesus through forgiveness, repentance of vows and curses and allowing Jesus to heal them. Search "Sandra Brown Timeline Tool" on YouTube. https://youtu.be/9lxMgu2KW6o

Jesus has covered all your negative experiences with his blood, they are washed clean. After covering your negative experiences with the Blood of Jesus, check and see if you still remember the pain or hurt of these times. If you do not hurt, REJOICE, God has healed you. Every good thing in our lives is the work of the Holy Spirit. If you do, REJOICE! Because God has started the healing process through the work of the Holy Spirit.

Continue the Healing Process with these 4 Steps

1. **Forgiveness -Matt 6:12; Eph 6:4**

   Forgive the people and yourself who hurt, abused, or wronged you (and /or others you care about). "I forgive myself and the others and I accept God's forgiveness and healing."

2. **Repentance - I John 1:9-10**

   Repent of any wrongdoings that you have done. "I repent of my reactions, and I confess that I was angry, wrong, selfish, and I receive the gifts of God's goodness in exchange."

3. **Renounce and recognize and vows or curses you have made.**

   "God, Forgive me for saying words like "I will never do that again!" or "I wish I were dead." "I give these vows and curses to Jesus, and I ask for good words to replace them." Break off any curses made. (Examples:"Damn them" or "I wish I were dead") Gal 3:13 Renounce any vows made. (Examples: "I will never do that again" or "I will never talk to them or trust him again") - John 3:17.

4. **Ask Jesus to come into your painful scenario.** Then, ask God to heal it completely; and next, receive God's blessings such as joy instead of sorrow; deeper understanding of God as a result of hardships. God can replace and restore what was taken and destroyed.

Finally, pray for God to seal the good work and that God would seal them from any backlash or evil. - Matt 6:13

Acknowledgments

Thank you to my OG Bible Study partner Kathryn, my Hebrew teacher Barbara, and to the wonderful women who were my weekly motivation to get each chapter done for Bible Study on Thursday at 10:00 am - Elizabeth, Vallee, Lois, Jaletta, Diana, and Laura. Your faithfulness, encouragement, perspective, and wisdom are gifts in my life. I especially loved that we had an Elizabeth and a Lois in our group- two women that I aspire to be more like.

A special thanks to each of my reviewers. Angie Moses, Karen Murdock, Julie Choi, Cathy Kasem, Joyce Rudisill, Nancy Summers, Felicia Bissell Murray and my mom, Sandy Brown. Each of you contributed in your own way through encouragement, proof reading, helping me formulate my thoughts and challenging me to think about how others would perceive what I had written. I am so grateful to call you all friend.

As I have reviewed the proofs of this Bible Study, I have realized that I must thank God for bringing some amazing women into my life through Mars Hill College. Over 20 years ago, I showed up as a freshman on the fourth floor of Edna Corpening Moore Dormitory and was blessed to live near Becky, Laura, Betts, Loren, Amee, and Karena. My sophomore year God brought Erica, Sarah, and Emily into my life. I cherish each of you girls, I marvel at God's provision so many years ago and his amazing grace evidenced in your friendship, wisdom, and faithfulness. You guys are so much a part of this book and my story.

Thanks to my wonderful husband, my super boys Chris and John and my delightful Hillary, her husband Jeremy and Jeremy Jr. for loving me and for being used by God to show me His amazing love, grace and kindness. I love you so much. I am so blessed to have you in my life and especially to be called wife, Mom and Mimi!

About the Author

Penny Noyes is a compulsive reader who spent most of her youth reading everything but the Bible. As a college freshman, she decided to read the Bible all the way through so that she would have a firsthand understanding of God's Word, rather than what other people believed, or said was in the Bible.

Since then, Penny has developed a passion for sharing stories from the Bible, encouraging others to study the Bible, and helping them apply it to their life. Her favorite audience is her wonderful husband, two boys, Chris and John and precious stepdaughter Hillary, son-in-law Jeremy and grandson Jeremy Jr and granddaughter Chloe. Penny lives in North Carolina Learn more about Penny at pennynoyes.com or on her Amazon author page.

OPEN DOOR PUBLISHING
Training Center for Missionaries and New Authors
Hendersonville, NC

Made in the USA
Coppell, TX
23 October 2022

85193099R00136